THE TERM STRUCTURE OF
INTEREST RATES
Expectations and Behavior Patterns

THE
TERM STRUCTURE
OF INTEREST RATES
Expectations and Behavior Patterns

BURTON GORDON MALKIEL

PRINCETON UNIVERSITY PRESS
PRINCETON, NEW JERSEY
1966

FOR

JUDITH A. MALKIEL

PREFACE

THE TERM STRUCTURE of interest rates has been one of the most active areas for economic research during the 1960's. As a continuing deficit in the balance of payments has forced United States governmental authorities to search for new policy instruments, theorists and statisticians alike have taken another look at the possibility of "twisting" the rate structure. Far from converging toward a single set of answers, however, this research has intensified preexisting controversy.

In this study I have attempted to construct a theory of the term structure in which expectations, transactions costs, and the maturity preferences of bond investors and issuers play major roles. In addition to formal aggregate statistical tests, considerable microeconomic evidence is developed to shed light on the actual behavior patterns of the various parties in the bond market. Differences from alternative theories are emphasized throughout the study, and implications for current monetary policy are suggested.

The present study is a revised and expanded version of Part I of my doctoral dissertation, "Problems in the Structure of Financial Markets," submitted to Princeton University in January 1964. In my revisions, I have tried to incorporate the most recent contributions to the field through the first half of 1965. Since this book includes an extensive discussion of some of the institutional arrangements of the bond market and of the behavior patterns of the most important participants in the market, a glossary of frequently used technical and colloquial terms is appended for the convenience of readers.

The help which I have been given in the course of this study has been so considerable that I sometimes think of my role as that of an intellectual intermediary. It would be impossible to express my gratitude adequately to the many who have helped me both within and outside the academic community. If the following acknowledgments appear perfunctory, it is only because an adequate accounting of the extent of my debt would appear almost maudlin. My greatest debt is to William J. Baumol. His influence is to be found throughout the entire study, and his help and direction have been literally invaluable. It would not be an exaggeration to say that he deserves a large share of the credit for whatever glimpses of lucidity may be found within these pages.

Lester V. Chandler introduced me to formal analysis of the term structure in his challenging graduate seminar in money and banking.

His generous counsel, criticism, and advice have materially benefited every chapter of this study. To Richard E. Quandt I owe a large share of the credit for training me in the rudimentary tools of mathematical analysis. His help in the mathematical and statistical portions of this book was often indispensable. I am particularly indebted for his generous assistance in programming certain necessary computer calculations.

Special mention must also be made of the contribution of Edward J. Kane. He read a final draft of this manuscript in its entirety and offered exceedingly valuable advice. Moreover, as a friend and collaborator in banking research, I continuously shared my problems with him and was grateful to have him as a sounding board for my ideas. In addition, I am indebted to Fritz Machlup both for prolonged intellectual stimulation and for the "Seminar on Research in Progress" which he initiated at Princeton. Four chapters of this study were dissected during these meetings and the discussions proved extremely fruitful. Moreover, he supported this research generously through the facilities of the International Finance Section. I am also thankful for valuable suggestions and encouragement from Nevins D. Baxter, Thomas J. Courchene, John G. Cragg, John G. Cross, Stephen M. Goldfeld, Robert E. Kuenne, James W. Land, Sir Arthur Lewis, Dudley G. Luckett, Franco Modigliani, Richard A. Musgrave, Harold T. Shapiro, and John H. Williamson.

Vital contributions to the study were made by several members of the financial community. Three men deserve especial mention. Sidney Homer of Salomon Brothers and Hutzler, the dean of bond analysts, was unusually generous with his time and advice over a prolonged period. Ralph Leach of Morgan Guaranty Trust Co., whose expertise in bank-portfolio management and the government-securities market is by now legendary, allowed me to share, vicariously, the wealth of his experience. Finally, the late John Ohlenbusch, one of the kindest men I have ever known, favored me with very helpful discussions of the investment problems of savings banks. It would be impossible to list all the professional financial people from whom I have learned. Nevertheless, I must at least mention my gratitude to Albert H. Hauser, Roger A. Lyon, George W. McKinney, Jr., William Nagle, Ralph Peters, and Donald B. Riefler.

During the course of this study, I have benefited from the help of several research assistants. My thanks are due to Beverly Land, Fedor Kalishevsky, Dennis Mueller, William Shaffer, Kenneth L.

Thompson, Peter von zur Muehlen, and Elizabeth Zenowich. I especially want to record my gratitude to Robert Lem and Åke Blomqvist, respectively my undergraduate and graduate research assistants during 1965. They both made immense contributions to the successful completion of this study. I must also mention here my thanks to Catherine Brown, Patricia Comeau, Helen Peek, and Patricia La Rue and the Princeton Secretarial Service for typing the various drafts of the manuscript, to William L. Hemphill, who assisted in the preparation of the index, and to Mary Fernholz for valuable editorial advice.

I have included in Chapters 3 and 7 primarily, but in other portions of the work as well, materials that originally appeared in the *Quarterly Journal of Economics, American Economic Review,* and *National Tax Journal.* Permission from the editors and publishers to use these materials is gratefully acknowledged. In Chapter 6, I have included the results of research done jointly with Edward J. Kane.

I wish to express my appreciation to the American Bankers Association, which supported my early work with a Stonier Fellowship, and to the National Science Foundation, which provided generous financial support for later parts of the study. My association with the Princeton University Press has been an extremely pleasant one thanks in large measure to the skill and patience of my editor Dorothy Hollmann.

Finally, the contribution of my wife, Judith A. Malkiel, was of inestimable importance. The usual uxorial acknowledgment of "cheerful encouragement" can scarcely begin to measure the extent of my gratitude. She has painstakingly edited every page of this manuscript and has assisted me during every phase of this undertaking. This accounting of my debt to her is the largest understatement of all.

Burton G. Malkiel

Princeton, New Jersey
March 1966

CONTENTS

CONTENTS

LIST OF FIGURES

LIST OF TABLES

THE TERM STRUCTURE OF
INTEREST RATES
Expectations and Behavior Patterns

CHAPTER 1

The Yield Curve: Methods of Construction
and Historical Patterns

ECONOMISTS often speak of "*the* rate of interest" as if it were a single datum readily observable in the real world. If one were, in fact, to look at actual market rates of interest on a single day, one would find what is at first glance a bewildering variety of yields for the obligations of different issuers and for different maturities of the bonds of the same issuer. We try to account for these variations by linking them to a number of differentiating factors, and we designate the systematic arrangement of the yield variations as "the structure of interest rates."

Perhaps the chief determinant of differential market rates of interest for bonds of the same maturity is the *credit risk* of the securities, the risk of default in promised payments of interest and principal. Other determinants of bond-yield differentials include marketability, coupon rate, tax status, sinking-fund activity, and certain features allowing the bond holder to convert his claims into common shares or to enjoy privileged subscription rights.[1] Indeed, the most important variables that explain the structure of market yields may be unrelated to the maturity of the issues involved. Nevertheless, perhaps the most intriguing structural relationship among market interest rates is the functional relationship among yields of securities which differ only in their term to maturity. This relationship, called "the term structure of interest rates," is the subject matter of this book.

1.1 *The Yield Curve*

The yield curve is the most widely used graphic device for examining the relationship between yield and term to maturity of comparable

---

[1] The determination of bond-yield differentials on securities of the same maturity has been studied by Lawrence Fisher, in "Determinants of Risk Premiums on Corporate Bonds," *Journal of Political Economy* 67 (June 1959), pp. 217–237; and by Peter E. Sloane, in "Determinants of Bond Yield Differentials," *Yale Economic Essays,* 3 (Spring 1963), pp. 3–55. A study of the effects of convertibility features on bond yields was recently completed by William J. Baumol, Burton G. Malkiel, and Richard E. Quandt, "The Valuation of Convertible Securities," *Quarterly Journal of Economics* 80 (February 1966), pp. 48–59.

debt securities.[2] It refers simply to a chart depicting the general functional relationship between the yield and the length of the loan. Along the abscissa we measure years to maturity and along the ordinate, annual yield to maturity. The yield curve depicts what is essentially a theoretical relationship for hypothetical securities identical in all respects except term to maturity. However, since no two securities, even of the same issue, are identical in all respects, empirically constructed yield curves cannot be more than an approximation of this relationship.

It would seem that at least the yield curves for United States Treasury securities might be unambiguous. Since Treasury obligations are not subject to any significant risk of default, the securities of all maturities might be expected to be homogeneous with respect to creditworthiness and safety. Nevertheless, during recent periods a myriad of special features have altered the yield relationships for certain government securities. Optional maturities differentiated some issues in the minds of the buyer. Some issues were partially tax exempt. Other securities could be "put" (sold back to the Treasury at a fixed price) at the option of the holder. Certain government securities have been traded relatively infrequently, and consequently the marketability of different issues has not been uniform. Most government securities in the estate of a decedent have been acceptable at par for payments of federal estate taxes irrespective of their current market price. Moreover, prices of maturing issues were often influenced by possible exchange privileges at call or maturity. Finally, as we shall see in later chapters, differential coupons on issues of the same maturity rendered the securities dissimilar in many important properties. Thus, even for governments—the most homogeneous group of securities—the determination of a yield-maturity relationship is not easily accomplished.

In practice, some arbitrary rules of thumb are usually devised to exclude those issues where special features lead to significant differences in yield. For example, the yields of taxable and nontaxable issues are never plotted together. In some cases it is decided to exclude callable issues where the figure apparently describing yield to maturity is spurious because of the possibility of early call. In other constructions, the term to maturity is considered to be measured by the earliest

---

[2] The yield to maturity for a bond is defined as the (annual) interest rate which makes the present value of the stream of future coupon payments and of the face value payable at maturity equal to the purchase price. It is defined algebraically in equation (3-1) of Chapter 3. Term to maturity refers to the date when the face value of the bond becomes due and payable.

call date if the bonds are selling above par, whereas the terminal date is taken to be the date of final maturity if the issue is selling at a discount from par. Securities are sometimes excluded if their coupons are markedly higher or lower than those of the majority of bonds outstanding at the time or if they have special redemption provisions. Finally, many analysts use only those issues outstanding in large quantities and enjoying the best marketability. Thus, issues which attract the strongest trading interest are used in deriving the yield curve.

A point is then plotted on the chart for each issue whose yield is to be used in constructing the curve. In drawing the yield curve,

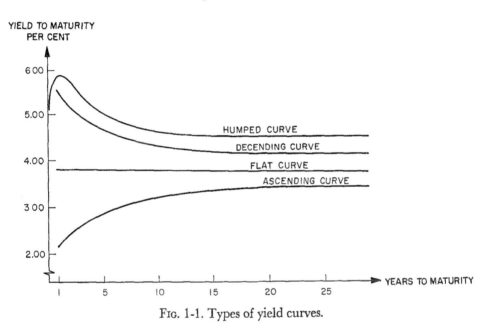

Fig. 1-1. Types of yield curves.

the relationship is sometimes constructed by connecting all of the separate dots representing the yield figures. The resulting locus is then likely to be a jagged line. An alternative procedure leaves the dots as a scatter pattern and employs a free and relatively smooth curve, which describes, in general, the indicated relationship. The latter technique is more aesthetically pleasing and is the more popular practice.[3]

[3] See, for example, "Market Interest Rates and Maturity of Issues," *Monthly Review,* Federal Reserve Bank of Kansas City (August 1954), p. 4. As we shall see in Chapter 2, however, the choice of method of fitting is not simply a matter of aesthetics. The method of construction and smoothing of the yield curve has an important bearing on the success of certain empirical tests.

Generally, smoothed empirical yield curves have approximated one of four forms. The curve may display the lowest interest rates on short-term issues and then rise at a diminishing rate until it approaches a horizontal line in the longest maturities, so that we have an "ascending curve." Alternatively, but somewhat less frequently, yields may be highest in the short-term area and then decrease at a diminishing rate until they level out, thus forming a "descending curve" (or what many bankers call a "reverse" curve). Still less frequently, yields on long and short issues are approximately equal, thus forming a horizontal line or a "flat yield curve." Finally, yields may rise in the early maturities, reach a peak (or hump), and then decline until they finally level out in later maturities.[4] Figure 1-1 shows the four types of yield relationships described above.

1.2   *The Durand Basic Yields*

While several different interest-rate time series exist for high-grade-bond yields in the United States, the Durand series of corporate-bond yields provides the only consistent history over a long period of time.[5] Durand had good reasons for employing corporate-bond yields, in preference to the yields of municipal and Federal obligations, in the construction of his series. Municipal-yield figures were distorted by the changing value of their tax exemption. Several difficulties also mar the usefulness of the Treasury-yield data. Not only did the tax status of Treasury issues change during the century, but there were also special privileges attached to some government issues. Moreover, until recently there were large gaps in the maturity continuum, making historical yield-curve comparisons extremely hazardous. The Durand data, on the other hand, provide a consistent annual record of high-grade-corporate-bond yields over the whole maturity spectrum in excess of one year.

---

[4] Such "humped" yield curves have usually been found only for government securities. As will be shown below, the method of construction of our long-term series of empirical corporate yield curves precludes the recognition of any hump in the early maturities.

[5] The Durand Series may be found in David Durand, *Basic Yields of Corporate Bonds, 1900–1942*, Technical Paper 3 (New York: National Bureau of Economic Research, 1942); David Durand and Willis J. Winn, *Basic Yields of Bonds, 1926–1947; Their Measurement and Pattern*, Technical Paper 6 (New York: National Bureau of Economic Research, 1947); *The Economic Almanac, 1953–1954* (New York: Thomas Y. Crowell Company, 1953); and David Durand, "A Quarterly Series of Corporate Basic Yields, 1952–1957, and Some Attendant Reservations," *The Journal of Finance* 13 (September 1958), pp. 348–356.

The so-called basic yields were meant to serve as an estimate of market yields to maturity on the highest grade of corporate bonds free from all extraneous influences. The yield series was based on an examination of prevailing (secondary) market yields for all important high-grade issues that were outstanding. Of course, not all of the outstanding bonds were actually used in constructing the curves. For example, yields of bonds with conversion features, prices substantially influenced by call provisions or sinking funds, etc., were eliminated. For each bond that was actually used, six price quotations were obtained—the high and low sales prices (not including transactions charges) during each of the first three months of the year.[6] The annual yield curves were derived from the averages of the high and low yields corresponding to these prices.

These average yields[7] were then plotted on graphs. The freehand curve was not, however, drawn in the regular way to describe the *general pattern of rates. Rather, the curve was drawn as an envelope* of (clusters of) the lowest yields plotted. Particular care was taken to check the lowest yields in order to eliminate those that contained spurious elements.

Durand's actual method of fitting the yield curve was somewhat Procrustean. In practice, he limited himself to the bottom three of the smooth basic yield-curve shapes depicted in Figure 1-1.[8] Where there was a hiatus between clusters of observations in particular maturity ranges, the yield curve was interpolated to fit the basic patterns. Especially noteworthy was the method of smoothing employed. Adjustments were made in the freehand curves until the successive differences between maturities became sufficiently regular.[9] Durand's desire to interpolate smooth curves resulted in yield-curve estimates with a considerable degree of artificiality.

As Durand noted himself, the short-term yield estimates are especially suspect:

> The short term basic yields are subject to numerous special errors in addition to those of the longer term yields. In the first place,

[6] Yields after 1942 were calculated using January and February prices, and since 1951 the yields are based on February prices.

[7] The yields were rounded down to the nearest 0.05 per cent.

[8] In some cases Durand's ascending yield curves would rise at a constant rate through the short-dated region.

[9] J. A. G. Grant was the first to call attention to the difficulties involved in the Durand method of smoothing. See J. A. G. Grant, "Meiselman on the Structure of Interest Rates: A British Test," *Economica* 31 (February 1964), p. 59.

THE YIELD CURVE

TABLE 1-1
Basic Yields by Maturity—Prime Corporate Bonds

February			Years to maturity				
	1	5	10	15	20	25	30
1900	3.97%[a]	3.36%[a]	3.30%	3.30%	3.30%	3.30%	3.30%
1901	3.25	3.25	3.25	3.25	3.25	3.25	3.25
1902	3.30[b]	3.30[b]	3.30[b]	3.30[b]	3.30[b]	3.30[b]	3.30[b]
1903	3.45	3.45	3.45	3.45	3.45	3.45	3.45
1904	3.60	3.60	3.60	3.60	3.60	3.60	3.60
1905	3.50	3.50	3.50	3.50	3.50	3.50	3.50
1906	4.75[a]	3.67[a]	3.55	3.55	3.55	3.55	3.55
1907	4.87[a]	3.87[a]	3.80	3.80	3.80	3.80	3.80
1908	5.10[a]	4.30[a]	4.02[a]	3.95	3.95	3.95	3.95
1909	4.03	3.97	3.91	3.86	3.82	3.79	3.77
1910	4.25	4.10	3.99	3.92	3.87	3.83	3.80
1911	4.09	4.05	4.01	3.97	3.94	3.92	3.90
1912	4.04	4.00	3.96	3.93	3.91	3.90	3.90
1913	4.74	4.31	4.12	4.06	4.02	4.00	4.00
1914	4.64	4.45	4.32	4.22	4.16	4.12	4.10
1915	4.47	4.39	4.31	4.25	4.20	4.17	4.15
1916	3.48	4.03	4.05	4.05	4.05	4.05	4.05
1917	4.05	4.05	4.05	4.05	4.05	4.05	4.05
1918	5.48	5.25	5.05	4.91	4.82	4.77	4.75
1919	5.58	5.16	4.97	4.87	4.81	4.77	4.75
1920	6.11	5.72	5.43	5.26	5.17	5.12	5.10
1921	6.94[b]	6.21	5.73	5.46	5.31	5.22	5.17
1922	5.31	5.19	5.06	4.95	4.85	4.77	4.71
1923	5.01	4.90	4.80	4.73	4.68	4.64	4.61
1924	5.02	4.90	4.80	4.73	4.69	4.67	4.66
1925	3.85	4.46	4.50	4.50	4.50	4.50	4.50
1926	4.40	4.40	4.40	4.40	4.40	4.40	4.40
1927	4.30	4.30	4.30	4.30	4.30	4.30	4.30
1928	4.05	4.05	4.05	4.05	4.05	4.05	4.05
1929	5.27	4.72	4.57	4.49	4.45	4.43	4.42
1930	4.40	4.40	4.40	4.40	4.40	4.40	4.40
1931	3.05	3.90	4.03	4.08	4.10	4.10	4.10
1932	3.99[a]	4.58[a]	4.70	4.70	4.70	4.70	4.70
1933	2.60[b]	3.68	4.00	4.07	4.11	4.14	4.15
1934	2.62[b]	3.48	3.70	3.83	3.91	3.96	3.99
1935	1.05	2.37	3.00	3.23	3.37	3.46	3.50
1936	0.61	1.86	2.64	2.88	3.04	3.14	3.20
1937	0.69	1.68	2.38	2.72	2.90	3.01	3.08
1938	0.85	1.97	2.60	2.81	2.91	2.97	3.00
1939	0.57	1.55	2.18	2.50	2.65	2.72	2.75

TABLE 1-1 (*continued*)

February	1	5	10	15	20	25	30
			Years to maturity				
1940	0.41%	1.28%	1.95%	2.34%	2.55%	2.65%	2.70%
1941	0.41	1.21	1.88	2.28	2.50	2.61	2.65
1942	0.81	1.50	2.16	2.47	2.61	2.64	2.65
1943	1.17	1.71	2.16	2.45	2.61	2.65	2.65
1944	1.08[b]	1.58	2.20	2.54	2.60	2.60	2.60
1945	1.02	1.53	2.14	2.45	2.55	2.55	2.55
1946	0.86[b]	1.32	1.88[b]	2.26	2.35	2.40	2.43
1947	1.05[b]	1.65	2.08[b]	2.30	2.40	2.46	2.50
1948	1.60	2.03	2.53	2.66	2.73	2.77	2.80
1949	1.60	1.92	2.32	2.54	2.62	2.68	2.74
1950	1.42[b]	1.90[b]	2.30	2.40	2.48	2.54	2.58
1951	2.05[b]	2.22[b]	2.39	2.51	2.59	2.63	2.67
1952	2.73[b]	2.73[b]	2.73	2.81	2.88	2.94	3.00
1953	2.62[b]	2.75[b]	2.88	2.97	3.05	3.11	3.15
1954	2.40	2.52	2.66	2.78	2.88	2.95	3.00
1955	2.60[c]	2.70	2.80	2.88	2.95	3.00	3.04
1956	2.70	2.78	2.86	2.93	2.99	3.04	3.09
1957	3.50[b]	3.50[b]	3.50	3.50	3.50[b]	3.60	3.68
1958	3.21[b]	3.25[b]	3.33	3.40	3.47	3.54	3.61
1959[c]	3.67	3.80	4.03	4.10	4.10	4.10	4.10
1960[c]	4.95	4.73	4.60	4.55	4.55	4.55	4.55
1961[c]	3.10	3.75	4.00	4.06	4.12	4.16	4.22
1962[c]	3.50	3.97	4.28	4.37	4.40	4.41	4.42
1963[c]	3.25	3.77	3.98	4.05	4.10	4.14	4.16
1964[c]	4.00	4.15	4.25	4.29	4.33	4.33	4.33
1965[c]	4.15	4.29	4.33	4.35	4.35	4.35	4.35

[a] Estimated by interpolation and therefore particularly subject to error.
[b] More than usually subject to error.
[c] Estimated by the use of methods similar to those employed by Durand.

Sources

1900–42   David Durand, *Basic Yields of Corporate Bonds, 1900–1942*, Technical Paper 3 (New York: National Bureau of Economic Research, 1942).

1943–47   David Durand and Willis J. Winn, *Basic Yields of Bonds, 1926–1947: Their Management and Pattern*, Technical Paper 6 (New York: National Bureau of Economic Research, 1947).

1948–52   *The Economic Almanac, 1953–1954* (New York: Thomas Y. Crowell Company, 1953).

1953–58   David Durand, "A Quarterly Series of Corporate Basic Yields, 1952–1957, and Some Attendant Reservations," *The Journal of Finance* 13 (September 1958).

1959–65   Sidney Homer, *A History of Interest Rates* (New Brunswick: Rutgers University Press, 1963) and from the private records of the author.

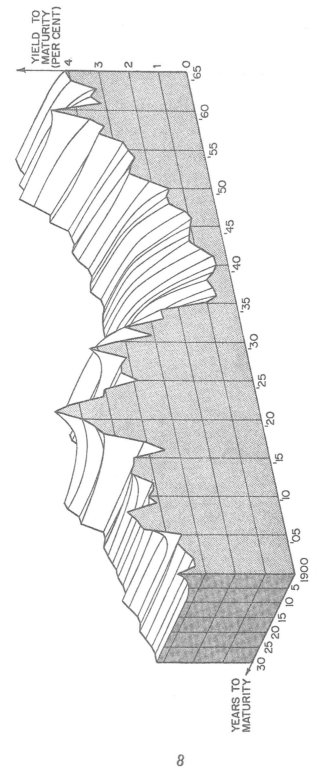

Fig. 1-2. Basic yields of corporate bonds by maturity, 1900–1965; perspective 1. Three-dimensional charts of time series of yield curves were first executed by Sidney Homer. See his *A History of Interest Rates*, pp. 380–381.

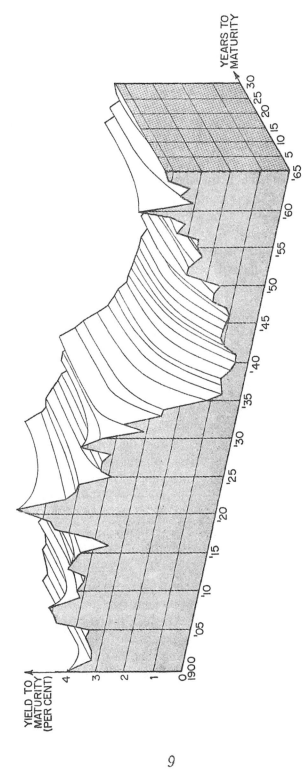

FIG. 1-3. Basic yields of corporates bonds by maturity, 1900–1965; perspective 2.

price fluctuations of an eighth of a point, the usual limit to which prices are quoted, have an important effect on the yield of a short term bond. For a price range of $99\frac{7}{8}$ to $100\frac{1}{8}$, the yield range for a 30-year, 4 per cent bond is 3.993 to 4.007 per cent, which is negligible; for a 1-year, 4 per cent bond the range is 3.88 to 4.13 per cent, which is appreciable; and for a 3-month, 4 per cent bond the range is 3.48 to 4.48 per cent, which is considerable. Furthermore, the short term bond yield is often equally sensitive to daily changes in term to maturity. At $101\frac{1}{8}$ a 3-month, 6 per cent bond yields 1.48 per cent. If the price remains constant for one week, the yield will be 1.12 per cent; if the price then falls to 101, the yield will rise to 1.64 per cent. Obviously, if short term yields are to be studied satisfactorily, they can be studied only on a day to day basis. Our practice of determining the yield from a three-month average price is patently unsatisfactory, and is justified by reasons of economy alone.[10]

Nor is Durand's averaging mechanism the only difficulty. The appropriateness of the figures themselves is also questionable, since short-term-bond values are sometimes influenced by exchange privileges. More important, Durand's estimates take no account of brokerage commissions. Durand based his yield estimates on actual sale prices, not including transactions charges. But, since an investor would have to pay brokerage charges in order to buy the bonds, his realized yield would be less. Moreover, the shorter the term to maturity of the issue, the more will yields calculated from sale prices overstate the realizable yields available to an investor.[11] Thus Durand was forced to admit that: "at 1 year to maturity the basic yield curve is presumably subject to an error of at least .25 per cent; and in the questionable years, such as 1932, an error of 1 per cent would not be surprising."[12]

Durand was well aware of these difficulties. We shall see that they will create obstacles for the utilization of the basic-yield curves in certain empirical tests. Nevertheless, the Durand data provide the only consistent time series of yield-curve relations during the present century. Moreover, for the purposes which the estimates were intended to serve, the basic yield curves are exceedingly valuable. Durand himself was perfectly frank in admitting that his data were designed only "to create a quick and crude impression of the term structure of

---

[10] Durand, *Basic Yields of Corporate Bonds,* pp. 12–13.

[11] A thorough examination of transactions charges is undertaken in Chapter 5.

[12] Durand, *Basic Yields of Corporate Bonds,* p. 14.

high-grade-bond yields at a moment of time; and for this they are adequate."[18]

Table 1-1 describes the Durand yield data from 1900 to 1958 and comparable basic-yield estimates from 1959 to 1965. Figures 1-2 and 1-3 depict in three dimensions the basic shapes of the Durand yield curves and thus the simultaneous fluctuations in the yields of all maturities. They are shown from two different perspectives because the peaks and troughs tend to obscure one another. Several conclusions may readily be drawn from an examination of these graphs. Short-term rates have clearly been far more volatile than long-term rates. In periods of rising interest rates they rise more than long rates and

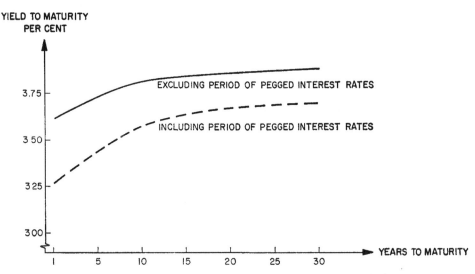

FIG. 1-4. Yield curves of average corporate rates 1900–1965.

in periods of falling rates they fall further. Moreover, the historical data suggest that descending curves are apt to be typical of periods when both long- and short-term rates are relatively high. Conversely, an ascending curve appears to have been characteristic of periods when relatively low rates prevailed for both maturity groups. Level curves have appeared most frequently when short- and long-term rates have been near or somewhat above the middle of the range between the historical highs and lows.

If we compute, for each term to maturity, average yields over the 66 years of history for the Durand basic yields, we can obtain a composite yield curve which should represent more or less normal conditions. Figure 1-4 presents the results of this calculation. We note

[18] Durand, "A Quarterly Series of Corporate Basic Yields . . . ," p. 348.

that the average yield curve is positively sloped and tends to flatten out as term to maturity is extended. Even if we exclude the data for the World War II and immediate postwar years when (government) rates were pegged, the composite yield curve retains its positive slope. Thus, the Durand data support the contention that a positively sloped yield curve is in some sense the more "normal" phenomenon, at least for the present century.

1.3 *Yield Relationships for Other Securities*

In obtaining a general picture of yield-maturity relationships, we should not restrict our observations to the Durand data. There is some indication that not all default risk has been eliminated from the Durand curves. Yield curves for U.S. Treasury securities have generally lain below the Durand curves. Moreover, the Durand yield curves are not well delineated in the very early maturities (up to a year and a half). Durand's estimates begin only with one-year issues, and, because of the existence of transactions costs, the yield estimates do not represent realizable yields. As mentioned above, this source of error is particularly serious for short-term issues. In addition, transactions charges tend to be considerably higher for corporate securities than for Treasury issues. While it is not possible to obtain a long series of government yield curves, we can at least examine some more recent curves to obtain a clearer picture of the shape of the term-structure curve in the very early maturities.

Figure 1-5 depicts the yield curves for Treasury securities for the years 1953 through 1966. Like the Durand yield curves they were smoothed to eliminate irregularities in successive differences between maturities. Unlike Durand's estimates, however, they are based on "asked" or offering (end of January) yields in the market, *net* of transactions charges to the buyer. The yield curves begin with the 30-day bill rate and end with the longest outstanding Treasury issue. Moreover, they are plotted using many issues that mature between one and two years. Consequently, we get a more reliable representation of the left-hand segment of the yield curve than was obtainable with the Durand data.

In general, these curves exhibit the same basic characteristics as do the Durand yield curves. During periods of low interest rates the curve is ascending throughout the first 10 to 15 years. In periods of high rates, on the other hand, the ascending portion of the curve is much shorter, and (during 1957, 1960, and 1966) the yield on short-term issues was little different from that on long-term issues.

12

Moreover, portions of the yield curve are found to be negatively sloped.[14] Even during periods when the complex of rates under five years was substantially higher than long-term rates, however, the slope of the yield curve in the very early maturities was always unmistakably positive. This had the effect of producing a conspicuously "humped" yield curve through many months of 1957, 1959, 1960, and 1966. It is not possible to identify curves that were "humped" using the Durand

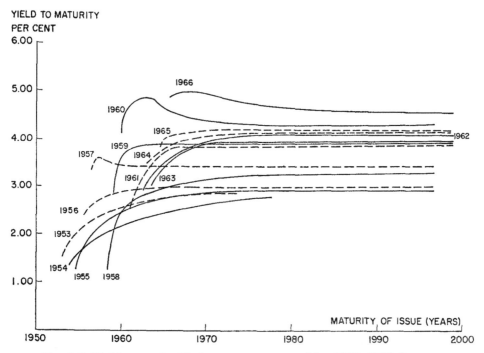

Fɪɢ. 1-5. Yield curves for U. S. government securities, 1953–1966. Source: *Treasury Bulletin* 1953–1966. The yield curves were adjusted to depict "asked" yields.

data since the hump seems always to involve the early maturities for which the Durand estimates are weakest.

Figure 1-6 presents sample yield curves for the outstanding commercial paper and debentures of General Motors Acceptance Corporation. We find that humped curves were prevalent during late 1959 and early 1960. Therefore, there is no reason to believe that humped yield curves are peculiar to U.S. Government issues.

Calculating an average government yield curve we find the same

[14] Even steeper negative segments were common throughout the late months of 1959 not covered by Figure 1-5.

13

general pattern as was present for the composite Durand data. Table 1-2 presents data on the average yields of government securities over the two reference cycles from August 1954 to February 1961 and from those of the Treasury–Federal Reserve Accord through January 1965. We note that, on the average, bill rates were almost 100 basis points[15] less than long-term bond yields. The cycles chosen included the years of peak rates where negatively sloped portions of the yield curve were found, so that the averages are not simply composed of

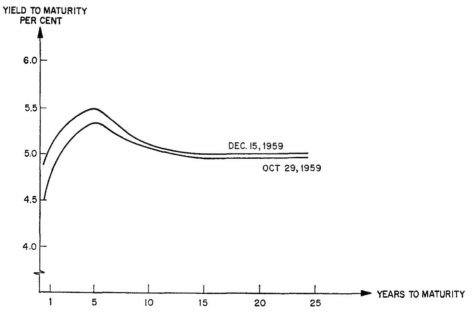

FIG. 1-6. Selected yield curves for the obligations of General Motors Acceptance Corporation during 1959.

yield curves whose slopes were always positive throughout. Thus, we find support for our earlier suggestion that the "normal" yield curves of recent history may be positively sloped.

In examining a longer period of interest-rate history both in the United States and abroad, we can discern patterns similar to those identified from the preceding corporate- and government-yield data. The cyclical behavior noted above of short relative to long rates has been confirmed for both the United States and England as far back as the middle of the nineteenth century. Reuben Kessel, for example, reports that from the Civil War until the First World War, U.S. short-

---

[15] A basis point equals 0.01 per cent.

TABLE 1-2
AVERAGE YIELDS OF U.S. TREASURY SECURITIES

	Bills	9- to 12-month governments	3- to 5-year governments	20-year governments
Aug. 1954 to April 1958	2.296	2.500	2.912	3.079
April 1958 to Feb. 1961	2.742	3.356	3.846	3.904
Unweighted average of the cycle averages, Aug. 1954 to Feb. 1961	2.519	2.928	3.379	3.492
Unweighted average of monthly yields, April 1951 to Jan. 1965	2.464	2.751	3.201	3.479

Source: Average yields over the reference cycle, Aug. 1954 to Feb. 1961 from Reuben Kessel, *The Cyclical Behavior of the Term Structure of Interest Rates*, Occasional Paper 91 (New York: National Bureau of Economic Research, December 1965), p. 62. Averages from April 1951 through January 1965 were calculated from yield estimates by Sidney Homer of the firm of Salomon Brothers & Hutzler.

term rates rose relative to long rates during periods of business expansion and fell relative to long rates during periods of business contraction.[16] Sir Ralph Hawtrey found the interest-rate differential between short and long rates varied cyclically over the same period in the United Kingdom. During depressions, when the level of rates was low, short rates were low relative to long rates. During periods of boom and high interest rates, the short rate tended to be high relative to the long rate.[17] Very scanty evidence over a much longer period of history suggests that these patterns may even have been common in medieval and Renaissance times. Sidney Homer found that when

[16] Reuben Kessel, *The Cyclical Behavior of the Term Structure of Interest Rates*, Occasional Paper 91 (New York: National Bureau of Economic Research, 1965), p. 74.

[17] Ralph G. Hawtrey, *A Century of Bank Rates* (London: Longmans, Green and Co., 1938), pp. 167ff. John R. Hicks, in "Mr. Hawtrey on Bank Rates and the Long Term Rate of Interest," *Manchester School* 10 (April 1939), p. 28, found, however, that short rates were on the average less than long rates in England from 1850 to 1930. This is not to deny that during some periods of history short-term interest rates have generally exceeded long-term rates. For example, in the United States from 1880 to 1920 commercial-paper rates were usually above the rates on high-grade railroad bonds. It should be noted that the entire period was one of relatively high rates. Nevertheless, we must treat this comparison with some caution. While both series represented yields of "prime" obligations, it is by no means certain that the quality of the issues was identical. Moreover, the commercial paper was not marketable, while the long-term issues were. Hence, these series do not offer a direct comparison of marketable short and long yields, as do the Durand and Treasury-security data.

15

interest rates tended to be very high, short rates were generally above long rates. When interest rates were relatively low, short rates were usually below long rates.[18]

1.4 *Recapitulation*

It is useful to summarize our historical survey of yield relationships, indirectly, by asking what desiderata a theory of the term structure of interest rates should fulfill.

1. The theory must explain the greater volatility of short-term rates. During periods of restricted credit conditions short rates rise more than long rates, while in periods of easy money they fall further.

2. The theory should be consistent with the fact that yield curves (or segments of curves) with negative slopes were likely to be typical of periods when both long and short rates are relatively high. Conversely, ascending curves appear to have been representative of periods when relatively low rates prevailed for both maturity groups. A level structure of rates has appeared most frequently when short- and long-term rates have been near the mid-point of the range between the historical highs and lows.

3. The theory must account for the pervasive tendency of the curve to level out as term to maturity increases and to develop what is called a "shoulder,"[19] irrespective of its general shape in the early maturities. Slopes with large absolute values occur only in the early maturities.

4. A fourth requirement is that the theory be capable of explaining why short-term rates over the current century tend to be lower than average long-term rates. While curves with descending segments are not uncommon, the typical relationship has been an ascending term structure.

5. Finally, the theory must indicate why the slope of the yield curve in the very early maturities is normally positive.

[18] Sidney Homer, *A History of Interest Rates* (New Brunswick: Rutgers University Press, 1963), pp. 141ff.

[19] This terminology appears in Roland I. Robinson, *The Management of Bank Funds* (New York: McGraw-Hill, 1951), pp. 320–332.

CHAPTER 2

The Traditional Expectations Theory and Its Critics

THE HISTORICAL PATTERNS of relationships between short-term and long-term yields have long intrigued both economic theorists and investment analysts. Despite the considerable attention devoted to the question, the theory of the term structure of interest rates is by no means settled. This chapter examines briefly the principal hypotheses which have been offered in attempts to explain the relationship of short to long rates. This will provide a background for a new theoretical apparatus which, it is hoped, will simultaneously constitute a useful framework for amending and reconciling our current bevy of theories and bring the beliefs of academic economists into closer conformity with the practices of bond traders and institutional investors.

2.1   The Traditional Expectations Theory

Among economists, the expectations theory of the term structure has long served as the basis for discussion. The proposition that expectations of the level of future interest rates influence the rate structure dates back at least to Irving Fisher.[1] Several writers during the 'thirties developed theories along this line.[2] The theory was further refined by J. R. Hicks, and perhaps its most articulate spokesman was F. A. Lutz.[3] More recently, the theory has been

[1] Irving Fisher, "Appreciation and Interest," *Publications of the American Economic Association* 11 (August 1896), pp. 23–29, 88–92; *The Nature of Capital and Income* (New York: The Macmillan Co., 1906), pp. 273–274; and *The Theory of Interest* (New York: The Macmillan Co., 1930), p. 210. We use the term "at least" advisedly. One can find anticipations of the expectations theory in Henry Sidgwick, *The Principles of Political Economy* (London: Macmillan, 1887), pp. 255–277 and even in J. B. Say, *A Treatise on Political Economy* (Philadelphia: Lippincott, Grambo & Co., 1853), pp. 343–354.

[2] See especially John Burr Williams, *Theory of Investment Value* (Amsterdam: North-Holland Publishing Company, 1956, 1st printing, 1938), pp. 115–118; Nicholas Kaldor, "Speculation and Economic Stability," *The Review of Economic Studies* 7 (October 1939), pp. 13–16, and Michael Kalecki, *Essays in the Theory of Economic Fluctuations* (London: G. Allen & Unwin, Ltd., 1939), pp. 112–113.

[3] J. R. Hicks, *Value and Capital* (London: Oxford at the Clarendon Press, 1939, 2nd ed. 1946), pp. 144–145; Friedrich A. Lutz, "The Structure of Interest Rates," *Quarterly Journal of Economics* 55 (November 1940), pp. 36–63, reprinted in American Economic Association, *Readings in the Theory of Income Distribution* (Homewood: R. D. Irwin, 1946), pp. 499–529. All future references to Lutz will cite page numbers in the A.E.A. *Readings*.

reinterpreted by J. W. Conard.[4] In the following exposition of the theory the Conard interpretation will be used.

In the pure or perfect-certainty variant of the traditional theory there are four usual assumptions:

1. All securities are riskless with respect to the payment of both interest and principal. Moreover, the theory abstracts from tax considerations, call features, differing coupons and other such "imperfections."

2. Investors hold with complete confidence a set of uniform expectations concerning *all* future short-term rates of interest, and their forecasts are accurate.

3. There are no transactions costs, and consequently switches among securities of different maturities are unimpeded.

4. The behavior of all market participants is motivated by no objective other than profit maximization, thus ensuring full use of every opportunity for profitable arbitrage among different maturities.

Under these conditions it follows that each investor will choose the security (or combination of securities) that maximizes his return for the period during which his funds are available. These circumstances lead to a unique set of equilibrium relationships among securities of different maturity. Let us illustrate such an equilibrium situation for the simple case where only two securities are outstanding: a one-year and a two-year bond. We call the yield realized by the investor over the time period for which he has funds to invest, the investor's "holding-period yield." Let us assume that the actual one-year rate $(_tR_1)$ is 2 per cent and the two-year rate $(_tR_2)$ is 3 per cent.[5] Further, we posit that next year's expected one-year rate $(_{t+1}r_1)$ is 4 per cent. Now let us examine the options open to an investor who has funds to invest for two years. He may buy a two-year bond from which he obtains an average annual yield of 3 per cent. Alternatively, he may buy a one-year bond and receive a 2 per cent return and next year reinvest the proceeds in another one-year issue to yield 4 per cent. In either case his average annual return is (approximately) 3 per cent.

[4] Joseph W. Conard, *Introduction to the Theory of Interest* (Berkeley: University of California Press, 1959), Part Three.

[5] We utilize the notation developed by David Meiselman in *The Term Structure of Interest Rates* (Englewood Cliffs: Prentice-Hall, 1962), p. 19. Capital R's represent actual market yields, while lower-case r's are expected rates. The prescripts represent the time period at which the rates are applicable and the subscripts stand for the maturity of the bonds.

Let us now look at the alternatives open to the investor who has funds at his disposal for only one year. If he buys a one-year issue, his annual holding-period return is 2 per cent. What return will he realize if he invests in a two-year bond and then sells the issue after holding it for one year? To answer this question we must first determine what price the two-year issue will have at the end of the holding period. Assume the (current) two-year issue is a 3 per cent coupon bond (selling now at par, i.e., 100). Since $_{t+1}r_1$ is expected to be 4 per cent, the price of the bond must fall to 99 next year. This is so because the price of a one-year, 3 per cent coupon bond, which has an internal rate of return (yield) of 4 per cent, is 99.[6] We may now compute the one-year-holding-period return with the aid of the following definitional equation:[7]

Holding-period yield

$$= \frac{\text{coupon interest received} + \text{capital gain (loss)}}{\text{purchase price}} . \quad (2\text{-}1)$$

Utilizing the data from our example we have

$$y_1 = \frac{3 + (99-100)}{100} = 2 \quad \text{per cent} ,$$

where y_1 refers to one-year-holding-period return. Thus, we see that the investor whose funds are available for one year obtains the same holding-period return whichever maturity he buys.

From this simple illustration, the whole game can be made clear. Since expectations are identical for all market participants, our hypothetical investors may be taken as representative of the entire market. Suppose now that the equilibrium conditions are not satisfied—that there are differences in yields for comparable periods. Consider first the investor with a long holding period. If successive investment in shorts were expected to yield more (less) than investment in longs, he would not want to purchase longs (shorts). He would want to buy that combination of securities which would give him the largest expected holding-period yield. *Mutatis mutandis*, the same argument applies for investors with short holding periods. But in trying to take advantage of a potentially larger holding-period yield available from any particular security, investors would

---

[6] $\text{Price} = \dfrac{\text{coupon payment} + \text{face value at maturity}}{1 + \text{yield}}.$

$P = \dfrac{3 + 100}{1.04} \approx 99.$ Our numerical examples are usually only approximately correct.

[7] See Lutz, *op. cit.*, p. 503.

tend to drive the price of that security up and its yield down. Such buying would continue until the price was bid up to the point where that security no longer had the largest expected yield. Investor interest might then be concentrated on the security that previously offered the next largest holding-period yield. By the same reasoning, the price of this issue would tend to be bid up until it also offered no extra opportunity for gain. This process would continue until all differentials in anticipated holding-period yields were completely eliminated for *each holding period*.

Our numerical example can help to clarify the equilibrating mechanism. Suppose, as before, that $_tR_1$ is 2 per cent and $_{t+1}r_1$ is 4 per cent, but that $_tR_2$ is $3\frac{1}{2}$ per cent. The investor with funds to invest for two years would find that successive investment in shorts would give a holding-period return of approximately 3 per cent, while investment in the two-year bond would give a $3\frac{1}{2}$ per cent return. Consequently, all two-year investors would want to invest in the two-year bond. Wealth holders with funds to invest for one year would make a similar comparison. Investing in one-year securities would yield a return of 2 per cent, but investing in two-year securities (and reselling them at the end of one year) would give a holding-period return of 3 per cent. This is so because the price of a two-year, $3\frac{1}{2}$ percent coupon bond at the end of one year would be $99.50 if one-year yields were then 4 per cent. Consequently, all investors would prefer to invest in two-year issues. Similarly, arbitrageurs would make a sure gain by simultaneously selling (short) one-year bonds (on which they pay 2 per cent) and buying two-year bonds (on which they receive a one-year-holding-period return of 3 per cent). All these transactions would bid up the price of two-year securities and drive down the price of one-year bonds. Yields would tend to rise on one-year securities and fall on two-year issues until holding-period yields were equalized.

In equilibrium, for a holding period of any given length, the holding-period yield must be the same regardless of the maturity of the security(ies) purchased. As will next be shown, from this crucial proposition it follows that long rates must turn out to be an average of present and future short-term rates of interest. Only when this is true can the long-term investor, for example, receive through successive investment in shorts the same holding-period yield he would earn by holding a long-term security to maturity.

In formalizing the theory, the bond market is considered analogous to a commodity-futures market.[8] The rate of interest for a

[8] This analogy was used by J. R. Hicks in *Value and Capital*, p. 146.

two-year loan is conceived as being compounded out of the "spot" rate for loans of one year and the expected "forward" rate of interest for one-year loans to be executed at the beginning of the second year. Let us write the two-year rate (the "long" rate) as $_tR_2$, the current one-year ("short") rate as $_tR_1$, and the forward one-year "short" rate as $_{t+1}r_1$. If our investor lends long, at the end of the two-year period every dollar of his investment will have grown to $(1 + {_tR_2})^2$. Similarly, two successive one-year loans would have given him $(1 + {_tR_1})(1 + {_{t+1}r_1})$. Since in equilibrium the two must be equal we must have

$$(1 + {_tR_2}) = \sqrt{(1 + {_tR_1})(1 + {_{t+1}r_1})} \ . \qquad (2\text{-}2)$$

In general, the relationship between long and short rates becomes

$$(1 + {_tR_N}) = [(1 + {_tR_1})(1 + {_{t+1}r_1}) \cdots (1 + {_{t+N-1}r_1})]^{1/N} \qquad (2\text{-}3)$$

or

$$(1 + {_tR_N}) = [(1 + {_tR_{N-1}})^{N-1}(1 + {_{t+N-1}r_1})]^{1/N}. \qquad (2\text{-}3a)$$

In this way, the system of market rates for various maturities can be reduced to a function of the current short rate and a series of relevant forward short rates.[9]

In all this analysis relative supplies of securities of different maturities have not been mentioned. The previous argument shows that, in the model of the expectations theory, changes in the maturity composition of the total outstanding debt are irrelevant for the determination of the rate structure. Unless they alter expectations, changes in relative supplies can have no long-run effect on the term structure, which is determined fully by expectations of future short-term interest rates in the manner shown by equation (2-3).

It is possible in this model to account for every sort of rate structure. If future short-term rates are expected to fall, then the long-term average of those rates must lie below the current short rate. Similarly, long rates will exceed the current short rate if future short rates are expected to rise. For example, if the yield curve is monotonically increasing, then

$$_tR_k > {_tR_{k-1}}, \qquad k = 2, 3, \ldots, N \ . \qquad (2\text{-}4)$$

For this to hold, it is sufficient but not necessary for all successive forward (one-year) rates to rise monotonically. All that is required

<hr/>

[9] Hicks assumes that all funds are retained in the investment until maturity, that is, that the coupon carried by the bond is zero. In the appendix to this chapter we shall examine the implications of the more realistic case where periodic coupon payments are made to the investor, and suggest the nature of difference involved.

is for each successive expected one-year rate to be greater than the previous year's long rate; that is, we require[10]

$$_{t+k-1}r_1 > {}_tR_{k-1} \; . \qquad (2\text{-}5)$$

By suitably restraining expected future rates, the theory is able to explain any pattern of rates whatsoever.

It is of course possible to look at the relationship between spot and forward rates the other way around. Rather than view the determination of actual market interest rates as being compounded out of present and expected forward short rates, we can look at the actual market rates at any point in time and ask what forward rates are implied by the term structure. The forward rate Φ for one-year loans during the period $t + 1$ that is implicit in the term structure may be expressed as

$$_{t+1}\Phi_1 = \frac{(1 + {}_tR_2)^2}{(1 + {}_tR_1)} - 1 \; . \qquad (2\text{-}6)$$

Thus, for example, if the actual one-year rate today is 4 per cent and the actual two-year rate is $4\frac{1}{2}$ per cent, we can calculate the forward rate on one-year loans to commence next year as approximately equal to 5 per cent. More generally, the implicit forward rates for one-year securities for any future period can be derived from

$$_{t+N-1}\Phi_1 = \frac{(1 + {}_tR_N)^N}{(1 + {}_tR_{N-1})^{N-1}} - 1 \; . \qquad (2\text{-}7)$$

This relationship is not a statement of economic behavior; it is, as Meiselman has pointed out, only a tautology.[11]

The pure expectations theory, however, does provide us with a proposition concerning forward rates that *is* an assertion about economic behavior. It maintains that the forward rates which can be derived from the term structure are *unbiased* estimates of expected rates; that is

$$_{t+N-1}\Phi_1 = {}_{t+N-1}r_1 \; . \qquad (2\text{-}8)$$

[10] PROOF: Rewriting (2-4) we have by hypothesis

$$1 + {}_tR_k > 1 + {}_tR_{k-1} \; .$$

Using (2-3a) we can rewrite the left-hand side of the inequality and obtain

$$[(1 + {}_tR_{k-1})^{k-1}(1 + {}_{t+k-1}r_1)]^{1/k} > 1 + {}_tR_{k-1} \; .$$

Therefore,

$$1 + {}_{t+k-1}r_1 > (1 + {}_tR_{k-1})^k / (1 + {}_tR_{k-1})^{k-1} = 1 + {}_tR_{k-1} \; ,$$

which is equivalent to (2-5).

[11] Meiselman, *op. cit.*, p. 4.

The arbitraging mechanism described above ensures that forward rates and expected rates are driven to equality.

2.2 *Criticisms of the Expectations Theory*

The short-rate expectations theory has been under vigorous attack. Many critics have questioned the theory's basic behavioral postulate, that is, that investors do in fact decide what bond maturity to invest in on the basis of their expectations of future short rates.[12]

Consider, for example, the case of a potential bond purchaser who desires to keep his funds invested for five years. The expectations theory postulates that he compares the expected yields of alternative asset holdings (or combinations of asset holdings) over the five-year holding period. Suppose someone considers investing seriatim in five one-year bonds. Calculation of the five-year-holding-period yield requires, of course, that the investor be able to estimate the successive one-year interest rates over the investment period. Or the investor might instead think about purchasing a six-year bond with the expectation of selling it at the end of five years. But in order to determine the selling price of the bond in five years he must estimate the one-year rate of interest for year six. The *reductio ad absurdum* of the argument has been offered in a well-known quip by Mrs. Robinson: If the investor happens to buy consols then he must "think that he knows exactly what the rates of interest will be every day from today until Kingdom Come."[13]

Critics of the traditional expectations approach, especially those close to the bond market, argue that investors are simply not capable of predicting interest rates for periods far into the future. More important, as Luckett points out, it is doubtful whether any bond investors believe they are capable of doing so. Thus, these critics would argue that it is inadmissable to invoke Machlup's famous automobile-driver parable to suggest that investors *act as if* they could estimate future short rates even if they do not actually think in these terms.[14] While there is nothing illicit in defining the

---

[12] See, for example, J. B. Williams, *op. cit.*, pp. 251–252; and Dudley G. Luckett, "Professor Lutz and the Structure of Interest Rates," *Quarterly Journal of Economics* 73 (Feburary 1959), pp. 140–141.

[13] Joan Robinson, "The Rate of Interest," *Econometrica* 19 (April 1951), p. 102n. Actually Mrs. Robinson's criticism is a bit unfair. As we shall show in the next chapter, it is perfectly plausible that investors make judgments about possible future prices of consols without estimating future short rates *ad infinitum*.

[14] Fritz Machlup, "Marginal Analysis and Empirical Research," *American Economic Review* 36 (September 1946), p. 534; reprinted in Richard Clemence, *Readings in*

elements influencing the decision-maker in terms he may never use himself, the short-rate expectational theory may be inappropriate even as an abstract formulation. Culbertson has concluded that the theory ". . . scarcely merits a second glance as it is obviously inconsistent with all we know about the way people do behave in debt markets . . . ."[15]

Luckett has also argued that the Lutz formulation of the expectations theory is internally inconsistent.[16] Lutz portrayed the investor as making a choice between holding a bond to maturity and investing seriatim in a succession of short-term securities at the forward short rates he expects will prevail. But Lutz then went on to say that the investor "may quite reasonably form an opinion about the future long rate which is inconsistent with his opinion about future short rates . . . [since the former] depends, not on what he thinks about future short rates, but what the 'market,' i.e., other people, think about them."[17] But then current long-term rates may not be determined by, nor even be consistent with, investors, expectations of forward short-term rates. Rather they will be determined by investors' collective judgments about future long-term rates. Consequently, Luckett concludes there is no logical basis to support the Lutzian behavioral mechanism that investors decide between short- and long-term securities on the basis of their forecasts of future short-term yields.[18]

2.2.a THE HICKSIAN LIQUIDITY-PREMIUM MODEL

Another line of criticism is directed at the naive extension of the perfect-certainty variant of the expectations theory to a world of uncertainty. Building on the Keynesian theory of "normal backwardation" in the futures market, Hicks was the first to argue that the pure expectations model required qualification. He suggested that even if short rates are expected to remain unchanged, the forward short rate can normally be expected to exceed the current

---

Economic Analysis, II (Cambridge: Addison-Wesley, 1950), p. 139; and Fritz Machlup, *Essays on Economic Semantics* (Englewood Cliffs: Prentice-Hall, 1963), p. 167.

[15] John M. Culbertson, "Discussion: Econometric Studies in Money Markets II," a paper delivered at the annual meeting of the Econometric Society, Pittsburgh, December 1962.

[16] See Luckett, *op. cit.*, pp. 139–140.

[17] Lutz, *op. cit.*, p. 514.

[18] We should point out, however, that Luckett's criticism is not directed against an expectations theory *per se* but rather against certain formulations of it. As we shall see in the next chapter, it is possible to construct an expectations theory with far less demanding behavioral postulates.

short rate by a risk premium that must be offered the holder of a bond to compensate him for assuming the risks of price fluctuation.[19]

There are really three components of the Hicksian argument. First, there is the assertion that many borrowers need funds over extensive future periods. These borrowers will have a "strong propensity" to borrow long to ensure a steady availability of funds. Secondly, on the lending side of the market Hicks assumed there was an opposite propensity. If there were no premium for long loans, most individuals and institutions would prefer to lend short to minimize the variance in the money value of their portfolios.[20] This leaves an imbalance or "constitutional weakness" in the pattern of supply and demand of loanable funds, one which speculators can be expected to offset. Hence, the final step in the Hicksian argument is the assertion that speculators likewise are averse to risk and must be paid a liquidity premium to induce them to purchase long-term securities. According to this analysis, in equilibrium implicit or forward rates will exceed expected rates. Thus, the "normal relationship" is for long rates (which are averages of current and forward short rates) to exceed short rates. Only if the short rate is considered abnormally high can long rates fall below short rates.[21]

The Hicksian liquidity premium is typically expressed as the amount by which a forward rate implied by the term structure is

[19] See J. M. Keynes, *A Treatise on Money* (New York: Harcourt, Brace, 1930), II, pp. 142–144; and Hicks, *op. cit.*, pp. 138–139, 144–147.

[20] Once uncertainty is introduced, unanticipated changes in one forward rate are typically accompanied by changes in a whole series of forward rates in the same direction. Thus, the variance of the money value of a portfolio will increase with the maturity of the securities included. Assuming that it is the variance of the money value of the bond portfolio that is the relevant measure of risk in investors' utility functions, then more recent models of portfolio selection may be used to help justify this assertion of Hicks. See, for example, James Tobin, "Liquidity Preference as Behavior Toward Risk," *Review of Economic Studies* 25 (February 1958), pp. 65–86; and Harry Markowitz, *Portfolio Selection: Efficient Diversification of Investments* (New York: Wiley, 1959).

[21] Hicks, *op. cit.*, p. 147. Others to concur with the Hicksian view include Daniel Marx, Jr., "The Structure of Interest Rates: Comment," *Quarterly Journal of Economics* 56 (November 1941), pp. 152–156; David W. Lusher, "The Structure of Interest Rates and the Keynesian Theory of Interest," *Journal of Political Economy* 50 (April 1942), p. 274; Abba P. Lerner, *The Economics of Control* (New York: MacMillan & Co., 1944), p. 343; G. L. S. Shackle, *Uncertainty in Economics* (Cambridge: Cambridge University Press, 1955), p. 121; D. H. Robertson, "Mr. Keynes and the Rate of Interest," *Essays in Monetary Theory* (London: P. S. King and Son, 1940), pp. 1–38; reprinted in A.E.A. (ed.) *Readings in the Theory of Income Distribution* (Philadelphia: The Blakiston Co., 1951), pp. 425–460; and, most recently, Reuben Kessel, *The Cyclical Behavior of the Term Structure of Interest Rates*, Occasional Paper 91 (New York: National Bureau of Economic Research, December 1965).

higher than the corresponding expected rate. The relationship between long and current and expected short rates becomes

$$(1 + {}_tR_N) = [(1 + {}_tR_1)(1 + {}_{t+1}r_1 + L_2)$$
$$\cdots (1 + {}_{t+N-1}r_1 + L_N)]^{1/N} , \quad (2\text{-}9)$$

where $L_2, L_3, \ldots, L_N$ are the Hicksian liquidity premiums for periods $2, 3, \ldots, N$. The forward short-term rates implicit in the term structure will be upward-biased or high estimators of expected future short rates. Forward rates in general may be expressed as

$$_{t+N-1}\Phi_1 = {}_{t+N-1}r_1 + L_N . \quad (2\text{-}10)$$

The theory of normal backwardation implies that when the present short rate is expected to remain unchanged in the future, the yield curve will be ascending (not flat). A sufficient but not a necessary condition for this to hold is that

$$0 < L_2 < L_3 < \cdots < L_N . \quad (2\text{-}11)$$

2.2.b THE HEDGING-PRESSURE (OR INSTITUTIONAL) HYPOTHESIS

Another group of critics of the expectations theory also sees the market as dominated by risk averters. But they point out that risk aversion will not necessarily produce normal backwardation. Attempts to hedge against risk may lead different investing institutions (with differing structures of claims against them) to place their funds in separate maturity ranges. As long as there are institutions that prefer to hold long-term assets and that require a "premium" to induce them to buy short-term issues, the net effect of lenders' risk aversion on the yield curve will be a purely empirical question.

Institutionalists have no trouble producing examples of financial intermediaries who are almost exclusively long-term investors. Life insurance companies, for example, write annuity contracts on the assumption that they will be able to earn a particular rate of return over the expected life of the contract. The payments that they offer to the annuitant, in essence, guarantee a specified earning rate over a long period. Therefore, the risk-averting insurance company will base its contracts on currently available yields to maturity in the long market, investing the proceeds from the sale of such contracts in the long market immediately. This will guarantee it a profit regardless of what happens to interest rates over the life of the contract.

Similarly, many pension funds find themselves in a wholly analogous situation. *Ceteris paribus*, these funds do *not* prefer investment in short-term securities, as the Hicksian model would assert. While investment in short-term issues ensures that the principal of the fund will be kept intact, such investments leave uncertain the fund's future income. Since such investors are more concerned with guaranteeing themselves *certainty of income* over the long run, risk aversion on their part should lead to a preference for long-term rather than short-term securities. Indeed, so long as the holding period of the pension fund is expected to be longer than the maturity of the securities being considered for investment, the fund gains no additional *certainty of principal* by buying the shorter security rather than another bond of longer maturity. On the other hand, since by purchasing the shorter asset the fund would suffer additional uncertainty of income over the holding period, it might well require a negative liquidity premium to purchase the short-term issue. Premiums necessary to induce the purchase of short-term securities have been called "solidity premiums" by Martin Bailey.[22]

Of course, the institutionalists are quick to admit that the behavior of some investors may well accord with the Hicksian liquidity-premium model. Commercial banks, for example, are faced with a structure of liabilities of which an overwhelming proportion are payable upon demand or on short notice. It is assumed that these institutions prefer marketable securities that serve as a reserve to meet deposit drains or increased loan demand to consist only of very short maturities. In this way commercial banks protect themselves against the risks of future interest-rate fluctuations, that is, against the risks of realizing capital losses on securities sold to meet fund requirements. Institutionalists assume that the market is dominated by investors whose desire to hedge leads to strong preferences for either principal certainty or income certainty. In its extreme form, this hedging-pressure hypothesis asserts that, regardless of relative interest rates, investors will never shift between the short and long markets. According to this hypothesis, the yield structure is determined by (the pressure of) supply and demand within each of the segmented markets, since securities of different maturities constitute noncompeting groups.

J. M. Culbertson is usually characterized as the leading modern exponent of a hedging-pressure explanation of the term structure.

---

[22] Martin J. Bailey, "Discussion," *American Economic Review, Papers and Proceedings* 54 (May 1964), p. 554.

Culbertson's argument stresses the impediments to mobility among maturity areas for the various participants on both sides of the market. But Culbertson's assault is not confined to the simplifying assumptions of the expectations theory; it is directed at its entire structure. He concludes that changes in the maturity structure of the supply of debt instruments, combined with changes in the flow of funds to various investing institutions, determine the term structure.[23] He views the expectations theory as nothing more than an academic curiosum of little relevance to the real world. Expectations, though perhaps relevant in affecting "the timing of rate adjustments," are an insignificant element in the determination of the rate structure.[24]

2.3   Early Empirical Attacks on the Expectations Hypothesis

Early empirical investigators of the expectations hypothesis approached the problem from a similar viewpoint. Their assumption was that if expectations did determine the rate structure, one ought to observe a correspondence between the forward short-term rates implied by the yield curve at a given moment of time and the short-term rates which later were actually observed. These investigators looked for evidence of accurate forecasts to support the expectations theory. The typical hypothesis tested may be written as

$$_{t+1}\Phi_{1,t} = {_{t+1}R_{1,t+1}} , \qquad (2\text{-}12)$$

where we now add second right-hand subscripts to indicate that the expected one-period rate is implied by the term structure during period t and the actual one-period rate is to be observed in the next period, $t + 1$.

Hickman, for example, compared actual short rates with those implied by the term structure during the period 1935–1942 and concluded that no correspondence could be found.[25] An inertia hypothesis $(_tR_{1,t} = {_{t+1}R_{1,t+1}})$ gave better predictions than the expectations theory. Indeed, Hickman found that the implicit prediction of the *direction* of movement of the one-year rate was accurate less

[23] In contrast, the reader will recall that the expectations model implies that relative supplies of debt instruments are irrelevant. See J. M. Culbertson, "The Term Structure of Interest Rates," *The Quarterly Journal of Economics* 71 (November 1957), pp. 485–517.

[24] J. M. Culbertson, "The Use of Monetary Policy," *The Southern Economic Journal* 22 (October 1961), pp. 130–137.

[25] William Braddock Hickman, "The Term Structure of Interest Rates: an Exploratory Analysis," (New York: National Bureau of Economic Research, 1943; mimeographed).

than half of the time. Similarly, Macaulay examined "call" and "time" money rates in the period before the existence of the Federal Reserve System in an attempt to find evidence of accurate forecasting. Unlike Hickman, he did find that investors were able partly to anticipate the pronounced seasonal pattern in call-money rates.[26] Macaulay found that 90-day rates usually moved up prior to the seasonal rise in call rates, as would be expected by the expectations theory. However, he found that they did not rise enough and that, apart from these seasonal influences, he could find no evidence of successful forecasting.

Culbertson performed a similar test.[27] We noted earlier that a basic result of the expectations theory was that, for a holding period of any given length, the holding-period yield should be the same regardless of the term of the security purchased. Thus, as a variant of equation (2-12) Culbertson calculated one-week and three-month holding-period yields for long-term Treasury bonds and short bills. He found that the realized holding-period yields for bonds and bills were not equal. He concluded that speculators could not be operating in the government-securities market and be predicting as badly as his results indicated. Consequently, he interpreted his findings as contradicting the expectations theory.[28]

How should one appraise the results of these tests? Two antithetical positions have been taken in the literature. Meiselman has argued that these tests examined propositions not implied by the expectations theory and hence that the theory was rejected on inappropriate grounds.[29] The expectations theory deals with *ex ante* interest rates, whereas the empirical tests have all been applied to *ex post* data. Anticipated and realized yields will not be equal except in a world of perfect certainty. Expectations need not be correct, yet they may still determine the shape of the yield curve in the manner asserted by the theory.

[26] Frederick R. Macaulay, *The Movements of Interest Rates, Bond Yields, and Stock Prices in the United States Since 1856* (New York: National Bureau of Economic Research, 1938), pp. 33–36.

[27] Culbertson, "The Term Structure of Interest Rates," *op. cit.*, p. 502.

[28] An additional test of this type was performed by Charls E. Walker, "Federal Reserve Policy and the Structure of Interest Rates on Government Securities," *Quarterly Journal of Economics* 68 (February 1954), p. 19. Walker found that during the period of market pegging, expectations-induced shifts from short to long securities were consistent with the theory. Nevertheless, at the same time, since the pegging of longs reduced the probability of capital loss on these issues, the shift to longs was also consistent with the Hicksian liquidity-premium hypothesis.

[29] Meiselman, *op. cit.*, pp. 10 and 12.

29

Other writers have been more sympathetic to the approach of the first empirical tests. They agree that these tests do not necessarily imply that the expectations theory is not an accurate description of investor behavior. But, then, they must imply that investors have done an unbelievably bad job of predicting future rates. One wonders, in view of this record, whether professionals would continue to attempt such forecasts. Conard summarized his position on this question as follows: "I, for one, would accept the view that it is unreasonable to presume the market is so consistently and grossly wrong in its expectations that poor foresight could wholly explain these observations."[30]

2.4 *Meiselman's Test Supporting the Expectations Hypothesis*

Meiselman was the first to provide an operational test of the expectations hypothesis which did not depend for its validity on accurate forecasting. The lack of independent evidence concerning expectations of future interest rates has been the chief obstacle to effective empirical testing of the expectations hypothesis. Meiselman's contribution was the construction of an error-learning model that describes how expectations might change over time to take account of new information. His test shows that ". . . *changes* in, rather than *levels* of interest rates can be related to factors which systematically cause revisions of expectations . . . ."[31] The task is made easier because, according to the theory tested, expectations of future short rates are already implicit in the term structure. The essence of Meiselman's test is to observe how these implied short rates change over time with the receipt of new information.

Meiselman's conceptual framework is easily grasped by continuing with the simple numerical example we presented in Section 2.1. Assume actual market rates today are

$$R_{1,t} = 2 \text{ per cent },$$
$$R_{2,t} = 3 \text{ per cent },\qquad (2\text{-}13)$$
$$R_{3,t} = 4 \text{ per cent }.$$

We know by (2-7) that these rates imply a unique set of forward short-term rates as follows:[32]

$$_{t+1}r_{1,t} = 4 \text{ per cent },$$
$$_{t+2}r_{1,t} = 6 \text{ per cent }.\qquad (2\text{-}13a)$$

---

[30] Conard, *op. cit.*, p. 339.

[31] Meiselman, *op. cit.*, p. 18.

[32] Again, for the sake of illustration, we use arithmetic rather than geometric averaging.

Now let us allow one year to pass and assume that next year's (actual) one-year rate $(_{t+1}R_{1,t+1})$ turns out to be 3 per cent (100 basis points lower than had been anticipated). An error-learning approach would suggest that investors respond to their error by lowering their forecasts of still unrealized forward rates. Thus, the market will systematically revise expectations of future short-term rates downward in response to the error made in forecasting the present one-year rate. Specifically, Meiselman's hypothesis is that $_{t+2}r_{1,t}$ will be greater than $_{t+2}r_{1,t+1}$; that is, the one-year rate predicted for period $t + 2$, which was 6 per cent at time t, will be revised downward at period $t + 1$. Similarly, if actual rates turn out to be higher than had been anticipated, the market will systematically revise upward expectations concerning short-term rates in the future. Since, under the expectations theory, longer rates are averages of present and forward short rates, forecasting errors cause the whole structure of rates to rise or fall.

The error-learning hypothesis applied to the rate structure (that is, forward short-term rates change on the basis of errors made in forecasting the current short-term rates) may be written as follows:

$$_{t+N}r_{1,t} - {}_{t+N}r_{1,t-1} = f(_{t}R_{1,t} - {}_{t}r_{1,t-1}) , \qquad (2\text{-}14)$$

or

$$\Delta_{t+N}r_{1,t} = g(E_t) ,$$

where E_t is the forecasting error, the difference between the actual one-year rate and the one-year rate that had been expected to prevail. Assuming the functional relationship to be at least approximately linear, Meiselman estimated the equation

$$\Delta_{t+N}r_{1,t} = a + bE_t + u_t , \qquad (2\text{-}14a)$$

employing the annual Durand data from 1901–1954. He found that changes in forward one-year rates were highly correlated with the forecasting error (Table 2-1).

Meiselman's tests show that a significant part of the *movements* of forward rates can be explained by errors in prediction of the current one-year rate. However, the correlation coefficients tend to vary inversely with the maturity of the dependent variable, that is, with the time period in the future for which forward (one-year) rates are being forecast. This can be taken to indicate that, while investors may try to make and adjust specific forecasts for rates in the immediate future, they are unlikely to attempt seriously to forecast short rates eight years hence. This interpretation would also explain why the *b* coefficient declines with maturity. Since near-term forecasts are taken more seriously than long-term predictions, the former are likely to be revised to a greater degree than the latter when expectations prove incorrect. A constant term equal to zero in equation (2-14a) is necessary for Meiselman to be able to identify forward rates with forecasts as the expectations theory implies (see equation 2-8). Were the constant term not equal to zero, then forward rates would be revised even when expectations prove correct. Meiselman also argued that a zero constant term was inconsistent with the

TABLE 2-1
MEISELMAN'S TEST OF THE ERROR-LEARNING MODEL
(REGRESSION RESULTS: EQUATION (2-14a)

N (in years)	Constant term *a* (and its standard error)	Regression coefficient *b*	Correlation coefficient
1	0.00 (0.02)	0.703	0.952
2	0.00 (0.03)	0.526	0.867
3	−0.01 (0.04)	0.403	0.768
4	−0.03 (0.04)	0.326	0.682
5	−0.02 (0.04)	0.277	0.642
6	−0.01 (0.03)	0.233	0.625
7	−0.02 (0.03)	0.239	0.631
8	0.01 (0.03)	0.208	0.590

Hicksian liquidity-premium model. He thus concluded that his tests provided impressive support for the pure expectations hypothesis after it is buttressed by the error-correction mechanism.

Meiselman deserves great credit for devising and executing an ingeniously simple empirical test of the expectations hypothesis which is not based on the assumption of accurate forecasting. The publication of his results came at a time when the expectational explanation of the term structure had come under increasingly severe attack. While not entirely appealing to intuition, his work did serve as an offset to the suspicion to which the expectations hypothesis had been subjected and served as the necessary catalyst to stimulate other much-needed empirical studies of the term structure. However, several shortcomings in Meiselman's work have come to light. It has been shown by both Kessel and Wood that Meiselman was wrong in asserting that his zero constant term contradicted the Hicksian liquidity-premium assumption.[33] This can easily be seen by substituting equation (2-10), the Hicksian expression for implied rates, in place of the relevant terms in Meiselman's test equation (2-14):

$$[_{t+N}r_{1,t} + L_{N+1}] - [_{t+N}r_{1,t-1} + L_{N+2}]$$
$$= a + b[R_{1,t} - (_t r_{1,t-1} + L_2)] . \quad (2\text{-}15)$$

Rearranging terms, we have

$$[_{t+N}r_{1,t} - {}_{t+N}r_{1,t-1}] + [L_{N+1} - L_{N+2}]$$
$$= a + b[R_{1,t} - {}_t r_{1,t-1}] - bL_2 . \quad (2\text{-}15a)$$

Meiselman asserts that if expectations are realized, that is, if the bracketed term on the right-hand side of (2-15a) is zero, then forward rates will not be revised; that is, the first bracketed term on the left-hand side of (2-15a) should equal zero. Let us assume that expectations are realized and ask if a zero constant term is then inconsistent with the Hicksian liquidity-premium argument. The answer is easily obtained by looking at the remaining terms of (2-15a):

$$L_{N+1} - L_{N+2} = a - bL_2 . \quad (2\text{-}16)$$

We know from (2-11) that if $a = 0$ both the right-hand and left-hand sides of (2-16) are negative. Thus even if the constant term is equal to zero, we are not forced into any contradiction by the liquidity-premium assumption.[34] We may conclude that Meisel-

---

[33] See Kessel, *op. cit.*, pp. 37 ff. and John H. Wood, "Expectations, Errors, and the Term Structure of Interest Rates," *The Journal of Political Economy* 71 (April 1963), p. 166.

[34] Indeed, the existence of Hicksian liquidity premiums may actually account in part for Meiselman's regression results. Suppose that the term structure is as described in (2-13) during two consecutive periods. This means that the implicit rates of (2-13a) are applicable to both periods. Under the Meiselman hypothesis, investors over-estimated the one-year rate for period two (4 per cent > 2 per cent) and, therefore, will revise downward their estimate of the one-year rate for period three, which indeed they appear to do (6 per cent, the original estimate for period 3, is revised to 4 per cent). Thus, if, for example, the yield curve were normally positively sloped, period after period, this could often produce precisely the movements in implicit rates which Meiselman claims follow from the error-learning model. We use the word "often" since it is, of course, possible to have a positively sloped yield curve even when not all forward rates increase with maturity [see (2-5)].

Similarly, it can be shown, as long as the yield curve retains roughly the same slope (positive or negative) from period to period, that synchronous movements in all rates will, in most cases, not alter this relationship. Thus, movements in implicit rates will tend to be positively correlated with the forecasting error, as Meiselman finds, irrespective of the validity of the postulated error-learning model.

man's estimates do not discriminate between the pure and liquidity-premium versions of the expectations hypothesis.

Other critics have suggested that certain characteristics of the Durand data call the tests seriously into question. Our discussion in Chapter 1 pointed out some of the shortcomings of the Durand basic-yield curves. We called attention to the poor delineation of the yield curve in the important early maturities and to the reasons why particularly the short-term yield estimates were subject to error. In addition, the method of fitting and smoothing the yield curve was emphasized. We should recall that Durand's yield curves were confined to three basic shapes and that each type of yield curve tended to be repeated from period to period. Only two positively sloped yield curves were fitted from 1900 through 1930. No negatively sloped curves arose in the Durand data from 1931 through 1954. We mentioned above (in note 34) how this characteristic of the Durand data would tend to improve Meiselman's regression results. It would therefore be interesting to test Meiselman's hypothesis on differently constructed yield curves to see if the results could be duplicated.

J. A. G. Grant has performed such a test on yield curves for British government securities. His yield curves were fitted essentially by connecting all the separate dots representing the yield figures for the 6 to 14 bonds actually used.[35] His yield curves thus give the appearance of a jagged line frequently punctuated by noticeable humps. As might be expected, implicit rates are not nearly so well behaved as in the smoothed curves. Grant finds that Meiselman's hypothesis cannot be relied upon as an efficient explanation of the term structure. Correlation coefficients tended to be low, and the sign of the forecasting error in individual years was not well synchronized with that of the change in implicit rates. Moreover, Grant's constant terms [the a in (2-14a)] were often positive and significantly different from zero. Positive constant terms are not consistent with the identification of implicit rates as expected rates.[36]

[35] J. A. G. Grant, "Meiselman on the Structure of Interest Rates: A British Test," *Economica* 31 (February 1964), p. 69.

[36] Grant's data are themselves subject to question, however. For example, he neglected to convert bill yields from a discount to a true yield-to-maturity basis, and he ignored all coupon differences except particularly large ones. The considerable effect of coupon differences on his resulting yield curves has been shown by Douglas Fisher, in "The Structure of Interest Rates: A Comment," *Economica* 31 (November 1964), pp. 412–419. It may well be that several of Grant's humps are themselves spurious. Nevertheless, it remains true that the method of construction of the Durand curves

Meiselman's test has also been performed on yield curves for U.S. Treasury securities. These yield curves were smoothed but differently constructed from the Durand basic yields. There are considerable differences in the curves, especially in the important early maturities where the Treasury curves typically have a pronounced positive slope. James Van Horne found that the data from U.S. Treasury yield curves imply positive constant terms.[37] Applying the error-learning model to monthly data on Treasury yields for the 1954–1963 period, Van Horne found that the estimated constant terms were consistently positive and significantly different from zero. A similar finding has been reported by Neil Wallace.[38] Both these results and Grant's are inconsistent with Meiselman's interpretation of forward rates as forecasts. A zero constant term, while not sufficient, is a necessary condition for Meiselman's hypothesis to hold.

2.5 Kessel's Empirical Findings Supporting the Hicksian Liquidity-Premium Model

We have noted in Section 2.3 above that early empirical investigators, such as Culbertson, rejected the expectations hypothesis because synchronous holding-period yields for securities of different maturities were not always equal. Meiselman correctly pointed out that expectations need not be realized in order for them to determine the rate structure in the manner asserted by the theory. Anticipated and realized yields will be equal only in a world of perfect certainty. Michaelson calculated the *average* holding-period yields for bills and bonds respectively over the (very short) period from which Culbertson's data were taken and concludes that the results do not contradict the expectations hypothesis.[39] Average differences between the realized short-term holding-period yields of bills and bonds did tend toward zero during the brief period for which the test was conducted. Thus, Michaelson

---

was particularly favorable to Meiselman's hypothesis. It can be shown that, by making differences between maturity sufficiently regular, one increases the likelihood that implicit rates will be well behaved.

[37] James Van Horne, "Interest Rate Risk and the Term Structure of Interest Rates," *Journal of Political Economy* 73 (June 1965), pp. 344–351.

[38] Neil Wallace, *The Term Structure of Interest Rates and the Maturity Composition of the Federal Debt*, unpublished Ph.D. dissertation submitted to the University of Chicago, December, 1964, pp. 24–27.

[39] Jacob B. Michaelson, "The Term Structure of Interest Rates: Comment," *Quarterly Journal of Economics* 77 (February 1963), pp. 166–174.

suggested that the realized holding-period yields could be considered to be composed of the sum of a single anticipated yield common to all securities and a random disturbance specific to each.

Kessel's study of the term structure, for the National Bureau of Economic Research, took the same approach. Kessel agrees that the existence of forecasting errors in no way invalidates the expectational explanation of the rate structure. Nevertheless, he holds that the distribution of forecasting errors ought to be symmetrical and that their mean should be zero over a long period of time. Kessel argues that the absence of symmetry ought to be a test of whether or not forward rates are expected rates. On the other hand, if liquidity premiums are present, the forward rates implicit in the term structure will exceed realized rates. Hence, Kessel argues that one can test the liquidity-premium model by looking at the magnitude and sign of Meiselman's error terms. Specifically, he posits that the frequency of negative error terms (the case where implicit rates are higher than the actual ones) should be significantly higher than the frequency of positive error terms and that their mean be negative. Utilizing the Wilcoxon two-sample and signed-rank tests, he confirms this hypothesis.[40]

Similar findings are reported for yield curves on government securities. Forward rates have systematically overstated realized rates, and the error terms are more negative the longer the maturity of the rate being predicted, at least within the range of very short maturities. The average error in predicting forward 14-day rates was 20 basis points while the average error in predicting forward 91-day rates was 70 basis points.[41] This finding is consistent with the formulation of the liquidity-premium model in equations (2-9) through (2-11).[42] The pure expectations hypothesis cannot provide an explanation of these data unless we think that investors continue to believe that interest rates will rise even though such forecasts lead to systematic errors.

[40] Kessel, *op. cit.*, p. 19. Significance levels of 6 and 2 per cent were produced using one tail of the normal distribution.

[41] Bills with precisely 182 and 91 days to maturity were used to compute the implicit 91-day rate, 91 days in advance. Bills with 28 and 14 days to maturity were used to compute the forward 14-day rate. See Kessel, *op. cit.*, p. 24. The time period under consideration was from January 1959 to March 1962. This period was chosen because Treasury bill rates were at the same level during the beginning and ending months.

[42] Kessel also finds (*ibid.*, p. 61) that, during the postwar period, 9- to 12-month government securities were more volatile over the cycle than 3-month bills, a finding that is also inconsistent with the expectations hypothesis except under the most bizarre assumptions concerning forecasting errors.

Kessel also reminds us that short-term rates have averaged considerably less than long rates over long periods of our history. Though this is not directly inconsistent with the pure expectations hypothesis, it does reduce its plausibility. Assuming that, over some reasonably long time period, investors would expect interest rates to rise about as often as they would expect them to fall, the pure expectations hypothesis would lead us to expect average yields on securities of different terms to maturity to be equal. We have already noted (Figure 1-4) that the average shape of the (Durand) yield curve over the past 66 years has been positively sloped even if we exclude the decade of pegged rates. Kessel reports that the yields on short-term government securities have averaged less than long-term yields over the past nine complete reference cycles, a period encompassing roughly 40 years.[43]

Meiselman commented on Kessel's work as follows: ". . . many of Kessel's substantive conclusions are based on a confusion between *ex ante* and *ex post*. It does not follow that the difference between forward and realized rates need be symmetrical about the correct forecasts for any given number of observations. The average yield curve within each cycle need not be flat . . . [but] would reflect secular expectations beyond the cycle in question and these can be for declining rates (1917–1920), or rising rates (more recent years)."[44]

Of course, it is true that in an uncertain world no one should expect anticipations to be verified precisely by subsequent events. But, if we can find investors consistently overestimating future short-term rates and not learning from their experience, then we must either reject the view that the market will continue to waste its scarce resources in fruitless attempts to predict future short rates as the model requires it to do, or we must admit that non-expectational elements play a significant role in determining the rate structure. When Kessel finds that over a period as long as 40 years implied rates have consistently been higher than actual rates, it is difficult to give much credence to the view that during this entire period speculators held expectations of secularly rising rates.

While the statistical evidence overwhelmingly supports the

[43] *Ibid.*, p. 71.

[44] David Meiselman, "Discussion: Econometric Studies in Money Markets II," a paper delivered at the annual meeting of the Econometric Society, Pittsburgh, December 1962.

proposition that short-term yields have typically been lower than those for long-term securities, it is much less clear that Kessel has found the single missing link needed to reconstruct the expectations hypothesis into a complete explanation of the term structure. We have seen earlier that risk aversion does not necessarily produce a positively sloped yield curve. For investors with long holding periods, risk aversion implies a *ceteris paribus* preference for long-term issues. Moreover, Kessel's "liquidity premia" are not constant—they vary over the interest-rate cycle. A more complete description of the determination of these "premia" is required, and independent evidence must be marshalled to explain the cause of their cyclical variability. Kessel's useful work clearly indicates that the expectations theory cannot fully account for empirical term structures. His case is less convincing that liquidity preference is sufficient to complete the explanation.

2.6 Conclusion: The Current State of Term-Structure Theory

As the reader can clearly see from this brief survey of the literature, rate-structure theory today is by no means settled. The traditional expectations analysis of the term structure has come under increasingly severe attack. Critics have disputed the basic behavioral assumptions of the analysis in an effort to undermine the very foundations of the theory. In the process, a very appealing and elegant model was put under suspicion.

David Meiselman's work constituted a clever defense of the expectations explanation of the rate structure. He accepted the criticism that some investors, because of risk aversion or other impediments to mobility, may be rigidly committed to certain maturity areas. Still, he argued that market excess-demand schedules for securities of each maturity tend to be infinitely elastic at rates consistent with expectations of future short rates, as the expectations analysis requires. He based his view on the belief that there is considerable overlapping in the maturities in which different transactors specialize, as well as a significant number of adequately financed speculators who are willing to switch freely from maturity to maturity on the basis of their mathematical expectation alone. As a result, the term structure of rates is forced into a pattern consistent with the expectations of the more mobile investors, and interest rates behave exactly as they would if all investors were prepared to switch freely from maturity to maturity. Meiselman concluded from his empirical tests that "as a matter of descriptive reality . . . speculators who are indifferent to uncertainty will bulk sufficiently large to determine market rates on the basis of their mathematical expectations alone."[45]

Several difficulties that beset Meiselman's work have subsequently been pointed out. Meiselman's view that his results are inconsistent with the liquidity-premium version of the expectations model is invalid. The results of his empirical test of the expectations hypothesis have shown it to be highly sensitive to the nature of the data he employed. Kessel's work, indicating that short-term yields have on the average been significantly below long-term yields, suggests at the very least that elements other than pure expectations must play an important role in a complete explanation of the facts. Kessel himself concluded that expectations and liquidity preference together shed more light on the behavior of the yield curve than does either hypothesis alone.

At the other end of the spectrum, Culbertson has remained intransigent and unconvinced. Culbertson rejects the expectations approach because it is not really an "explanatory" theory, especially because it is both implausible and inconsistent with the way we know people behave in debt markets. He chides his modern colleagues for looking for casual correlations instead of causes.

> They are willing to select a limited body of data of their own choosing, to apply tests of their own choosing, and if their hypothesis has 'explanatory power' in that it produces a good correlation, to proclaim that their theory is supported and should be accepted. The degrees of freedom for the investigator that are involved in this procedure, especially in connection with highly intercorrelated macro-economic data, clearly are such that one can find some support for any of a large number of theories. This, of course, permits one to choose the theory that he wants to believe, which brings us to the essential reason why my modern colleagues defend the expectational theory, because they prefer it. It fits in with the methodological bias of our times.[46]

Culbertson goes on to reconfirm his adherence to the view that the short and long markets are effectively separated.

Lest the reader conclude that such polarity of views characterizes all who have worked on these problems, we should mention several investigators who have come to what is an essentially eclectic position. Conard accepted the basic expectational position but

[45] Meiselman, *The Term Structure of Interest Rates*, p. 10.
[46] Culbertson, "Discussion . . ."

asserted that it must be modified to account for the effects of risk aversion and market segmentation. While he found no evidence that downward-sloping yield curves have been characteristic of times when the supply and demand for longs and shorts were "abnormal," he believed that changes in the relative supply of debt instruments may cause both temporary and permanent alterations in the shape of the curve. In particular, he conjectured that the positive slope of the curve in recent years may reflect, in part, the supply situation, and he pointed out that the "supply of shorts may be none too large in relation to the desire for them by institutions wishing to meet liquidity requirements."[47] Moreover, some empirical studies have found that both expectations and changes in the supply of private and government securities outstanding help to explain variation in the interest-rate spread between short-term and long-term rates.[48] Because these studies are directly relevant to a basic policy problem—the ability of the monetary authorities to influence deliberately the term structure by changes in supplies of the various maturities—and because the theoretical basis for these empirical tests will be developed in later chapters, it is best to defer a discussion of this work until Chapter 8.

This completes our brief review of the literature on the term structure. The reader will note, as this study progresses, that most of the ingredients necessary for a complete theory of the rate structure have already been presented. The new elements which will be added are perhaps not subversive of the old theory. Yet the modified and expanded theory that will be developed with their aid will be shown to differ significantly from the received one, both in its logic and its implications about reality.

APPENDIX TO CHAPTER 2

Yields to Maturity, Long Rates, and Implied Forward Rates[1]

We have noted in Section 2.1 that the traditional expectations theory conceives of (unity plus) the long rate as a geometric average of (unity plus) the current and expected future short-term rates of interest. In this appendix we shall investigate the relationship

---

[47] Conard, *op. cit.*, p. 333.

[48] See Wallace, *op. cit.*, and Robert Haney Scott, "Liquidity and the Term Structure of Interest Rates," *Quarterly Journal of Economics* 79 (February 1965), pp. 135–145.

[1] The following discussion relies heavily on the work of Neil Wallace, "The Term Structure of Interest Rates and the Maturity Composition of the Federal Debt," unpublished Ph.D. dissertation submitted to the University of Chicago, December 1964, Chapter 1.

between that concept of the long rate and the conventionally used yield to maturity of a bond. We shall see that the two concepts are identical only under very special circumstances. We shall also demonstrate a finding emphasized by Neil Wallace, that yields to maturity are not sufficient in themselves to derive the forward rates of interest actually embodied in the term structure.

2A.1   The Yield to Maturity of a Bond

Conventionally, the yield to maturity of a bond maturing in N years $(_tR_N^*)$ is calculated as the internal rate of return which makes the present values of all the coupons C to be received as interest and of the principal amount F to be repaid at maturity, equal to the market price of the bond P,

$$P = \frac{C}{(1 + _tR_N^*)} + \frac{C}{(1 + _tR_N^*)^2} + \cdots + \frac{C}{(1 + _tR_N^*)^N}$$
$$+ \frac{F}{(1 + _tR_N^*)^N} \cdot \quad \text{(2A-1)}$$

We thus speak of a bond whose principal amount will be repaid in N years as having N years to maturity. But note that, in effect, the purchaser of such a bond has made a one-year loan of C dollars, a two-year loan of C dollars, . . . , and an N-year loan of $C + F$ dollars. The conventional definition of maturity does not take into account that such a bond represents a composite of several different loans with dissimilar terms to maturity. But if the concept of maturity is not free of ambiguities, the concept of yield to maturity cannot be unambiguous either. This can easily be demonstrated by assuming that an investor buys a bond maturing in N years and reinvests all coupons immediately upon receipt. Assume further that the investor withdraws his coupons plus accumulated interest when the principal amount of the bond becomes due and payable in N years. Would the investor receive $_tR_N^*$ as an N-year-holding-period return? In general, the answer is no. It would be true only if the intermediate coupon receipts could be reinvested at the rate $_tR_N^*$. Indeed, this is the implicit assumption behind the calculation of an internal rate of return if any sense is to be made of the criterion as an appropriate means to rank investments.

The conventional calculation of an internal rate of return, in effect, assumes that all streams received in advance of the final maturity date of the longest project considered could be reinvested at the marginal efficiency rate. Otherwise, the internal rate of return would not unambiguously rank investment opportunities in order of their desirability. Consider, for example, two investments, A and B with final maturity dates 20 years from now and with identical internal rates of return of 5 per cent. Suppose that investment A makes no intermediate payments—all funds are retained in the investment until maturity. Investment B, on the other hand, provides a stream of periodic payments in advance of the final payment in 20 years. If the intermediate payment stream from B can be reinvested at a rate of return of 6 per cent, then an investor would, *ceteris paribus*, prefer B to A. If, on the other hand, the intermediate payments from B could be reinvested only at 4 per cent, the investor would prefer A, which compounds all earnings from his investment at a rate of 5 per cent.[2]

As this suggests, except under very special circumstances, the conventional internal-rate-of-return calculation is inconsistent with the assumptions of the traditional expectations theory. For a coupon-paying security, the two approaches coincide only when it happens that all forward rates are identically equal to the current short rate. Only the final coupon and principal payment have actually been accumulated as a result of N years compounding at the internal rate of return. In general, intermediate coupon receipts cannot be reinvested at $_tR_N^*$. For example, the coupon received in the penultimate year of the bond's life can be reinvested at a rate $_{t+N-1}r_1$. The true N-year holding period for an investor who reinvests his coupon receipts may, therefore, not be equal to $_tR_N^*$.

2A.2   *The True N-Year-Holding-Period Return*

Let us consider next a wealth holder who invests one dollar today in a bond which pays out no coupons, and keeps his money invested until the maturity of the bond in N years. In year N, his investment will be worth $\prod_{j=0}^{N-1} (1 + {}_{t+j}r_1)$ and his average annual

[2] In the literature of capital budgeting, several writers have called attention to such difficulties with the internal rate of return. See for example Jack Hirshleifer, "On the Theory of the Optimal Investment Decision," *Journal of Political Economy* 66 (August 1958), pp. 329–352; James H. Lorie and Leonard J. Savage, "Three Problems in Rationing Capital," *Journal of Business* 28 (October 1955), pp. 229–239; Armen A. Alchian, "The Rate of Interest, Fisher's Rate of Return over Cost and Keynes' Internal Rate of Return," *American Economic Review* 45 (December 1955), pp. 938–943; Ezra Solomon, "The Arithmetic of Capital-Budgeting Decisions," *Journal of Business* 29 (April 1956), pp. 124–129; Ed Renshaw, "A Note on the Arithmetic of Capital Budgeting Decisions," *Journal of Business* 30 (July 1957), pp. 193–201; and Romney Robinson, "The Rate of Interest, Fisher's Rate of Return over Cost, and Keynes' Internal Rate of Return: Comment," *American Economic Review* 46 (December 1956), pp. 972–973. These articles are all reprinted in Ezra Solomon, *The Management of Corporate Capital* (Illinois: Free Press of Glencoe, 1959).

yield over the N-year holding period will be

$$\left[\prod_{j=0}^{N-1} (1 + {}_{t+j}r_1)\right]^{1/N} = 1 + {}_tR_N .\qquad (2A-2)$$

The reader will recall that this is the Hicks equation (2-3) for the relationship between long and short rates and, consequently, we shall call ${}_tR_N$ the Hicksian average long rate, which gives the true holding-period return for an investment which is left to accumulate for N years.

2A.3   The Market Price of a Bond

Under the assumptions about market behavior described in Section 2.1, the price should be equal to the present value of C dollars to be received in one year, C dollars to be received in two years, and $(C + F)$ dollars to be received in N years. Employing the relevant expected short rates during the life of the bond to discount each coupon payment (and thus taking account of the fact that for each separate holding period, yields must be the same on all investments, regardless of term) the "correct" bond formula becomes

$$P = \frac{C}{(1 + {}_tr_1)} + \frac{C}{\displaystyle\prod_{j=0}^{1} (1 + {}_{t+j}r_1)} + \cdots$$

$$+ \frac{C}{\displaystyle\prod_{j=0}^{N-1} (1 + {}_{t+j}r_1)} + \frac{F}{\displaystyle\prod_{j=0}^{N-1} (1 + {}_{t+j}r_1)} \cdot \quad (2A-3)[3]$$

[3] It is easy to show that (2A-3) correctly takes account of the actual opportunities available to the investor who reinvests his coupons. Consider the case of a two-year bond where the investor reinvests his first coupon (C_1) at next year's expected one-year rate $({}_{t+1}r_1)$.

Pay out today	Receive at the end of year two
P	$C_1(1 + {}_{t+1}r_1) + C_2 + F$

Discounting the amount to be received at the end of year two by $(1 + {}_tR_2)^2 = (1 + {}_tr_1)(1 + {}_{t+1}r_1)$ we have

$$P = \frac{C_1}{(1 + {}_tr_1)} + \frac{C_2 + F}{(1 + {}_tr_1)(1 + {}_{t+1}r_1)} .$$

Note that this differs from the conventional bond formula (2A-1) which would discount both C_1 and $C_2 + F$ by unity plus ${}_tR_2^*$ to the appropriate power.

2A.4 Yields to Maturity, Holding-Period Yields, and Forward Rates

We may now examine the relationship which holds between the conventionally calculated N-year rate and the true N-year-holding-period yield, on the one hand, and present and forward short-term rates of interest on the other. First, let us assume that no coupons are paid ($C = 0$)—all funds are retained in the investment until maturity. Equating the last terms on the right-hand sides of (2A-1) and (2A-3) we obtain

$$(1 + {_tR_N^*})^N = \prod_{j=0}^{N-1} (1 + {_{t+j}r_1}) = (1 + {_tR_N})^N ,$$

which is, of course, the Hicks equation (2-3) for the relationship between long and short rates. We find that the yield to maturity equals the true N-year-holding-period yield, and long rates are a simple geometric average of present and forward short rates.[4]

When coupon payments are made, however, the yield to maturity ($_tR_N^*$) and the true N-year-holding-period return ($_tR_N$) will not, in general, be equal as we suggested earlier. Consider, for example, the case where the yield curve is positively sloped and all forward rates rise with maturity, that is $1 + {_{t+j}r_1} > 1 + {_{t+j-1}r_1}$, $j = 1, \ldots , N - 1$. This implies

$$\left[\prod_{j=0}^{N-1} (1 + {_{t+j}r_1}) \right]^{1/N} = 1 + {_tR_N} > \left[\prod_{j=0}^{l} (1 + {_{t+j}r_1}) \right]^{1/l+1} , \quad (2A\text{-}4)$$

$$l = 1, \ldots , \quad N - 2$$

We see that the true N-year-holding-period return (Hicksian average long rate) is larger than the average rates for all shorter periods. Suppose we employed $_tR_N$ to discount the entire stream of future payments in (2A-3) and called the resulting hypothetical present value P_H. It would follow, of course, from (2A-4) that $P_H < P$, where P is the market price of the bond. We conclude that $_tR_N$ must be greater than $_tR_N^*$, the yield to maturity, which, by definition, will discount the payment stream so that its present value is exactly P. Thus, we see that, with an ascending structure of forward rates, the yield to maturity of an N-year bond will be less than the true N-year-holding-period return. Conversely, for a descending structure of forward rates it can similarly be shown that $_tR_N$ must be less than $_tR_N^*$.

[4] Similarly, if all forward rates of interest are equal, the yield to maturity will also measure the true N-year-holding-period yield.

We can also demonstrate that the (percentage) difference between the yield to maturity of an N-year bond and the N-year-holding-period return will increase with the size of the coupon on the bond. We shall proceed as follows. We first show that the (percentage) difference between P_H (the hypothetical present value of the bond if the entire payment stream is discounted by the true N-year-holding-period return) and P (the market price of the bond as determined by equation 2A-3) increases with C. We shall then show that this implies that the differential between $_tR_N$ and $_tR_N^*$ increases as well. To simplify the notation we let

$$\left[\frac{1}{1+{}_tr_1}+\cdots+\frac{1}{\displaystyle\prod_{j=0}^{N-1}(1+{}_{t+j}r_1)}\right]=a_{\overline{N}|_{t}\!r_1},$$

$$\left[\frac{1}{1+{}_tR_N}+\cdots+\frac{1}{(1+{}_tR_N)^N}\right]=a_{\overline{N}|_tR_N}, \qquad (2A\text{-}5)$$

and

$$\frac{F}{\displaystyle\prod_{j=0}^{N-1}(1+{}_{t+j}r_1)}=\frac{F}{(1+{}_tR_N)^N}=\tilde{F}.$$

Using the definitions in (2A-5), we may then write

$$P_H = Ca_{\overline{N}|_tR_N}+\tilde{F} \qquad (2A\text{-}5a)$$

and

$$P = Ca_{\overline{N}|_{t}\!r_1}+\tilde{F}.$$

We wish to show

$$\frac{\partial|(P_H-P)/P_H|}{\partial C}>0. \qquad (2A\text{-}6)$$

Rewriting (2A-6) we have

$$\frac{\partial[(P_H-P)/P_H)]}{\partial C}=\frac{\partial[1-(P/P_H)]}{\partial C}=-\frac{\partial(P/P_H)}{\partial C}. \qquad (2A\text{-}6a)$$

Substituting the definitions of (2A-5a) into (2A-6a) and differentiating we obtain

$$-\frac{\partial(P/P_H)}{\partial C}=-\frac{\partial[(Ca_{\overline{N}|_{t}\!r_1}+\tilde{F})/(Ca_{\overline{N}|_tR_N}+\tilde{F})]}{\partial C}$$

$$=-\frac{\tilde{F}(a_{\overline{N}|_{t}\!r_1}-a_{\overline{N}|_tR_N})}{P_H^2}. \qquad (2A\text{-}7)$$

Since $P_H \gtrless P$ implies $a_{\overline{N}|_tR_N} \gtrless a_{\overline{N}|_{t}\!r_1}$, it follows that $\partial[(P_H-P)/P_H]/\partial C \gtrless 0$ as $P_H-P \gtrless 0$. Thus, the absolute

45

value of the (percentage) difference between P_H and P is an increasing function of the size of the coupon.

What remains to be shown is that the (percentage) difference between $_tR_N^*$ and $_tR_N$ also increases with the size of the coupon. In Theorem 5 of Chapter 3 we shall demonstrate that the larger is C, the smaller will be the (percentage) change in P_H for a given (percentage) change in the discount rate $_tR_N$, that is

$$\partial \left(\frac{\partial P_H}{\partial_t R_N} \cdot \frac{_t R_N}{P_H} \right) \Big/ \partial C > 0$$

for all finite $N \geqq 2.$[5] Looking at the matter the other way around, to produce a given percentage price change, the discount rate must change more the larger is the coupon on the bond. Therefore, it follows that the differential between $_tR_N$ (the discount rate producing P_H) and $_tR_N^*$ (the discount rate producing P) must grow, *a fortiori*, with the size of the coupon. Not only does the absolute value of the percentage gap between P_H and P increase with the size of the coupon, but the difference between $_tR_N$ and $_tR_N^*$ which is implied by a given gap is also an increasing function of C. We conclude that the larger is the coupon on the bond, the greater will be the difference between the yield to maturity of an N-year bond and the true N-year-holding-period yield.[6]

We have seen that when coupon payments are made, the yield to maturity and true N-year holding period will not, in general, be equal. Moreover, without knowledge of the size of the coupon, we usually cannot express the yield to maturity in terms of a set of forward short rates. An exception is the special case when a bond sells at par $(P = F)$. In this case the coupon rate on the bond (C/P) will equal the yield to maturity $_tR_N^*.$[7] If we now multiply (2A-3) by $\prod_{j=0}^{N-1} (1 + _{t+j}r_1)$, divide by P, and substitute $_tR_N^*$ for C/P we have

$$\prod_{j=0}^{N-1} (1 + _{t+j}r_1) - 1 = {}_tR_N^* \left[\prod_{j=1}^{N-1} (1 + _{t+j}r_1) \right.$$
$$\left. + \prod_{j=2}^{N-1} (1 + _{t+j}r_1) + \cdots + (1 + _{t+N-1}r_1) + 1 \right]. \quad (2A\text{-}8)$$

[5] This conclusion follows since the simple derivative $\partial P_H / \partial_t R_N < 0$ as is shown in Theorem 1 of Chapter 3.

[6] It can also be shown that the difference between yields to maturity and the geometric average of current and forward short-term rates of interest will tend to be greater the longer the term to maturity.

[7] This is shown in Chapter 3 below. See equation (3-4a).

$$_tR_N^* =$$

$$\frac{\displaystyle\prod_{j=0}^{N-1} (1 + {}_{t+j}r_1) - 1}{\displaystyle\prod_{j=1}^{N-1} (1 + {}_{t+j}r_1) + \prod_{j=2}^{N-1} (1 + {}_{t+j}r_1) + \cdots + (1 + {}_{t+N-1}r_1) + 1}.$$

This is the formula given by Lutz for the relationship between long and short rates.[8] But note that this equation is correct only for the case of bonds selling at par.

2A.5 *Some Numerical Examples*

To show the order of magnitude of the differences we have been discussing, consider the following case.

Assume the schedule of current and forward short rates as follows.

$$
\begin{aligned}
{}_t r_1 &= 1 \text{ per cent} \\
{}_{t+1} r_1 &= 2 \text{ per cent} \\
{}_{t+2} r_1 &= 3 \text{ per cent} \\
{}_{t+3} r_1 &= 4 \text{ per cent} \\
{}_{t+4} r_1 &= 5 \text{ per cent}
\end{aligned}
\qquad (2A\text{-}9)
$$

Utilizing these data we can solve equation (2A-3) for the price of a bond where each payment is discounted by a rate which reflects the true opportunity cost of the funds over the relevant period. Columns 1 and 2 of Table 2A-1 show the prices of hypothetical five-year and four-year bonds which differ in their coupons. In columns 3 and 4, these prices are converted into yields to maturity (internal rates of return) by means of the conventional bond formula (2A-1).

When the coupon is zero we find that the yields to maturity of five-year and four-year bonds are 2.990% and 2.494% respectively. In this case the entire investment in the bonds is left to accumulate over the full N-year period. Here the Hicksian average long rate, which takes the geometric mean of (unity plus) the current and forward short-term rates of interest, coincides with the internal rate of return. Moreover, as we have shown above, once coupons are paid on the bonds in question, the internal rates of return (yields to maturity) differ from the true N-year-holding-period yields given by the Hicks formula. The calculations also illustrate how the difference between conventionally calculated

[8] Friedrich A. Lutz, "The Structure of Interest Rates," in American Economic Association, *Readings in the Theory of Income Distribution* (Homewood: R. D. Irwin, 1946), p. 500n.

rates and average long rates given by the Hicks equation will be greater the larger is the coupon on the bond. (See columns 3 and 4 of Table 2A-1.)

TABLE 2A-1
HYPOTHETICAL PRICES AND YIELDS

[Calculated using forward rates of equation (2A-9)]

Annual coupon	(1) (2) Price of bond calculated from equation (2A-3)		(3) (4) Internal rate of return (yield to maturity)	
	5-year bond	4-year bond	5-year bond	4-year bond
6.00	$114.336	$113.473	2.880%	2.425%
4.00	104.991	105.854	2.913	2.446
2.00	95.646	98.235	2.949	2.469
0	86.302	90.617	2.990	2.494

The reader will observe, however, that the differences tend to be small, despite the fact that in our example the yield curve was assumed to have a large positive slope. Nevertheless, we shall see that even small differences in internal rates of return can make very large differences in the estimation of implicit forward rates.

2A.6 *Calculation of Forward Rates from the Term Structure*

We have shown that the relationship between current and forward short rates and yields to maturity depends on the coupon of the bond and is not unique. Therefore, if only the yields to maturity of securities are known, as is the case with the Durand data, there exists no unambiguous way to derive the forward rates of interest actually embodied in the term structure. Remember that when we use the Hicks formula for calculating forward rates [equation (2-7)] our inputs are simply the two adjacent long rates of interest calculated by the traditional yield-to-maturity method. This will, in general, give an incorrect result since the same forward rates of return may imply different yields to maturity for long bonds with different coupons. But if the market yields to maturity are the only known quantities, all we can do is make some assumption about the coupons and then calculate the forward rate of return implied by these yields. When the Hicks formula is used, the assumption is made that the coupon is zero. We shall illustrate the calculation by estimating forward rates of return for year five ($_{t+4}r_1$) using the yields to maturity of bonds with different coupons presented in Table 2A-1. Remember that the true one-year rate for year five is 5 per cent. Table 2A-2 presents the various estimates.

TABLE 2A-2

IMPLICIT FORWARD RATE FOR YEAR 5 ($_{t+4}r_1$) AS CALCULATED FROM
MARKET YIELDS OF TABLE 2A-1 USING THE
HICKS FORMULA [EQUATION (2-7)]

Annual coupon on 4-year bond

		0	$2.00	$4.00	$6.00
Annual	0	5.000	5.103	5.197	5 282
coupon on	$2.00	4.791	4.894	4.988	5.073
5-year	$4.00	4 606	4.709	4.802	4.887
bond	$6.00	4.441	4.544	4.637	4.722

We note once again that, when neither bond has a coupon, it is correct to apply the Hicks formula, and we obtain the appropriate forward rate (5 per cent). On the other hand, whenever there are coupons on either the four- or the five-year bond from which the forward rate is calculated, we find that the inaccuracies of our estimates are substantial. In cases where the coupons on the four- and five-year bonds used in the calculation are quite disparate, possible errors of over 50 basis points may be introduced.

CHAPTER 3

An Alternative Formulation of the Expectations Theory*

WE BEGIN our construction of an over-all theory of the term structure with a reformulation of the expectations theory. This study takes the position that the traditional expectational approach is, in principle, correct and of substantial importance in understanding the actual behavior of market interest rates of securities with different terms to maturity. Nevertheless, the yield-maturity relationship may be more convincingly described and more clearly perceived when *explicit* recognition is given to bond prices. In this chapter, the nexus between market interest rates and bond prices is examined rigorously. Then the traditional theory will be recast in terms consistent with the practices of bond investors and traders. Even the nature of the motivation of bond investors seems better described by the mechanism delineated in this chapter than by the traditional view. Expectations will be introduced through explicit expected price changes rather than expected future short rates. Moreover, a short planning period will be substituted for the long-run horizon implicit in the received analysis.

Three building blocks serve as the foundations of the analysis: (1) the mathematics of bond-price movements; (2) the assumption that investors have an expectation of a "normal range" of interest rates; (3) expectations proper, that is, a belief by investors that a particular course of future interest-rate movements is likely.

In this chapter, we examine how these three elements (which will be referred to simply as "factor one," etc.) in various combinations restrict the possible shape of the yield curve, or, to look at the matter another way, we shall ask what degrees of freedom are left for other factors in determining the term structure of interest rates.

3.1 *Factor One: The Mathematics of Bond-Price Movements*

Economists have typically formulated theories of the structure of interest rates in terms of bond yields rather than bond prices. Keynes probably came closest to an explicit realization of the effect of price

* Large parts of Sections 3.1 through 3.6 of this chapter were taken from my article, "Expectations, Bond Prices, and the Term Structure of Interest Rates," *Quarterly Journal of Economics* 76 (May 1962), pp. 197–218.

risks as a major determinant of the desire for liquidity and, therefore, of interest rates.[1] Even Keynes, however, did not adequately call attention to the precise relationship between changes in bond yields and bond prices. Keynes argued that with a long-term rate of interest of 4 per cent, if it were feared that the rate would rise faster than 0.16 per cent, per annum, then cash would be preferred to bonds. He reasoned that the fall in bond prices associated with the rise in the interest rate would more than offset the coupon interest received.[2] Keynes was not careful to point out, however, that his analysis is approximately correct only in the case of a perpetual bond. If the issue in question were a ten-year (4 per cent coupon) bond, it would take a 0.50 per cent rise in yields to satisfy his argument. For a five-year bond, rates would have to rise by more than 0.91 per cent to wipe out an amount of capital equivalent to the interest received. I feel the implication of yield changes on bond prices has usually received neither adequate nor sufficiently careful attention in the literature. Bonds are traded in terms of price, not yield. They are bought and sold by speculators, long-term investors, and financial institutions, all acutely conscious of price movements. I hope to show that a rigorous examination of the nexus between changes in bond yields and changes in market prices can be enormously helpful in understanding the actual fluctuations of yields in the bond markets.[3]

By themselves, mathematical theorems concerning the response of bond prices to hypothetical changes in interest rates tell us nothing about the term structure. However, they will enable us later in the chapter to derive more fully the implications of some simple assumptions on the nature of expectations.

There is, of course, a rigid connection between a set of expected yields and the prices of bonds of different maturities. In what follows, with the exception of Theorem 5, we shall proceed on two simple assumptions: (1) that all securities with which we are concerned carry the same coupon and (2) that the present short rate and all forward short-term rates of the traditional analysis are identical (that is, that the yield curve is always perfectly flat). Therefore, if the

---

[1] J. M. Keynes, *The General Theory of Employment, Interest and Money* (New York: Harcourt, Brace, 1935), Chapter 15.

[2] *Ibid.*, p. 202.

[3] The need for a study of the term structure of interest rates to go behind the yields themselves and consider bond prices has been suggested, but not explored, by David Durand. See David Durand, *Basic Yields of Corporate Bonds, 1906–1942*, Technical Paper 3 (New York: National Bureau of Economic Research, 1942), p. 19.

present short-term interest rate rises by a certain amount, it is assumed that expected future short-term rates and, hence, all long rates go up by precisely the same amount. Of course, this is not what happens in practice—yield curves are not all horizontal, as we have seen, and yield changes are not equal for all maturities. Nevertheless, it is important to have this special case as a reference point. In fact, one of the main functions of this unrealistic case is to help us to see precisely why the yield curve takes the shapes it does.[4]

Market practitioners consider the value of a bond to be determined by four elements: (1) the face value of the bond, that is, the principal amount to be paid at maturity, which we denote by F; (2) the coupon or interest paid periodically to the bondholder, denoted by

[4] In the perfect-foresight version of the traditional expectations approach it is assumed that all future short rates are known with certainty. Thus, even though the short rate may change from period to period, these changes are fully anticipated and, consequently, no alteration is called for in forecasts of forward rates. It follows that, over any time interval, if holding-period yields are to be equal, price changes must also be approximately equal on all securities regardless of term.

Once uncertainty is introduced, however, there is no reason to believe that expectations of future short-term rates of interest are perfectly inelastic, that is, independent of changes in the spot short-term rate. It would seem reasonable to suppose that if investors do, in fact, make forecasts of forward short-term rates into the future, such forecasts would be strongly influenced by changes in the level of the short-term market rate. Consequently, changes in the spot short rate are typically accompanied by changes in a whole series of forward rates in the same direction.

There is no lack of empirical support for such a conjecture. Indeed, Meiselman's hypothesis that investors revise their forecasts of forward rates in response to errors made in forecasting the current short-term rate, may be regarded as a special case of an elastic-expectations hypothesis. John Wood has tested a more general elastic-expectations model where forward rates are assumed to be linearly related to the level of the current short rate. Employing the Durand data, Wood confirms that the whole series of forward rates moves in the same direction as the short-term spot rate. "The results indicate that, while long-term rates may be expected to change less than short-term rates . . . movements in long rates will not by any means be insignificant. See John H. Wood, "The Expectations Hypothesis, The Yield Curve, and Monetary Policy," *Quarterly Journal of Economics* 78 (August 1964), pp. 468–469.

Consequently, on both a priori and empirical grounds, we find there are good reasons to believe that market interest rates will exhibit significant fluctuations for all maturities. It would seem useful then to ask what kind of price changes would be realized by holders of bonds of alternative maturities as a result of these movements in market rates. We emphasize, however, that this does not mean we believe that long yields in fact turn out to be as volatile as short yields. We shall see that investor behavior focused on *potential* price changes will tend to limit the scope of actual yield fluctuations on long-term bonds, and the theorems demonstrated below will be useful in illuminating this result.

C; (3) the internal rate of return, i, which is referred to as the net return per period or, where we assume annual compounding, the annual yield to maturity;[5] and (4) N, the number of years to maturity. As mentioned earlier, the yield to maturity i is simply that discount rate which makes the sum of the present values of all the coupons to be received as interest and of the principal amount to be paid at maturity equal to the purchase price.[6]

$$P = \frac{C}{(1+i)} + \frac{C}{(1+i)^2} + \cdots + \frac{C}{(1+i)^N} + \frac{F}{(1+i)^N} \cdot$$

$$(3\text{-}1)$$

Summing the geometric progression and simplifying we obtain

$$P = \frac{C}{i}\left[1 - \frac{1}{(1+i)^N}\right] + \frac{F}{(1+i)^N} \cdot \qquad (3\text{-}2)$$

As N approaches infinity the expression approaches the limit C/i. Thus, for a perpetual bond paying \$1.00 per annum, the market value becomes simply the reciprocal of the market rate of interest.

It will be useful to review certain well-known preliminary relationships. Rewriting (3-2) above as

$$P = \frac{C}{i} + \frac{(F - C/i)}{(1+i)^N} \qquad (3\text{-}3)$$

and defining the nominal or stated rate of yield (i_0) as

$$i_0 = C/F \qquad (3\text{-}4)$$

we can observe that when the market yield to maturity i is equal to the nominal yield then

$$C/i = F \qquad \text{and} \qquad P = F ; \qquad (3\text{-}4a)$$

the bond sells at par. When $i > i_0$, then

$$C/i < F \qquad \text{and} \qquad P < F ; \qquad (3\text{-}4b)$$

the bond sells at a discount. When $i < i_0$, then

$$C/i > F \qquad \text{and} \qquad P > F ; \qquad (3\text{-}4c)$$

the bond sells at a premium.

[5] We have previously referred to the internal rate of return as $_tR_N^*$. We shall use the simpler notation i throughout this chapter, however, in order to simplify the algebra.

[6] Books of so-called bond tables (often referred to as "basis books") are constructed on the same principle and embody semi-annual compounding. In this study the *Acme Tables of Bond Values* (Boston: Financial Publishing Company, 1923) have been used.

We may now proceed to examine the relationship between yield changes and bond-price movements. The first of our results is quite obvious, but it is needed for some of our later calculations.

THEOREM 1: *Bond prices move inversely to bond yields.*

PROOF: Differentiating (3-1) with respect to i we obtain

$$\frac{\partial P}{\partial i} = -\frac{C}{(1+i)^2} - \frac{2C}{(1+i)^3} - \cdots$$
$$- \frac{NC}{(1+i)^{N+1}} - \frac{NF}{(1+i)^{N+1}} < 0 . \quad (3\text{-}5)$$

THEOREM 2: *For a given change in yield from the nominal yield, changes in bond prices are greater, the longer the term to maturity.*

PROOF: We wish to evaluate $\partial[P(i) - P(i_0)]/\partial N$. But $\partial P(i_0)/\partial N = 0$ since for $i = i_0$, $P = F$, a constant, by (3-4a). Therefore, it is sufficient to evaluate the sign of $\partial P(i)/\partial N$. Rewriting (3-2) we have

$$P = \frac{C}{i} - (1+i)^{-N}\left[\frac{C}{i} - F\right] .$$

Differentiating with respect to N we obtain

$$\frac{\partial P}{\partial N} = \left[\frac{C}{i} - F\right][1+i]^{-N}[\ln(1+i)] . \quad (3\text{-}6)$$

When $i < i_0$, the bond sells at a premium,

$$\left[\frac{C}{i} - F\right] > 0 \quad (3\text{-}6a)$$

from (3-4c), and therefore $\partial P/\partial N > 0$. Therefore, if the market yield is below the nominal yield, i_0, the price of the bond P will be higher the longer the time to maturity.

When $i > i_0$, the bond sells at a discount,

$$\left[\frac{C}{i} - F\right] < 0 \quad (3\text{-}6b)$$

from (3-4b), and therefore $\partial P/\partial N < 0$. Thus if the market yield is above the nominal yield, the price P of the bond will be lower as the length of time to maturity increases. Since the absolute and percentage change in bond prices is measured by the difference between the derived P and the constant F ($F = 100$), we find that bond-price movements are amplified as time to maturity is increased. Thus the effect of a given change in yield from the nominal yield will be larger, the longer the term to maturity.

This theorem is not generally true when yield changes are measured from a base other than the nominal yield. In particular, when bonds are selling at a discount (their initial yield to maturity being greater than the nominal yield) it is possible to find cases where longer-term securities are actually less sensitive to a given change in market interest rates than are shorter issues. In view of the limited practical importance of this point, we shall defer a discussion of it to the Appendix of this chapter.

THEOREM 3: *The percentage price changes described in Theorem 2 increase at a diminishing rate as N increases.*

PROOF: Differentiating (3-6) with respect to N we obtain

$$\frac{\partial^2 P}{\partial N^2} = -\left[\frac{C}{i} - F\right][\ln(1+i)]^2[(1+i)^{-N}] . \qquad (3\text{-}7)$$

Repeating the same argument as above, we have for i below the nominal rate, i_0, $\partial^2 P/\partial N^2 < 0$. The percentage price rise from par increases with N, but at a diminishing rate. Similarly, for i above i_0, $\partial^2 P/\partial N^2 > 0$. The percentage price decline from par increases with N at a diminishing rate.

THEOREM 4: *Price movements resulting from equal absolute (or, what is the same, from equal proportionate) increases and decreases in yield are asymmetric; that is, a decrease in yields raises bond prices more than the same increase in yields lowers prices.*

PROOF: We will see presently that in order to prove asymmetry it is sufficient to show that $\partial^2 P/\partial i^2 > 0$. To derive the inequality we differentiate (3-5) with respect to i and obtain

$$\frac{\partial^2 P}{\partial i^2} = \frac{2C}{(1+i)^3} + \frac{2.3C}{(1+i)^4} + \cdots + \frac{N(N+1)C}{(1+i)^{N+2}}$$
$$+ \frac{N(N+1)F}{(1+i)^{N+2}} > 0 . \qquad (3\text{-}8)$$

Thus, the slope of the function $P = f(i)$ becomes less negative as i increases. Consequently, for any i', the average slope of the function over the range between i' and $(i' - \Delta i)$ is steeper than over the range between i' and $(i' + \Delta i)$. Therefore, an increase, say 10 per cent, in yield will result in a smaller absolute and percentage price decline than a 10 per cent decrease in yield will raise bond prices.

THEOREM 5: *The higher the coupon carried by the bond, the smaller will be the percentage price fluctuation for a given percentage change in yield except for one-year securities and consols.*

PROOF: We wish to prove $\partial \left[\frac{\partial P}{\partial i} \cdot \frac{i}{P} \right] \Big/ \partial C > 0$, for all finite $N \geqq 2$.

(Recall that $\partial P / \partial i < 0$.) Differentiating (3-2) with respect to i we obtain:

$$\frac{\partial P}{\partial i} = \frac{-C(1 + i)^{N+1} + C(1 + i + Ni) - FNi^2}{i^2(1 + i)^{N+1}} .$$

Multiplying through by i/P (where we use expression (3-2) for P) and simplifying we obtain:

$$\frac{\partial P}{\partial i} \cdot \frac{i}{P} = \frac{-C(1 + i)^{N+1} + C(1 + i + Ni) - FNi^2}{C(1 + i)^{N+1} - C(1 + i) + Fi(1 + i)} . \quad (3\text{-}9)$$

Let us write $\Delta(N) = (1 + i)[C(1 + i)^N - C + Fi]^2$ so that

$$\frac{Fi}{(1 + i)[C(1 + i)^N - C + Fi]^2}$$
$$= \frac{Fi}{\Delta(N)} > 0 \text{ for all finite } N . \quad (3\text{-}10)$$

Differentiating (3-9) with respect to C we obtain:

$$\partial \left[\frac{\partial P}{\partial i} \cdot \frac{i}{P} \right] \Big/ \partial C = \frac{Fi}{\Delta(N)} [1 + i + (1 + i)^N(Ni - 1 - i)] . \quad (3\text{-}11)$$

When $N = 1$, (3-11) $= 0$. (3-11) is positive for all finite $N \geqq 2$, as will now be shown by induction. Write

$$\phi(N) = 1 + i + (1 + i)^N(Ni - 1 - i) .$$

First note that for $N = 2$, $\phi(N) = (i^2 + i^3) > 0$ for all $i > 0$. We now prove that $\phi(N)$ is an increasing function of N, so that since $\phi(N) > 0$ for $N = 2$, $\phi(N) > 0$ for $N > 2$.

$$\phi(N + 1) = 1 + i + (1 + i)^N(1 + i)(Ni - 1) , \text{ that is,}$$
$$\phi(N + 1) = \phi(N) + Ni^2(1 + i)^N$$
$$\therefore \phi(N + 1) > \phi(N) \text{ for all } N > 0, i > 0 .$$

Thus we conclude

$$\phi(N) > 0 \text{ for all finite } N \geqq 2 . \quad (3\text{-}12)$$

Hence, since (3-11) can be written $Fi/\Delta(N) \cdot \phi(N)$, we conclude by (3-10) and (3-12) that

$$\partial \left[\frac{\partial P}{\partial i} \cdot \frac{i}{P} \right] \Big/ \partial C > 0 . \quad \text{Q.E.D.}$$

But note that when $N \to \infty$, $Fi/\Delta(N) \to 0$ and (3-11) $\to 0$.

Table 3-1 gives numerical illustrations of several of the relationships described by the theorems. The greater absolute and diminishing marginal volatility of long-term bond prices is patently revealed. A 2-year bond is shown to rise or fall about twice as far from par as a 1-year bond. Similarly, a 4-year bond fluctuates almost twice as much as a 2-year security. A 64-year bond will not, however, fluctuate in price significantly more than a 32-year bond, particularly for an increase in yield. Thus, the implications for an investor of an extention

TABLE 3-1

SELECTED PRICE DATA FOR A BOND WITH NOMINAL YIELD (i_0) 3 PER CENT[a]

Years to maturity (N)	Price (P) to yield 4% (i) to maturity	Loss incurred if market yields rise from i_0 to 4%	Marginal loss incurred by extending maturity one add'l year	Price (P) to yield 2% (i) to maturity	Gain realized if market yields fall from i_0 to 2%	Marginal gain realized by extending maturity one add'l year
1	99.029	0.971%	.971%	100.985	0.985%	.985%
2	98.096	1.904	.933	101.951	1.951	.966
4	96.337	3.663	.862	103.826	3.826	.928
8	93.211	6.789	.736	107.359	7.359	.857
16	88.266	11.734	.536	113.635	13.635	.731
32	82.039	17.961	.285	123.551	23.551	.531
64	76.982	23.018	.080	136.009	36.009	.281
consol	75.000	25.000	.000	150.000	50.000	.000

[a] All examples assume semi-annual compounding.

in the maturity of his bond portfolio can be quite different depending on the maturity range of the curve to which it is applicable.[7] Furthermore, an asymmetry of price movements is revealed from one side

[7] Frederick R. Macaulay has argued that years to maturity is a very inadequate measure of the true length of a loan. It tells only the date of the final payment and nothing about the size and frequency of all intermediate payments. In the case of a very-long-term bond, the importance of the maturity date may be so small as to be negligible. Macaulay uses the term "duration" to describe the true length of the bond. The duration of any loan is simply the weighted average of the maturities of the individual loans that correspond to each future payment. The present values of the individual payments are used as weights. As bonds lengthen in time to maturity, true length or duration increases at a decreasing rate. A 25-year bond is surprisingly little different from a 50-year bond, but a 6-year bond is approximately twice as long as a 3-year issue. This is consistent with and helps explain the actual price relationships described by our theorems. See Frederick R. Macaulay, *The Movements of Interest Rates, Bond Yields, and Stock Prices in the United States since 1856* (New York: National Bureau of Economic Research, 1938), pp. 44–53.

57

of the par axis to the other. There is a natural cushion that exists simply in the mathematics of bond prices and that limits a long-term bond's price decline as yields rise.[8] Typical price curves for an equal increase and decrease in all yields from the nominal yield are depicted in Figure 3-1.

Throughout the remainder of this study we shall utilize these relationships to help explain several characteristics of the yield curve. At this point we can at least indicate the direction in which the preceding analysis will take us. We noted in Chapter 1 that in empiri-

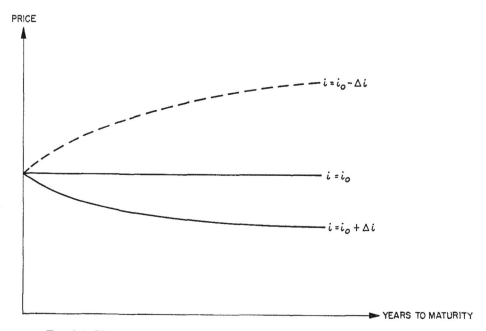

FIG. 3-1. Hypothetical price curves. The curves show the prices for bonds of different maturities resulting from an equal increase and decrease in yields. All bonds are assumed to have a coupon rate equal to the nominal yield.

cal yield curves the portion that is *not* flat invariably occurs in the earlier maturities. Our hypothetical price curves can help provide

[8] Another important factor is the tax implication of bond discounts. The effective after-tax yield to maturity is much larger for a discount bond selling at a given yield to maturity than for a bond selling at par with the same pre-tax yield. In the case of the discount bond, part of the yield to maturity is taxed at preferential capital-gains rates. In addition, the remoteness of possible call features lends added attraction to deep-discount bonds. Of course, in the tradition of term-structure theory, we abstract from these considerations in the basic model.

an explanation for this phenomenon. We note that for a given change in yields, the potential price fluctuations for long-term bonds are roughly similar over a wide range of maturities. In terms of the relationships displayed in Figure 3-1, the price curves tend to flatten out as term to maturity increases. Hence, bonds of longer maturities, which are mathematically almost equivalent securities in terms of price responsiveness to changes in the level of interest rates, may plausibly be expected to be close substitutes whose yields would consequently be very similar. Conversely, in the short and intermediate range of the maturity spectrum, the extension of maturity even for a few years implies considerably different price risks and opportunities for capital gains. Thus, it is reasonable to expect that in these areas of the yield curve, bonds of different terms to maturity would be more likely to differ in value in response to expected changes in the level of interest rates.[9]

Moreover, it can be shown that the mathematics of price movements can help to explain the characteristic slopes of the yield curve even if factors other than expectations are accorded a major role in determining the rate structure. For example, to the extent that (Hicksian) liquidity premiums influence the yield curve, we shall show (in Section 3.6) why their effect will be observed mainly in the early maturities. Furthermore, even under an institutional theory of the term structure, we shall find in Chapter 7 that the bond-price relationships may help explain the limited volatility of long rates. We shall demonstrate these results specifically in the analytic models which follow.

3.2 *Factor Two: The Normal Range of Interest Rates*

We now approach the very difficult area of expectations. Fortunately, our *modus operandi* enables us to move gingerly at first. We shall begin by introducing the theoretical construct, "the expected normal range of interest rates." This range will be defined in terms of the level rather than the structure of rates. Our problem is one of finding some correspondence between our *ex ante* theoretical construct and the observable *ex post* empirical data at our disposal, that

---

[9] All of this argument has been based on the assumption that anticipated yield changes are equal for all maturities. In Section 3.4 we shall show that the argument still remains valid even when this is not the case. It is interesting to compare the above explanation of the flattening out of the yield curve with that offered by Lutz. To form a "shoulder," short rates would have to be expected to change in the near future and then reach a certain level where they would stay constant.

is, the historical level of rates.[10] As a first approximation, the aggregate of individuals comprising the "market" will be assumed to believe that the historical range of interest rates will prevail in the future. We shall assume, in the examples which follow, that the expected normal range for government bonds is roughly between 2 per cent and 5 per cent.

First, let us suppose that interest rates for securities of all maturities are fixed at $4\frac{1}{2}$ per cent by the arbitrary decree of a *deus ex machina*. For simplicity, we shall consider that all bonds carry coupons of $4\frac{1}{2}$ per cent and, therefore, the prices of all securities are fixed at par. Now, in stages, we shall examine the effects of removing completely all controls from the market. In the first stage, we shall assume the "market" has formed no expectation as to whether bond prices will rise or fall. However, in consonance with our normal-range construct, investors must be aware of the fact that, in terms of potential bond-price movements, this level of rates leaves less to be feared than hoped. The worst situation that could confront an investor is for him to suffer capital losses corresponding to a rise in interest rates to 5 per cent. On the other hand, rates could fall to 2 per cent and still lie within the normal range. The resulting capital gains would be substantial, especially on longer-term securities.

We must now introduce explicitly some planning horizon over which the investor compares alternative investment strategies. Recall that the traditional expectations theory had the investor estimate the likely course of events in the bond market for a period at least as long as the time during which he had funds available for investment. We noted that several critics have argued that the planning horizons of bond investors were typically much shorter than those suggested by the traditional analysis. Especially those close to the actual investment process of financial institutions doubted that expectations were held and acted upon for any but a very short horizon. The point has been clearly stated by Michaelson. "In the most general case, the end of a portfolio planning horizon is not a fixed point in chronological time marking the liquidation date of the portfolio: it is rather a planning dimension setting the span of time over which alternative courses of action are compared."[11] As we suggested at the beginning

---

[10] Our method here follows that used by Milton Friedman, in *A Theory of the Consumption Function* (Princeton: Princeton University Press, 1957), Chapter 3.

[11] Jacob B. Michaelson, "Holding Period Yields on U.S. Government Securities and the Term Structure of Interest Rates," *The Journal of Finance* 20 (September 1965), p. 460.

of this chapter, our alternative formulation of the expectations theory will substitute a relatively short planning period for the long-run horizon implicit in the traditional analysis. For the sake of illustration, we shall choose one year as the relevant horizon. It will be shown later that the one-year outlook appears to be consistent with the actual planning practices of many institutional bond investors.

Let us return now to the alternatives facing our illustrative investor. The current level of rates is $4\frac{1}{2}$ per cent, and the extremes of the normal range are 2 and 5 per cent. Historical interest-rate movements would suggest, however, that a drastic drop in the level of rates to the lowest bound of the normal range has been associated with secular rather than cyclical movements. Thus, investors could not reasonably anticipate that the lower end of the normal range would be realized within, say, one year. Under these circumstances we might believe that a plausible one-year normal range might be between 5 per cent and $3\frac{1}{2}$ per cent. In the next chapter we shall suggest several alternative methods by which the normal range might actually be estimated. At this stage, we simply wish to explore the effects of a subjective expectation of a normal range on the structure of rates. The critical assumption is that the investor has more to gain than to fear. Therefore, whatever the expected normal fluctuations for the coming year may be, our assumption demands that the "market" believe that these will be contained in a range where the lower limit is further from $4\frac{1}{2}$ per cent than the upper limit. Again we must remind our reader, however, that investors have collectively made no judgment as to the likelihood of interest rates in general moving up or down. The situation is viewed as one of neither certainty nor even risk. We only assert that constraints exist as to the range of possible outcomes. In Shackle's terms, there is "bounded uncertainty" thereby permitting meaningful choices to be made.[12]

Columns 2 through 5 of Table 3-2 summarize the resulting price action of bonds of varying maturities if in one year yields should move uniformly to the extremities of the one-year normal range. Thus, investors collectively are faced with the matrix consisting of the array of percentage gains and losses (negative gains) contained in columns 3 and 5, which we can call states of nature A and B. We next assume, as a first approximation, that utility is linear in gains. Furthermore, we postulate that investors' preferences can be represented by a von Neumann–Morgenstern utility index. We may now choose that par-

[12] G. L. S. Shackle, *Decision, Order and Time in Human Affairs* (Cambridge: Cambridge University Press, 1961).

ticular relationship where the utility numbers are made equal to the gains.[13] There are at least two grounds upon which one could quarrel with this assumption. In the first place, it is doubtful that utility is linear in money. Second, and in addition to the possibility of diminishing marginal utility of money payoffs, it may well be that losses *per se* are especially unpleasant, particularly for institutional investing officers. Thus, on both counts the disutility of money losses will be greater than the utility of equal gains. We shall examine later the implications of the relaxation of this assumption of linearity, but, as an initial approximation, we shall consider that the unadjusted

TABLE 3-2

OUTCOMES FOR ALTERNATIVE INVESTMENT STRATEGIES OVER THE PLANNING HORIZON
($4\frac{1}{2}$ per cent coupon bonds—interest rates near upper bound of normal range)

(1)	(2)	(3)	(4)	(5)	(6)	(7)	(8)	(9)
N	Market price of bond if interest rates rise to 5% in 1 year[a]	Resulting capital loss (%) A	Market price bond if interest rates fall to $3\frac{1}{2}$% in one year	Resulting price appreciation (%) B	Math. expectation of gain (p:A,B) $p = 0.50$	Market prices equalizing math. expectation of gain (Col. 6) among maturities	Derived structure of rates from Col. 7	Derived structure of rates (p:A,B) $p = 0.25$
1	100.00[b]	—	100.00[b]	—	—	100.00	4.50	4.50
$1\frac{1}{2}$	99.76	−0.24	100.49	+0.49	+0.13	100.13	4.41	4.29
2	99.52	−0.48	100.97	+0.97	+0.25	100.25	4.37	4.18
5	98.21	−1.79	103.70	+3.70	+0.96	100.96	4.28	3.98
10	96.41	−3.59	107.66	+7.66	+2.04	102.04	4 25	3.91
20	93.91	−6.09	113.79	+13.79	+3.85	103.85	4.21	3.86
50	90.89	−9.11	123.35	+23.35	+7 12	107.12	4.16	3.82
Consol	90 00	−10 00	128 66	+28.66	+9.33	109.33	4.12	3.78

[a] Price in one year to yield 5 per cent from "present plus one year" to maturity.
[b] In one year a one-year security matures at par.

gains and losses make up the game matrix facing our collective investor.

We may now proceed to consider this situation as a classical example of a game against nature. The investor must choose among several acts (that is, the array of maturities available to him) where the

[13] See John von Neumann and Oskar Morgenstern, *Theory of Games and Economic Behavior*, 3rd ed. (Princeton: Princeton University Press, 1953), pp. 15–31. The index chosen has minus 100 as its zero point. Minus 100 is the worst possible outcome. The investor cannot lose more than his investment. No such limitation exists for his gains.

desirability of each act depends on the state of nature that will prevail. We have postulated that the decision-maker believes that one state of nature (either A or B) will occur, but he does not know the relative probabilities of each. The standard literature on decision theory suggests a group of criteria to deal with these types of problems.[14] The theoretical justification for the utilization of any one of these is shaky. We shall select the Laplace (or Bayes) principle of insufficient reason to solve the game matrix.[15] This criterion asserts that since the decision-maker is ignorant of the probabilities of the different possible states of nature, he should treat them all as equally likely. He will then assign to each act X_i its expected utility index

$$\frac{U_{i1} + \cdots + U_{in}}{n}$$

and choose that act with the largest index. In our case, which has only two states of nature, this is equivalent to attaching a probability of 0.50 to each state.

Unfortunately, from an empirical point of view, this principle encounters serious difficulties. There is really an infinite number of states of nature which could be regarded as "equally likely." For example, yields might remain unchanged, rise 0.5 per cent, fall 0.5 per cent, etc. Why should the extremes of our one-year normal range be singled out as the natural parametrization of the states for which this criterion is appropriate? Our answer is simply that for our pruposes it makes no difference which states of nature we select so long as they conform to our critical assumption which demands that equally likely states leave the investor more to hope than fear. By selecting the extremes of the possible range of price movements we achieve the same result as would be obtained by use of the uniform distribution over the entire range. The narrower the expected range of fluctuations, the smaller will be the derived yield differentials. But the differences in

[14] See John W. Milnor, "Games Against Nature," in Thrall, Coombs, and Davis, eds., *Decision Processes* (New York: John Wiley, 1957), pp. 49–60; or R. Duncan Luce and Howard Raiffa, *Games and Decisions* (New York: John Wiley, 1957), pp. 275–326.

[15] The Hurwicz solution, which utilizes a subjective "optimism-pessimism index," is inconsistent with our assumption that our representative investor has made no judgment as to the likelihood of interest rates moving up or down. Application of the Wald "minimax" criterion is tantamount to saying that normal backwardation will always force investors to buy the shortest security available if there exists any possibility of loss. Similarly, the Savage "minimax regret" criterion would lead investors to confine their purchases toward the long end of the yield curve. These latter two criteria may be rejected on empirical grounds because they are not in accord with the normal behavior of bond investors.

results will be only differences in degree. If, however, investors believe that there will be no range of fluctuation during the coming year, then the derived yield curve will be horizontal, which is precisely what we would expect.

We may now proceed quickly to some results. Column 6 of Table 3-2 presents the mathematical expectation of gain for each maturity. Longer-term securities are clearly more desirable to our collective investor than short-term issues.[16] Hence the bond market will not remain at the equilibrium which was formerly imposed upon it by decree. Assuming that the prices of long-term securities are bid up to remove the differences in opportunities for gain among maturities, the prices listed in Column 7 will be realized in the market.[17] At these prices, the derived yields to maturity listed in Column 8 will represent the new equilibrium term structure of rates.[18] There will be no net tendency to shift from one maturity to another from a partial-equilibrium, comparative-statics point of view.[19] We have, therefore, explained a descending yield curve when the level of rates is near the upper limit of its normal range.

From this simple illustration, we may move to some general conclusions. We assert that our assumption attributing to investors a belief in a normal range of interest-rate variations (basic explanatory factor two) in conjunction with the mathematics of bond-price movements (factor one) are sufficient by themselves to determine the signs of

[16] One additional element serving to dampen potential price fluctuations of short-term securities should be noted. The passage of time changes the maturity of the security, and this diminishes the issue's characteristic price fluctuations. The passage of one year cuts the potential volatility of a two-year bond approximately in half.

[17] There are, of course, several ways in which the market could equalize the mathematical expectation of gain among maturities. We shall return to this point.

[18] We should actually equalize the (discounted) value of the expected price appreciation (depreciation) and the coupons to be received during the holding period, all as a percentage of the purchase price paid for the bond. In our examples we have eliminated the entire (undiscounted) mathematical expectation of gain (loss), but the value of the two coupons as a percentage of the market price of the securities will not be equalized. Our approximation was used to permit simplicity of computation. The differences in the derived yield are generally in the order of magnitude of 0.01 per cent and therefore have no effect on our results.

[19] We must assume, however, that investors' expectations as to what constitutes the normal one-year range are tied to the level of the one-year short rate and are, therefore, unchanged. Otherwise, the structure of rates derived after the process of adjustment is likely to set up changed expectations concerning the one-year normal range and further adjustments would be required. This restriction is not, in general, necessary, as we shall show in note 28 *infra*.

both the first and second derivative of the yield curve. When interest rates are near what they assume to be the upper bound of the normal range, investors will have more to hope than fear in terms of the possibilities for capital gains and losses. Hence, long-term bonds will be more attractive than short-term securities. If investors seek to equalize the mathematical expectation of gain over the horizon period, long-term securities must yield less than shorts.

Alternatively, if interest rates are near the lower bound of the normal range, investors will have more to fear than hope. Possible capital gains will be small, but potential capital losses over the horizon period will loom large. In this situation, if investors seek to equalize the mathematical expectation of gain among maturities an ascending curve will result. In either case, because equal potential changes in yields imply roughly similar changes in bond prices for most longer-term bonds, the yields of these securities will turn out to be approximately equal. Hence, whatever the slope of the yield curve in the early maturities, the curve will eventually level out. Note, however, that expectations have been introduced only to the extent of assuming that the normal range of the past will continue into the future.

3.3 *Factor Three: Expectations Proper*

Having started with almost complete uncertainty as the foundation of our analytical model, it is now incumbent on us to introduce expectations in a less passive manner. By expectations proper (factor three) we simply mean that investors may believe that a certain course of interest-rate movements is more likely than any other, or they may make specific forecasts of future interest rates. Assume that, at a time when interest rates appear to be high relative to the normal range, investors also attach a higher subjective probability to that state of nature in which interest rates fall. This transforms our game matrix from a game against nature into one in the domain of decision-making under risk. We can now associate with state of nature A, the probability p, and with state B, the probability $(1 - p)$. The new utility index for each act X_i becomes $U_{iA}(p) + U_{iB}(1 - p)$ and again the decision-maker will choose that act having the maximum utility index. If we assume that the "market" attaches a probability of 0.75 to the state of nature in which rates fall, Column 9 (Table 3-2 presents the new derived yield-maturity curve. We notice that the specific expectations introduced have made the curve descend more sharply than before. Nevertheless, the new curve shows the same tendency to level out as term to maturity is extended.

Table 3-3 describes a similar case starting from an initial fixed interest-rate level of $2\frac{1}{2}$ per cent for all maturities. All bonds are assumed to bear a $2\frac{1}{2}$ per cent coupon. As in our first example, the one-year normal range is postulated to be between 2 per cent and $3\frac{1}{2}$ per cent. In this case, investors have more to fear than hope. The result (Column 8) is an ascending yield curve, which becomes flat for long-term maturities. One curious result should be noted. We find that our theoretical apparatus indicates that a consol should yield less than a 50-year dated issue despite the fact that the general shape of

TABLE 3-3

OUTCOMES FOR ALTERNATIVE INVESTMENT STRATEGIES OVER THE PLANNING HORIZON

($2\frac{1}{2}$ Per cent coupon bonds—interest rates near lower bound of normal range)

(1)	(2)	(3)	(4)	(5)	(6)	(7)	(8)	(9)
	Market price of bond if interest rates fall to 2% in one year	Resulting price appreciation (%)	Market price of bond if interest rates rise to $3\frac{1}{2}$% in one year	Resulting capital loss (%)	Math. expectation of loss (p:A,B) $p = 0.25$	Market prices which equalize math. expectation of loss (Col. 6) among maturities	Derived structure (from Col. 7)	Derived structure with exp. of greater fluctuations in short rates
N		A		B				
1	100.00	—	100.00	—	—	100.00	2.50	2 50
$1\frac{1}{2}$	100.25	+0.25	99.51	−0.49	−0.31	99.69	2.71	2.76
2	100.49	+0.49	99.03	−0.97	−0.61	99.39	2.81	2.87
5	101.91	+1.91	96.30	−3.70	−2.30	97.70	3.00	3.09
10	104.10	+4.10	92.34	−7.66	−4.72	95.28	3.05	3.15
20	107.87	+7.87	86 21	−13.79	−8.38	91.62	3.06	3.15
50	115.57	+15.57	76.65	−23.35	−13.62	86.38	3.03	3.12
Consol	125.00	+25.00	71.40	−28.60	−15.20	84 80	2.95	3.07

the yield curve is ascending. This is not a peculiarity of the particular numerical example chosen. The same result will be obtained for any p, $0.01 \leq p \leq 1$, that is, except where there is essentially no prospect for gain. This "anomaly" results solely from the mathematics of bond prices.[20] Furthermore, our finding is consistent with the empirical evi-

[20] This relationship can be explained with the aid of Theorem 4. Note that the asymmetry of bond-price movements provides a natural cushion limiting a consol's potential price decline, whereas no such restraint exists to dampen the consol's possible price appreciation. (Cf. Columns 3 and 5 for a 50-year and a perpetual bond). Thus, even though the mathematical expectation of

dence. British consols have typically sold to yield less than long-term dated issues, irrespective of the general shape of the yield curve.[21] It is one of the strengths of our theory that it is consistent with some of the more bizarre relationships of the yield curve. Thus, we see that our basic explanatory factor three, expectations proper, may accentuate (or in other cases counteract)[22] the effects of factors one and two in determining the sign of the first derivative of the yield curve. It does not, however, change the sign of the second derivative.

3.4 The Self-fulfilling Prophesy and the Greater Volatility of Short Rates

Let us now push our expectational analysis one step further. The empirical evidence reviewed in Chapter 1 discloses that short-term interest rates have exhibited greater volatility than long-term rates. Indeed, our theoretical apparatus indicates that this will occur because explanatory factors one and two alone are sufficient to cause an ascending curve to be formed when interest rates are low relative to the historical range, and a descending curve when rates are relatively high. Thus, at the $2\frac{1}{2}$ per cent rate level an ascending curve is likely to be formed by the market. This is not because investors would expect rates to rise from such a low level (although that might well be the case) but solely because, at that level, the potential price gains and losses inherent in the mathematics of bond-price movements give investors more to fear than hope, given their notion of the normal range. In fact, even if investors think it somewhat *less* likely that rates will rise rather than fall, an ascending curve might still be

---

loss (Column 6) is greatest for a perpetual bond, it is not so great as would be required to equalize the derived yields of Column 8. (Cf. Columns 4 and 7 for a 50-year and a perpetual bond.)

[21] We do not suggest that this can be explained entirely by the mathematics of differential potential price behavior. Undoubtedly another powerful determinant is the greater protection from call offered by the deeper discount.

[22] We should point out, however, that it is quite possible, for example, to have a descending yield curve even when investors believe it is more likely that rates will rise rather than fall. To illustrate such a possibility, consider our first example, where rates were arbitrarily set at $4\frac{1}{2}$ per cent and the upper and lower bounds of the normal range were assumed to be 5 and $3\frac{1}{2}$ per cent respectively. Even if we assume that investors attached a probability of $\frac{2}{3}$ to the state of nature in which rates rose and $\frac{1}{3}$ to the state in which rates fell, the yield curve would still have a slight negative slope. Consols would yield 4.37 per cent, 13 basis points less than one-year issues. Thus, in circumstances where the level of rates is close to one of the bounds of the normal range it may be very difficult for factor three to counteract the effect of the normal range assumption in determining the slope of the yield curve.

formed. This is so because the lower the level of rates, the greater will be the positive slope of the curve as a result of factors one and two alone. Thus, as we argued above, it would be more difficult for factor three working mildly in the opposite direction to counteract this.

In light of these observations, let us examine the implicit assumptions of Columns 2 and 4, Table 3-3. It is assumed that the yield curve will be flat at the 2 per cent and the $3\frac{1}{2}$ per cent level, implying uniform changes in the whole complex of rates. Is this assumption tenable? A logical extension of our argument indicates that the assumption is inconsistent with the workings of the model. This is so because, as we have shown above, if interest rates were at the 2 per cent level it is likely that an ascending (not a flat) yield curve would be formed by the market. Similarly, at very high levels of rates it is likely that a descending yield curve would be formed. Consequently, even on a priori grounds, and irrespective of what the specific expectations of rate changes happen to be (that is, abstracting from explanatory factor 3), it seems likely that investors would expect short rates to fluctuate more than long rates. Thus, the normal range, within which interest rates could be expected to fluctuate within the next year, should be narrower toward the longer end of the maturity spectrum.

Therefore, we are neither begging the question nor guilty of circular reasoning if we hypothesize that investors will consider the normal range for short rates to be wider than that for long rates. Thus, instead of assuming that 2 per cent will be the lower limit to which all interest rates can fall, we could assume that short rates would fall 75 basis points to 1.75 per cent but long rates would decline only 25 basis points to 2.25 per cent. Similarly, for the upper limit we shall allow short rates to rise to 4 per cent while long rates rise to 3.50 per cent. Intermediate rates would be scaled accordingly between the two limits. All other assumptions remain identical with those in our previous illustrations. We find in Column 9, Table 3-3, that an ascending yield curve is again formed, but in this case it traces a more sharply upward course than in our previous example. We conclude that to the extent that we can tell on a priori grounds that long rates should fluctuate less than short rates, this tends to set up expectations which are self-fulfilling and exaggerate the relationship.[23]

---

[23] Even so, under the specific assumptions postulated, the prices of long-term bonds are still more volatile than the prices of shorter securities.

3.5 *Introduction of Hicksian Risk Aversion into the Basic Model*

We can easily modify our basic model to provide an explanation for the presence of Hicksian liquidity premiums. To admit such qualifications we need only assume that losses are weighted more heavily than equivalent gains by the investors' utility functions. This will have the effect of making the slope of ascending yield curves steeper and the slope of the descending curves flatter. For example, if in the game matrix presented in Table 3-2 we double the negative utility values of all losses, we still obtain a descending yield curve which falls from 4.50 per cent to 4.31 per cent (for $p = 0.50$). The comparable yield curve derived (in Column 8 of Table 3-2) under the same assumptions, but not accounting for risk aversion, fell from 4.50 per cent to 4.12 per cent. Both curves start at 4.50 per cent but differ by 19 basis points at the longest end of the maturity spectrum. By comparing the two derived yield curves at other points on the maturity axis we can ascertain whether or not the slope of the yield curve is distorted evenly throughout its length. Such a comparison reveals that the entire 19 basis-point differential occurs by the fifth year and remains constant thereafter. A difference of 13 basis points results by the end of the second year. Thus, to the extent that Hicksian risk aversion influences the slope of the yield curve, the differential effect on the slope of the curve is felt mainly in the early maturities. This is so because of the diminishing marginal risk which an investor takes on in extending maturity beyond the earliest year.[24]

Perhaps the easiest way of demonstrating this finding is to admit Hicksian liquidity premiums in a situation where the yield curve would otherwise be flat throughout. Such a curve would be formed with the level of rates set at 3.50 per cent and the upper and lower bounds of the (one-year) normal range set at 4.00 per cent and 3.00 per cent respectively. We assume investors are agnostic concerning the likelihood of rates moving up or down; that is, we abstract from factor three: expectations proper. In this case, the yield curve will be level at 3.50 per cent, as drawn in Figure 3-2. If we now admit

---

[24] Two of our bond-price theorems combine to give us this result. We know (by Theorem 2) that, for an equal change in yields, possible losses are greater the longer the term to maturity, but by Theorem 3 we understand that possible losses increase with the maturity purchased but at a diminishing rate. Thus, the *additional* risk of loss increases sharply at the early end of the yield-maturity spectrum, for example, in extending the maturity of the bond purchased from one year to two years. But the difference in possible losses from a 21- to a 22-year issue is negligible and, consequently, so is the differential risk.

Hicksian risk aversion by doubling the utility value of all losses, the yield curve first ascends relatively sharply, approaches its maximum height near the five-year maturity range, and then becomes level. Thus, we see graphically that the effect of the Keynes-Hicks modification will be to distort the slope of the yield curve only in the early maturities.

Note that in this analysis we may generate Hicksian liquidity premiums even if the expected investment period of investors is very long. A rationalization of this phenomenon has been offered by Michaelson.[25] Michaelson argues that a strategy of simply matching the security purchased with the anticipated holding period is not free of risk. Such a strategy may involve the purchase of securities at

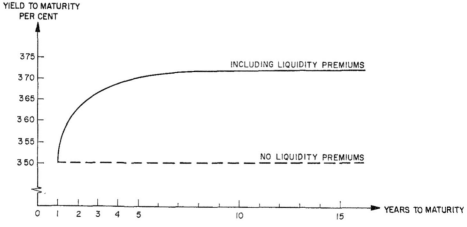

FIG. 3-2. Hicksian liquidity premiums and the slope of the yield curve.

prices which may turn out to be disadvantageous within a period short enough to be encompassed by the planning horizon. We have seen that unexpected changes in real factors in the economy tend to produce synchronous movements in yields for the whole spectrum of maturities. Consequently, an investor with a long holding period who simply invests all fund flows in the long-term market will, at times, be subjected to substantial capital losses on his purchases. In Michaelson's terms, there is a "very real opportunity cost of failing to time the purchase of long-term bonds better than could be achieved by chance alone."[26] As long as the horizon over which alternative strategies are compared is short, it is possible to rationalize liquidity

---

[25] Michaelson, op. cit., pp. 460–463.
[26] Ibid., p. 462.

premiums even for investors whose investment periods may be indefinitely long.

3.6 Altering Some Additional Assumptions

Next, we might relax the implicit assumption of the invariance of the normal range. Is it not plausible that investors' expectations will be influenced to a greater degree by the more immediate past? Thus, when interest rates have been low for a considerable period of time, investors will come to reduce their idea of a normal range. The effect of this suggestion is to make it possible for expectations to form a descending curve at a lower level of interest rates (when rates in the immediate past have been particularly low) than would be possible had proximate rates been at a higher level. Thus, for example, the yield curve on government securities in late 1957 descended gently at a level of interest rates of about 3.90 per cent. Yet, during the early summers of 1960 and 1961 and again during periods of 1964 and 1965, when the level of rates was again at 3.90 per cent, the curve was either relatively flat or rising. One difference was that investors in the 1960's had become accustomed to a significantly higher level of interest rates, and, therefore, their expectations as to what would constitute a normal range of rates were considerably changed from those they held in 1957. We shall make use of this modification in the empirical tests to follow. Investors will be assumed to form expectations of the appropriate normal range of interest rates partly on the basis of an average of rates that span a period of history in the experience of the typical decision-maker.[27]

[27] We noted in Chapter 2 that expectational theories have often been criticized on the basis of an empirical analysis of holding-period yields. In Tables 3-2 and 3-3 we derived hypothetical rate structures on the assumption that investors will act in such a way that the mathematical expectations of gain or loss are equalized among maturities. But even if an expectational analysis constructed in this manner could provide a complete explanation of the actual rate structure in the market, empirical investigations would not, in general, reveal identical holding-period yields for securities of different terms to maturity. Only in the unusual event that yields move exactly to the yield figures given by the mathematical expectation of our collective investor will holding-period yields be equalized. Since the mathematical expectation is compounded of several variables, including individual attitudes toward risk aversion, past interest rates, expected future rates, etc., a resulting equality of holding-period yields should hardly be expected. In particular, to the extent that (Hicksian) risk aversion and the normal-range assumption are important determinants, *ex post* holding-period yields will not correspond to *ex ante* specific expectations if these are held at all. During a continued period of low rates, the yield curve may always be positively sloped even if investors actually expect rates to fall further. This will be so to the extent that liquidity premiums influence the yield curve and because low rate

In our examples we have employed only two illustrative values of p, 0.50 and 0.75. If investors attach a probability greater than 0.75 to the possibility that bond prices will rise (fall), a more sharply descending (ascending) curve will result. And if coupons on existing maturities are not all identical, we can expect different price reactions, all of which will obey Theorem 5. These price reactions will then alter the yield-maturity pattern, for bonds will now be more or less attractive to the investor depending upon their coupons. This is one reason for the many kinks frequently observed in the yield curve for government securities. A model cast in terms of price changes can deal effectively with this type of adjustment.

The introduction of considerations such as call features and the special tax advantages of discount bonds strengthens our analytical findings. When interest rates fall to low levels, many long-term bonds rise in price to where they sell at premiums over their call prices. This diminishes their attractiveness and tends to raise the yields of these long-term securities. Alternatively, high interest rates and accompanying low bond prices free the bondholder from call risks, and deep bond discounts lend added attraction because of their higher effective after-tax yields.

Finally, let us consider alternative methods of equalizing the mathematical expectation of gain among securities of various maturities. In our examples, we equalized opportunities for gain by eliminating them; that is, we allowed all bond prices to rise or fall so that the entire expectation of differential gain was removed. It is interesting to examine what would happen if investors sold shorts and bought longs when prices were expected to rise. In this case short-term bond prices would fall and, consequently, long-term prices would not have to rise as much as in our examples in order to equalize holding-period yields over the horizon period. The resulting level of rates would be higher than in our example solution. Furthermore, it can be shown that the yield curve would become steeper, because even small price declines in the short-term area would have a greater effect in raising short yields than the smaller increases in price in the long-term area would tend to raise long yields.[28]

---

levels leave investors more to fear than hope. The *possibilities* of capital losses far exceed the potential gains should rates fall farther. It may well be that forecasts of rate *changes* (explanatory factor three) are so difficult to make that they are not even attempted. In this case, an attempt to verify the modified expectations hypothesis utilizing *ex post* data would perforce be unsuccessful.

[28] When we allow alternative methods of equalizing mathematical expectations of gains and losses, we need no longer assume that the one-year normal range

As will be argued specifically in later chapters, we have no quarrel with the position taken by Culbertson and others that changes in the maturity structure of the supply of debt instruments are important determinants of the rate structure. It is useful, however, to look behind these changes to examine the possible role that expectations may play in causing those disturbances which are accused of impeding expectations on the demand side from determining the shape of the yield curve. An analysis of the introduction of expectations to the supply side of the market is completely analogous to our previous argument. If issuers of securities believe that interest rates are relatively high compared with their expectations of what constitutes a normal range, they will tend, to whatever extent possible, to issue short-term securities rather than longer bonds. Conversely, if rates appear attractive, issuers will take advantage of the opportunity and issue long-term securities. The motivation of issuers cannot be cast in terms of price risks but must rather be explained by considering the desire to minimize long-run financing costs. In Chapter 6 we shall present evidence to show that the timing of long-term borrowing and refunding is, to an important extent, flexible.

The pressures on the bond market from both the demand and supply sides are reinforcing in their effect. When interest rates are believed to be high in relation to historical precedent, investors will prefer to buy long-term bonds while issuers will prefer to sell short-term securities. Conversely, low interest rates will encourage investors to buy shorts and issuers to sell longs.

In the foregoing analysis, we have opened, with care, the Pandora box of expectations, and the direction, if not the magnitude, of their effect is unambiguous.

3.7 Reconciliation of the Alternative Formulation with the Traditional Theory[29]

We have seen that our alternative formulation of the expectations theory has relied on behavioral postulates which differ widely from

---

is tied to the level of the one-year short rate. If investors are allowed to arbitrage by selling shorts and buying longs when yields are expected to fall, then the level of rates (assuming it is a function of both long and short rates) may not be changed after the adjustment. Short rates will be higher but long rates will be lower, so that the one-year normal range may remain unchanged and, therefore, no further adjustment is required. If we assume that the level of rates (and therefore the one-year range) does change, we cannot tell a priori whether it will be higher or lower, and, consequently, it is impossible to make any definite statement about the secondary adjustments in the term structure that will occur.

[29] This section relies heavily on the work of Dudley G. Luckett in "Meiselman on Expectations" (mimeographed, 1965).

those of the traditional theory. In this section, we shall show that, despite these differences, the alternative model of the theory gives precisely the same implications as does the traditional analysis.

The crucial result of our model is that expected holding-period yields are equalized over the horizon period of investors. The behavioral mechanism by which this is accomplished, however, is entirely different from that of the traditional analysis. The Hicks-Lutz theory portrays investors as deciding between short- and long-term bonds on the basis of their expectations of a whole series of forward short-term rates. The model described in this chapter postulates that investors choose between the different maturities on the basis of potential capital gains and losses over a very near-term planning horizon. Investors were assumed to make no forecast of forward short-term interest rates several years into the future. Indeed, in the first formulation of the alternative model, investors were taken to be agnostic regarding future interest-rate movements. The only expectation they held was that interest rates would continue to fluctuate within their normal range. They sought to equalize, over a short horizon period, the expected value of potential price fluctuations for securities of different terms to maturity. Consequently, investors, in effect, estimated the expected value of the price of each security at the end of the horizon period.

In later formulations of the model, where specific expectations as to future rates (expectations proper) were introduced, these expectations were near-term in character and applied to the whole family of interest rates. Investors were taken to formulate short-term forecasts of long-term interest rates rather than long-term forecasts of short-term interest rates. In all versions of the alternative formulation of the model, however, the crucial results were that future bond prices were estimated and that holding-period yields were equalized over the horizon period. As long as expected holding-period yields are equalized for any one holding period, then we can show that the market is implicitly estimating a set of forward long-term rates as well as a whole series of forward short-term rates. Thus, even with the weak assumptions described herein, we can generate a set of interest-rate relationships with properties identical to those of the traditional expectations model. More specifically, in terms of our notation, we have shown how investor expectations may be expressed in terms of their beliefs about next year's price of a two-year security, $_{t+1}P_{t+2}$, next year's price of a three year bond, $_{t+1}P_{t+3}$, etc. We want to show that implicit in this estimate is a stream of anticipated one-year interest rates $_{t+1}r_1$, $_{t+2}r_1$,

. . . , the data employed by the classical expectations model. That is, we shall show that given any set of expected *prices* for next year, there is a unique stream of future one-year interest rates that is consistent with it.

We begin by noting that since holding-period yields are equalized for all securities over the next year, the yield on one-year bonds is determined. Moreover, once investors have, in effect, estimated the expected value of next year's price, $_{t+1}P_{t+2}$, for a bond which currently has two years to run, they have also *implicitly* estimated the one-year rate $_{t+1}r_1$ which is expected to obtain next year. Since we know next year's price, the coupon of the bond, C, and its face value, F, we can find the only forward rate for next year consistent with these figures by means of the expression

$$_{t+1}P_{t+2} = \frac{(C + F)}{(1 + {}_{t+1}r_1)} . \qquad (3\text{-}13)$$

Similarly, investors have also estimated the price of a three-year security, next year. This estimate together with the value of $_{t+1}r_1$ derived from (3-13) above may be used to find $_{t+2}r_{1,t}$ with the aid of the equation

$$_{t+1}P_{t+3,t} = \frac{C}{(1 + {}_{t+1}r_{1,t})} + \frac{C + F}{(1 + {}_{t+1}r_{1,t})(1 + {}_{t+2}r_{1,t})} . \qquad (3\text{-}13a)$$

In the same manner, a whole set of forward rates can be obtained that have identical properties with those of the Hicks-Lutz formulation. Thus, even though the two approaches start from very different behavioral assumptions, the final results of the two approaches are indistinguishable. Consequently, we can feel assured that, even if the analysis of this chapter provides a more accurate representation of the actual market processes, the traditional expectations approach can serve as a valid basis for the development of a more comprehensive theory of the term structure.

Thus we see that our alternative formulation of the expectations theory can generate a consistent pattern of forward short-term rates with properties identical to those of the traditional analysis. As long as investors act in a way that makes anticipated holding-period yields equal over one (short) horizon period, the result is the same as it would be if investors were making forecasts of forward rates far into the future.

Along these lines, Dudley Luckett has shown that Meiselman's regression results, which we described in the preceding chapter, are completely consistent with the view that investors attempt to maximize short-term returns by estimating the expected value of long-term rates, one year hence.[30] Luckett's argument proceeds as follows: Any two adjacent market interest rates can be used to derive an implied forward short-term rate by means of the Hicks formula[31]

$$1 + {}_{t+N}r_{1,t} = \frac{(1 + {}_tR_{N+1})^{N+1}}{(1 + {}_tR_N)^N} . \qquad (3\text{-}14)$$

Taking logs of (3-14) we have

$$\ln (1 + {}_{t+N}r_{1,t}) = (N + 1) \ln (1 + {}_tR_{N+1})$$
$$- N \ln (1 + {}_tR_N) . \qquad (3\text{-}14a)$$

Since, for small r, $\ln (1 + r) \approx r$, we may approximate (3-14a) by

$${}_{t+N}r_1 = (N + 1)({}_tR_{N+1}) - N({}_tR_N) . \qquad (3\text{-}14b)$$

Since any two adjacent *expected* long-term rates also imply a forward one-period rate, we may also write

$${}_{t+N}r_{1,t-1} = (N + 1)({}_tr_{N+1,t-1}) - N({}_tr_{N,t-1}) . \qquad (3\text{-}14c)$$

We may now define the errors made in forecasting adjacent long-term rates as

$$E_N = {}_tR_N - {}_tr_{N,t-1} , \qquad (3\text{-}15)$$

and

$$E_{N+1} = {}_tR_{N+1} - {}_tr_{N+1,t-1} . \qquad (3\text{-}15a)$$

Subtracting (3-14c) from (3-14b), and utilizing the definitions (3-15) and (3-15a) we obtain

$${}_{t+N}r_{1,t} - {}_{t+N}r_{1,t-1} = N + 1(E_{N+1}) - N(E_N) . \qquad (3\text{-}16)$$

Thus, we find that the change in expected forward short-term interest rates can be written as a function of the errors made in forecasting long-term rates.

Assuming that investors form their estimates of the expected value of long rates in the next period by the mechanism we have described above, errors in forecasting adjacent long rates will tend to be closely related. As long as these errors are systematically related, it is possible to derive Meiselman's model. For example, let $N = 1$ and assume

$$E_2 = \alpha + \beta E , \qquad (3\text{-}17)$$

[30] Dudley G. Luckett, *op. cit.*
[31] We abstract from the complications introduced in the Appendix to Chapter 2.

Substituting (3-17) into (3-16) we have for $N = 1$

$$_{t+1}r_{1,t} - _{t+1}r_{1,t-1} = 2\alpha + (2\beta - 1)E \ . \qquad (3\text{-}18)$$

If $a = 2\alpha$ and $b = 2\beta - 1$ then we have

$$_{t+1}r_{1,t} - _{t+1}r_{1,t-1} = a + b(_tR_1 - _tr_{1,t-1}) \ , \qquad (3\text{-}18a)$$

which is, of course, precisely the model tested by Meiselman. If there is a high correlation between adjacent forecasting errors for long rates one year ahead, then there will be a high correlation between the change in one-year forward rates and the forecasting error for one-year rates.

Luckett summarizes his argument as follows: "A sufficient condition for Meiselman's error-learning model to show significant correlations (and hence to constitute 'striking evidence' for the Hicks-Lutz theory) is that all errors of forecasting long-term rates be systematically related. . . ."[32] Employing the Durand data, Luckett finds, in fact, that there is a very high correlation among short-term forecasting errors for all maturities and concludes:

> Thus, Meiselman's statistical results are equally consistent with either the Hicks-Lutz or Malkiel theories. While expectations obviously do play a significant role in determining the rate structure, it cannot yet be regarded as established fact that investors decide the price they are willing to pay for 20-year bonds today on the basis of what they fancy the Federal Funds market will be doing each day for the next twenty years.[33]

3.8 Recapitulation

We shall now summarize our findings and underline the advantages of the model that has been presented. First, we have shown that an explicit examination of theoretical bond-price movements takes us part of the way toward an understanding of the observable structure of market interest rates. The inevitable tendency of the yield curve to flatten out as term to maturity is extended was explained and later demonstrated. Next, we derived from our model an ascending and descending yield curve with behavioral assumptions far less demanding than those in the traditional theory. In fact, expectations were introduced only in the assumption that future interest-rate fluctuations are believed certain to be contained within the range which has existed in the past. At a level of interest rates close to the upper

---

[32] Luckett, *op. cit.*
[33] *Ibid.*

end of the historical range we could explain a descending yield curve even where investors have formed no expectations as to the probable direction of interest-rate changes. When later we introduced stronger elements of foresight, our model had imparted to it the advantage of closer conformity with the practices of bond investors who have always considered the traditional theory unrealistic. Furthermore, the Keynes-Hicks modifications were easily assimilated into the analytical framework. Finally, our model could be modified to take account of differences in yield that result from coupon differences, call features, and tax advantages of discount bonds.

It will be useful to enumerate the salient differences between this approach and the traditional theory. First, instead of requiring definite and explicit expectations about the course of future short rates, the model substitutes the less demanding assumption of a normal range of yield fluctuations and a short planning period over which alternative strategies are compared. Moreover, if stronger elements of foresight are introduced, expectations of rate changes need only be *near-term* in character and concern long rates as much as short. Thus, unlike the received analysis, the model is concerned more with fluctuations in the long rate during the short run than with the short rate's behavior over the long run. Third, we deal explicitly with prices rather than yields. This not only affords added insights into the behavior of the rate structure, but, as we shall demonstrate in Chapter 6, is a more effective description from a behavioral point of view, as it conforms closely to the actual practices of investing institutions. Finally, since the model suggests the way investors may determine the normal range, it lends itself unusually well to empirical testing. These tests are conducted in the following Chapter. Thus, at least we have clothed the traditional expectational theory with new raiment which fits more closely the investing practices of bond investors and makes the theory both simpler in its assumptions and more amenable to modification.

Despite considerable differences in the behavioral postulates of the present and traditional models, we were able to show that the two approaches yield results that are indistinguishable from each other. As long as investors act to equalize the expected value of holding-period yields over one (short) horizon period, it is possible to derive the same consistent set of interest-rate relationships as were implied in the traditional analysis. Consequently, despite our amendments, the relationships of the Hicks-Lutz analysis may still serve as the foundation upon which we may build a more comprehensive theory, where factors other than expectations are accorded a major role in influencing the term structure.

APPENDIX TO CHAPTER 3

Effects of a Change in Market Interest Rates on Bond Prices

We remarked in the text that Theorem 2 (showing that the potential price volatility of a bond increases with maturity) did not hold in the general case where interest-rate changes are no longer measured from the nominal yield. In this appendix we show that for certain long-term, deep-discount bonds, price volatility *in response to an equal change in all market yields* may actually decrease with maturity.

In order to prove that bond-price movements are amplified as time to maturity increases, we must show that the "cross" partial derivative $\partial^2 P/\partial i\partial N < 0$, i.e., the slope of the function $P = f(i)$, becomes more negative as N increases. Differentiating (3-2) with respect to N and i we have

$$\frac{\partial^2 P}{\partial i\partial N} = -\frac{C}{i^2}\left[(1+i)^{-N}\ln(1+i)\right]$$

$$- N(1+i)^{-N-1}\left(\frac{C}{i}-F\right)(\ln(1+i))$$

$$+ \frac{1}{(1+i)}(1+i)^{-N}\left(\frac{C}{i}-F\right). \quad (3A\text{-}1)$$

It can easily be shown from (3A-1) that $\partial^2 P/\partial i\partial N < 0$ whenever the bond sells at a premium, that is, if $[(C/i)-F] > 0$. In this case, the second term of (3A-1) is negative. Hence, we need only show that the absolute value of the (negative) first term is greater than that of the (positive) third term. Factoring $(1+i)^{-N} > 0$ from both terms, we need only demonstrate that

$$\frac{C}{i^2}\ln(1+i) > \left[\frac{C}{i}-F\right]\frac{1}{1+i}. \quad (3A\text{-}2)$$

Rearranging terms, we may write (3A − 2) as

$$\frac{Fi^2}{C(1+i)} + \ln(1+i) > \frac{i}{1+i}. \quad (3A\text{-}3)$$

Since $\ln(1+i) > i/(1+i)$,[1] this inequality is easily established. Thus, the theorem holds generally for all bonds selling at a premium.

[1] This can easily be shown by expanding $\ln(1+i)$ by Taylor's series.

TABLE 3A-1

EFFECTS OF A CHANGE IN MARKET INTEREST RATES ON BOND PRICES
(Maturity Value $100; Coupon Rate 2%)

Years to maturity	Price		Fall in price	Percentage fall in price
	5.40% yield	5.50% yield		
1	96.734	96.639	0.094	0.097
5	85.274	84.880	0.394	0.462
10	73.992	73.352	0.640	0.865
15	65.349	64.564	0.785	1.202
20	58.727	57.863	0.864	1.471
25	53.654	52.755	0.900	1.677
30	49.768	48.860	0.908	1.824
35	46.790	45.891	0.899	1.922
40	44.509	43.627	0.882	1.981
45	42.762	41.902	0.860	2.011
50	41.423	40.586	0.837	2.021
55	40.397	39.583	0.815	2.016
60	39.611	38.818	0.794	2.003
65	39.009	38.235	0.775	1.985
70	38.548	37.790	0.758	1.966
75	38.195	37.451	0.743	1.946
100	37.343	36.644	0.699	1.871
∞	37.037	36.364	0.673	1.818

When the bond sells at a discount, however, the sign of (3A–1) is no longer negative for all values of the parameters.

Table 3A-1 presents an illustrative calculation of the price volatility

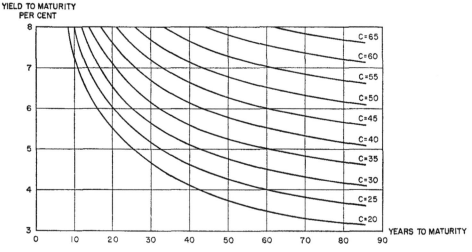

FIG. 3A-1. Combinations of yield, coupon, and maturity where the price volatility of a bond reaches a maximum.

of a 2 per cent coupon bond with alternative maturity dates. We note that when market yields increase from 5.40 per cent to 5.50 per cent, the resulting fall in price (column 3) increases with maturity, up to a maximum maturity of about 30 years. After 30 years, however, the price sensitivity of the bond actually declines with maturity. Column 4 shows that the percentage fall in price reaches a maximum at a maturity of about 55 years and declines thereafter.

Figure 3A-1 graphs some representative combinations of coupon values, maturity, and market yields for which the price sensitivity of bonds reaches a maximum. In other words, the curves show various combinations of parameters where the "cross" partial (3A-1) equals zero. While these particular combinations of parameters are seldom found in practice, they do demonstrate that it can be dangerous to accept, without analysis, some of the "obvious" and "universally known" propositions of the market place.

CHAPTER 4

An Empirical Test of the Reformulated
Expectations Hypothesis[1]

In Chapter 3 we introduced three basic factors that help to explain the slope of the yield curve: the mathematics of bond-price movements, the expectation of a normal range of interest rates, and expectations proper. We found that the first two determinants were sufficient, by themselves, to generate yield curves having any of the basic qualitative characteristics found in the Durand data. Of course, the nature of expectations proper may at times counteract the effect on the slope of a belief in the normal range whose operation is constrained by the mathematics of bond-price movements. But we have seen that if interest rates are near one of the bounds of the normal range, it will be difficult for specific expectations working in the opposite direction to alter the slope of the yield curve. Moreover, it is just as likely that expectations proper will intensify the effect of the first two factors. Thus, in the absence of any independent quantitative evidence concerning investors' expectations of the likelihood of rates rising or falling, it is appropriate to provide a test of an expectations hypothesis that ignores the effects of expectations proper.[2]

The hypothesis we wish to test may be stated as follows: When the level of interest rates is near the upper bound of the normal range of interest rates, the spread between long and short rates should be relatively small (algebraically), perhaps negative. When the level of rates is near the lower bound of the normal range, the long-short yield spread should be relatively large. Taking the long rate as representative of the general level of rates, we may write this postulated relationship as

$$L - S = h \left[\frac{L - L_{LN}}{L_{UN} - L_{LN}} \right] . \tag{4-1}$$

[1] This work used computer facilities supported in part by National Science Foundation Grant NSF-GP579.

[2] Of course, if specific expectations about future rate movements are themselves a function of the relationship between current rates and the normal range, then our tests might be considered to encompass all three explanatory factors described in the preceding chapter. For example, investors might believe that when rates are high relative to their normal range of variation there is a greater probability that they will fall and vice versa. If the reader wishes, he may interpret these results accordingly.

82

L refers to the long and *S* to the short rate, and the subscripts indicate the upper (UN) and the lower (LN) bound of the normal range of interest rates. As long as the current long rate does not fall outside the normal range, the fraction of the right-hand side will always be between 0 and 1, depending upon the height of the current long rate.

Equation (4-1) employs the long rate as a surrogate for the level of interest rates. The equation presumes that, whenever the long rate is high relative to the normal range for long rates, interest rates in general are high relative to their normal range.[3] On this presumption, when interest rates in general are high relative to their normal range, our hypothesis implies that the short rate will tend to be high relative to the long rate.

4.1 *Formulation of a Specific Hypothesis*

Equation (4-1) is not in operational form. Before it can be tested explicitly, the normal range must first be defined. In this section, we suggest a method that might plausibly be taken by investors in determining the extremes of the normal range, and on this basis we formulate a specific testable hypothesis.

In an *ex post* sense, the extremes of the normal range of interest rates are easy to determine. Utilizing the Durand data since 1900, we can say that the highest 30-year rate that ever prevailed was 5.17 per cent (in 1921) and the lowest (excluding the period of interest-rate pegging) 2.65 per cent (in 1941). There are two difficulties, however, with the utilization of these limits in our empirical work. In the first place, we seek *ex ante*, not *ex post*, extremes. It is one thing to argue that investors *today* may consider these extremes to bound the normal range for the highest quality corporate bonds. It is quite another matter to assert that an investor during 1920 could have foreseen accurately that interest-rate fluctuations for long-term bonds would be contained within that range. Thus, it is necessary to construct a normal range on the basis of information already in the possession of bond investors. Moreover, as we suggested in Section 3.7, it is plausible that investors'

---

[3] Of course, any number of other plausible hypotheses could have been tested. Another, which was tried, took the short-long spread to be a function of the position of the short rate within the normal range for short rates. This test yielded the same type of result as was obtained for the hypothesis discussed in the text. Notice that we could not use both the long and short rates to indicate the level of rates. Had we done so, we would have been predicting the short-long spread, already knowing the magnitude of both rates and hence their difference.

expectations will be more heavily influenced by the experience of the more immediate past. When interest rates have been low for a considerable period of time, investors may come to reduce the limits of what they consider to be the normal range. Thus we suggest, as an initial hypothesis, that investors at any point in time examine only actual interest-rate fluctuations over, say, the past 15 years in forming their expectation of the normal range of interest-rate fluctuations.

We suggest further that investors form their expectations of the limits of the normal range as if they took the average of rates over some period in the immediate past and added a specified number of standard deviations to either side of the average. The standard deviations would be calculated over a very long period of bond-market history and be considered constant from year to year. The average rate to which they would be applied would vary from period to period, because it would be continuously corrected by receipt of the most recent information. As each new year's information is added, the oldest year's observation would be eliminated. The number of standard deviations to be added would be determined by the confidence limits set by investors and their typical horizon period.[4] Thus, we may write the upper and lower bounds of the normal range as seen by investors as follows:

$$
\begin{aligned}
L_{UN} &= L_A + K\sigma \\
L_{LN} &= L_A - K\sigma
\end{aligned}
\qquad (4\text{-}2)
$$

where L_A is defined as the moving average of long-term interest rates over a specified period of years in the past. Substituting (4-2) into (4-1) we have the amended hypothesis

$$
L - S = h\left[\frac{L - L_A + K\sigma}{2K\sigma}\right]. \qquad (4\text{-}3)
$$

Under the assumption of unvarying σ, the right-hand side of (4-3) contains the constants $K\sigma$ and $2K\sigma$. Thus, as a nearly equivalent hypothesis we propose:

$$
L - S = H(L - L_A) \qquad (4\text{-}4)
$$

---

[4] The shorter the investors' horizon period, the less likely is it that rates can move to the extremes of the historical range. This is only to say that what might be considered an appropriate five-year normal range would undoubtedly be too wide for an investor whose planning horizon is three months.

where H and h are related by a linear transformation. Assuming the function H is itself linear, we may write:

$$L - S = a + b(L - L_\text{A}) . \qquad (4\text{-}5)$$

Our theoretical work in Chapter 3 suggests first that there is a significant correlation between the short- and long-rate differential and the distance of the long rate from the past average of long rates. Moreover, we posit that the b coefficient is negative and significantly different from zero. This is so because when rates are considered to be near the top of the normal range (that is, well above the mid-point of the range), basic explanatory factors one and two will cause long rates to be low relative to short rates. Inversely, when rates are considered to be near the bottom of the normal range, it is our hypothesis that long rates will be high relative to short rates. In the previous chapter we offered repeated illustrations of these relationships. The current tests seek to examine whether or not the long-short rate differential actually behaves in a manner consistent with the reformulated expectations hypothesis.

4.2 Some Preliminary Results

To execute an initial test of the hypothesis (4-5), we chose 15 years as a reasonable time period over which expectations of normal rates might be formed. The spreads between short and long rates at time t were regressed against the difference between the long rate during period t and the 15-year average of long rates ending in period $t - 1$. The short rate used was the Durand series of one-year rates presented in Table 1-1 above. The long rate was identified with the Durand 30-year rate. The test was limited to the period 1900 through 1942.

The years after 1942, through 1951, were considered inappropriate since interest rates were pegged throughout this time span.[5] Undoubtedly expectations continued to play a part in determining how far prices rose above their support levels. Nevertheless, these expectations concerned the likelihood that the pegging operations would continue, not the expectations of a normal range of interest rates. For much the same reason, we were unable to use data from the period following 1951. Since the average of long rates during the 1940's was artificially determined, an investor during 1952

[5] For a discussion and interpretation of Federal Reserve policymaking over this period, see Lester V. Chandler, *Inflation in the United States, 1940–1948* (New York: Harper and Bros., 1951), pp. 181ff.

would probably not have formed his expectations of the normal range in a free market from an average of long rates including those of the period of pegging.

Applying ordinary least-squares analysis to the Durand data through 1942, we obtain the following equation:

$$L - S = 0.335 - 1.585(L - L_A) . \qquad (4\text{-}6)$$
$$(0.095) \quad (0.125)$$

The correlation coefficient is 0.927, and the b coefficient is negative and significantly different from zero. Moreover, the positive constant term implies that when the long rate equals the long average, the yield curve will be positively sloped.

Unfortunately, this simple test has two difficulties which mar its usefulness for our purposes. First, as the reader has undoubtedly noticed, the long rate appears on both sides of the equation. As the long rate goes up, both $(L - S)$ and $(L - L_A)$ tend to rise. This biases the test against us, because our hypothesis is one of *negative* correlation. Naturally, this tends to introduce bias into the regression coefficients themselves. A second difficulty is that both constructed time series of differentials contain a significant degree of serial correlation. Unlike the first difficulty, this may work to the benefit of our hypothesis. Hence, the high correlation coefficient may well be misleading. For these reasons we were forced to abandon hypothesis (4-5) in favor of a different statement of the relationship.

4.3   An Alternative Test of the Expectations Hypothesis

Fortunately, both difficulties noted above are easily corrected. To avoid the bias introduced by the appearance of the long rate on both sides of the equation, we need simply solve (4-5) explicitly for S.

$$S = -a + (1 - b)L + bL_A . \qquad (4\text{-}7)$$

Leaving $(1 - b)$ completely unrestricted, we may then perform a multiple regression where the long rate and average of long rates are the independent variables and the short rate is the dependent variable. Since (4-7) does not include the lagged dependent variable, an unbiased estimate of its coefficients may be obtained by ordinary regression analysis. The results are:

$$S = -1.894 + 2.606L - 1.233L_A . \qquad (4\text{-}8)$$
$$(1.294) \quad (0.125) \quad (0.317)$$

As expected, our estimate of b falls, and the (multiple) correlation coefficient is raised to 0.972. To avoid the problem of serial correlation in the time series, we took first differences of equation (4-7) and then performed a separate multiple regression. The results were:

$$\Delta S = 0.000 + 2.446\ \Delta L - 1.599\ \Delta L_A\ , \qquad (4\text{-}9)$$
$$ (0.091) \quad (0.314) \qquad (1.161)$$

and the multiple correlation coefficient falls only to 0.847.

Two further tests were then performed to determine whether the differencing operation had successfully removed the autocorrelation from the time series. The first was a modification of a test procedure suggested by Orcutt and James to adjust for serial correlation in simple regression problems.[6] The Orcutt-James test adjusts the degrees of freedom used in significance tests according to the degree of serial correlation in the dependent and independent variables. As an adaptation of the test, we propose to treat the actual change in the short rate (ΔS) as the dependent variable and the calculated change in the short rate (ΔS_C) as the independent variable.[7] We find both the ΔS and ΔS_C series are essentially free of autocorrelation. The correlation coefficients between a series of the actual observations and a series constructed of the actual observations lagged one year are 0.18 for ΔS and 0.19 for ΔS_C. The Orcutt-James procedure uses these autocorrelation coefficients to adjust the number of observations downward. If there is significant autocorrelation in the series, the effective number of independent observations is reduced, and hence the significance of the correlation coefficient is attenuated. In our case, the autocorrelation coefficients are so low that the effective number of observations is reduced by less than three.[8] The multiple correlation coefficient is still significant at the one per cent level of significance. Thus we conclude that our high correlation is not spurious (that is, it is not produced by a high degree of autocorrelation in the time series).

[6] See G. H. Orcutt and S. F. James, "Testing the Significance of Correlation between Time Series," *Biometrika* 35 (1948), pp. 397–413.

[7] As a heuristic justification, we suggest that the short rate calculated from the two independent variables (the long rate and the long average) will tend to be autocorrelated to the extent that there is serial correlation in the independent variables.

[8] The number of observations in the differenced series is 26. By our adaptation of the Orcutt-James test, the effective number n of independent observations is given by

$$\frac{1}{n-1} = \frac{1 + [r(\Delta S)][r(\Delta S_C)]}{N[1 - r(\Delta S)r(\Delta S_C)]}\ .$$

Substituting the relevant values into the above equation, we find $n = 23.3$.

The Orcutt-James test does not, of course, relieve us of the necessity of testing for serial correlation in the residuals. It is possible that the residuals may be highly intercorrelated despite the fact that serial correlation was absent from the variables themselves. The residuals were analyzed by calculating the Durbin-Watson statistic (d').[9] For the regression on the first differences of the time series we have $d' = 2.28$ and $4 - d' = 1.72$. For $N = 27$ and two independent variables the upper limit for d' is 1.56 at the 5 per cent confidence level. Since both d' and $4 - d'$ are greater than the upper limit, we may safely assume that there is no serial correlation in the residuals. This suggests that we have been able to avoid the serious problems that most frequently beset the estimation of relationships from time-series data.[10]

4.4 *Reconciliation of the Alternative Hypothesis with the Theory*[11]

One further step remains. We must now ensure that our alternative hypothesis is indeed equivalent to the original hypothesis derived from the theory. Recall that we fitted equation (4-7) to the data, leaving $(1 - b)$ completely unrestricted. In this section we show that our results are in fact equivalent to a statement of the original hypothesis, which requires that the coefficients of the long and long average rates must add to unity.

Here, we employ a test described by Tintner.[12] The point of the test is to determine whether the restriction on the sum of the coefficients (that is, that they add to unity) is valid. This is accomplished by comparing two sums: (1) the sum of the squares of the deviations from the regression equation (4-9) fitted by the method of least squares and (2) the sum of the squares of the deviations from a new regression equation fitted by applying the restriction.

---

[9] See J. Durbin and G. S. Watson, "Testing for Serial Correlation in Least Squares Regression: II," *Biometrika* 38 (1951), pp. 159–178. The statistic d' is given by

$$d' = \sum_{t=2}^{N} (d_t - d_{t-1})^2 \bigg/ \sum_{t=1}^{N} d_t^2 \, ,$$

where $d_t (t = 1, \ldots, n)$ denote the residuals from the fitted-least-squares regression.

[10] For an excellent discussion of the consequences of autocorrelated disturbances, see J. Johnston, *Econometric Methods* (New York: McGraw-Hill, 1963), pp. 177–200.

[11] This section is somewhat more technical than the rest of the chapter and may be skipped, without loss of continuity, after reading the initial paragraph.

[12] Gerhard Tintner, *Econometrics* (New York: John Wiley and Sons, 1952), pp. 89–92. Tintner, in turn, credits S. S. Wilks, *Mathematical Statistics* (Princeton: Princeton University Press, 1945), pp. 124 ff., with the procedure.

We denote the new regression coefficients to be fitted under the restriction as K_0, K_2 and K_3. We have to minimize the sum of squares of deviations,

$$Q_2 = \sum_{t=1}^{27} (X_{1t} - K_0 - K_2 X_{2t} - K_3 X_{3t})^2 \qquad (4\text{-}10)$$

subject to the restriction

$$K_2 + K_3 = 1 .$$

The constrained minimum of (4-10) is the same as the minimum of the function

$$\theta = Q_2 + \lambda(K_2 + K_3 - 1)$$

where λ is a Lagrange multiplier. K_2, K_3, and λ may now be determined from a set of so-called "normal equations."[13] We find $K_2 = 2.39$, $K_3 = -1.39$, and the sum of the squares of the residuals for the restricted equation, $Q = 5.21$.

We now proceed to test whether the sum of the squares of the residuals is the same for both equations, that is, whether $Q_2 = Q_1$. In this way, we test the hypothesis that the sum of the regression coefficients is actually unity. We form the function

$$F = \frac{(Q_2 - Q_1)(N - p)}{Q_1}$$

where N represents the number of observations and p the total number of variables (dependent and independent). This is distributed like Snedecor's F, with 1 and 24 degrees of freedom. In our case, $F = 0.331$, whereas at the 1 per cent level of significance the critical value of F is 7.82. Consequently the empirical F is not significant. The hypothesis that the regression coefficients add to unity need not be rejected. We conclude that the original hypothesis is supported by the data.

4.5 *Some Supplementary Tests*

While these results are extremely encouraging for our modified expectations hypothesis, several questions remain. One can ask, for example, why 15 years should be singled out as the appropriate time span for the formulation of the normal range of interest rates. Moreover, even if 15 years were the proper time period, investors might still place more emphasis on interest rates in recent years in

---

[13] Tintner, *op. cit.*, p. 90.

formulating their ideas of the normal range of interest rates. In addition, we might question whether investors disregard more distant market history in formulating their interest-rate expectations. Do they, for example, ignore the historic range of interest-rate fluctuations prior to the past 15 years? Surely one can think of a number of plausible methods by which investors could formulate the normal range. It is then important to test the sensitivity of our results to alternative formulations of the normal range. Finally, in view of the difficulties encountered by Meiselman's hypothesis when confronted with alternative interest-rate time series, it is appropriate to ask whether our hypothesis is sensitive to the set of data chosen. Can it be supported by calculations utilizing United States Treasury yields and British government yields? In this section we shall present the results of tests of several alternative specifications of our reformulated expectations hypothesis utilizing different sets of interest-rate time series.

4.5.a INTRODUCTION OF A WEIGHTED MOVING AVERAGE

Table 4-1 presents regression results for the Durand corporate data, using a 15-year time period to formulate the (mid-point of the) normal range of interest rates. In addition to the simple-moving-average case described in Section 4.3, three alternative methods of calculating the long average rate (L_A) were examined. The first alternative was to construct an exponentially weighted moving average of past long rates as the basis upon which expectations of the normal range might be formed. The mid-point of the normal range for period t was computed by

$$L_{A,t} = \sum_{i=1}^{15} {}_{t-i}R_{30}\lambda^i \Big/ \sum_{i=1}^{15} \lambda^i . \qquad (4\text{-}11)$$

λ was allowed to vary from 0.9 to 0.1. When we allowed λ to take on the value of 0.9, this gave the long rate in the preceding year approximately four times the weight of the long rate 15 years previously in determining the long average.[14] The rationale for this procedure lies in our conjecture that investors may shape their expectations so as to lay heavier emphasis on the more immediate past in shaping their expectations.

---

[14] In contrast, the simple moving averages described earlier give equal weight to each of the preceding 15 years; that is, $\lambda = 1$. Only the regression results for $\lambda = 0.9$ are reported in Table 4-1.

TABLE 4-1

REGRESSION RESULTS: DURAND DATA (1900–1942), 15-YEAR AVERAGES

$$S = a_0 + a_1 L + a_2 L_A$$

Data	Method of calculating long average rate	$\hat{a}_0$	$\hat{a}_1$	$\hat{a}_2$	$\hat{a}_1 + \hat{a}_2$	F[a]	R[b]	d'[c]
Raw data	Simple moving average ($\lambda = 1$)	−1.876 (1.319)	2.606 (0.128)	−1.238 (0.323)	1.368	1.600	.969	0.888
Transformed data ($\hat{\rho} = 0.573$)	Simple moving average ($\lambda = 1$)		2.544 (0.209)	−1.310 (0.636)	1.234	0.185	.924	1.852
Raw data	Weighted moving average ($\lambda = 0.9$)	−2.863 (1.226)	2.812 (0.164)	−1.201 (0.360)	1.611	5.157	.966	0.846
Transformed data ($\hat{\rho} = 0.595$)	Weighted moving average ($\lambda = 0.9$)		2.631 (0.250)	−1.029 (0.599)	1.602	1.719	.917	1.843
Raw data	0.5 (simple moving average) + 0.5 (AHL)	0.504 (1.973)	2.611 (0.130)	−1.843 (0.498)	0.768	0.272	.968	0.858
Transformed data ($\hat{\rho} = 0.589$)	0.5 (simple moving average) + 0.5 (AHL)		2.563 (0.218)	−2.042 (1.023)	0.521	0.296	.921	1.799
Raw data	0.5 (weighted moving average, $\lambda = 0.9$) + 0.5 (AHL)	−0.266 (1.954)	2.767 (0.156)	−1.809 (0.541)	0.958	0.009	.966	0.823
Transformed data ($\hat{\rho} = 0.606$)	0.5 (weighted moving average, $\lambda = 0.9$) + 0.5 (AHL)		2.634 (0.252)	−1.724 (0.981)	0.910	0.013	.915	1.807

[a] Test that the regression coefficients satisfy the constraint $\hat{a}_1 + \hat{a}_2 = 1$.

[b] The multiple correlation coefficient.

[c] The Durbin-Watson statistic.

The choice of the second and third alternatives was motivated by the supposition that the (mid-point of the) long-run historic range of interest-rate fluctuations also plays a part in determining the normal range. In measuring the historic range, we went back 20 years prior to the beginning of the Durand series and found the high and low yields from 1880 until period $t - 1$, the year preceding each observation. This historic range was then adjusted whenever a rate was observed to fall outside of the previous range. While equivalent interest-rate data prior to the initial date of our series were not available, we felt that Macaulay's high-grade railroad bond averages were sufficiently comparable to the Durand basic yields to permit their use.[15] The mid-point of the historic range and the moving average over the past 15 years were then consolidated by simply taking the weighted sum of the two, where we arbitrarily selected weights of 0.5. Both the simple and weighted moving averages were used in connection with the mid-point of the historic range, and multiple regressions were performed with each combination.[16]

We found that when regressions were carried out with raw data, the residuals turned out to be significantly serially correlated, as indicated by the Durbin-Watson statistic d'. Consequently, it was necessary to transform the raw time series. Instead of using first differences, as we did in Section 4.3, the following data transformation was undertaken. We first computed the simple-least-squares residuals $\hat{\mu}_{1915}$, $\hat{\mu}_{1916}$, . . . , $\hat{\mu}_{1942}$. Then, assuming that the autoregressive scheme is a first-order one,

$$\mu_t = \rho\mu_{t-1} + \epsilon_t ,$$

we estimated ρ by computing the least-squares regression

$$\hat{\mu}_t = \hat{\rho}\hat{\mu}_{t-1} + e_t . \qquad (4\text{-}12)$$

The regression coefficient $\hat{\rho}$ was used to compute the transformed variables $(S_t - \hat{\rho}S_{t-1})$, $(L_t - \hat{\rho}L_{t-1})$, and $(L_{A,t} - \hat{\rho}L_{A,t-1})$. A simple-least-squares regression was then calculated utilizing the transformed variables.[17] The results of each regression on the

---

[15] See Frederick R. Macaulay, *The Movements of Interest Rates, Bond Yields, and Stock Prices in the United States since 1856* (New York: National Bureau of Economic Research, 1938), pp. A142ff.

[16] When we combine the mid-point of the historic range and the weighted moving average, we are, in effect, putting heavy emphasis on both the last few years and the historic range.

[17] A description of this procedure appears in Johnston, *op. cit.*, p. 194.

transformed variables are shown in Table 4-1 directly below the regression results for the original variables.

While we shall defer a full interpretation of the test results until the next section, it should be noted that all the four alternatives reported work well. The regression coefficients are quite stable (before and after data transformation), multiple correlation coefficients remain high, and none of the calculated empirical F's is significant. The alternatives that seem to work best (using the insignificance of the empirical F as a criterion) are those where both a moving average and the long-run historical range are used in calculating the mid-point of the normal range. We did find, however, that as the value of λ was allowed to decrease, the significance of the long average rate was attenuated. For example, the t-value associated with the coefficient of L_A when $\lambda = 1$ was 3.83 (2.06 after data transformation). The corresponding t-value when $\lambda = 0.1$ was 1.81 (1.04 after data transformation). These tests indicated that, in the case of a finite 15-year lag, a value of λ close to unity appears to yield the most satisfactory results.

4.5.b   USE OF SHORTER MOVING AVERAGES AND THE HISTORICAL RANGE

Table 4-2 presents the results of tests utilizing 10-year moving averages and the historical range of interest-rate fluctuations in the calculation of the long average rate. Data from the 1900–1942 period are first used alone and then combined with data from the 1951–1965 period. As mentioned earlier, we did not feel that the period of interest-rate pegging (1942–1951) could appropriately be included in the test. This also meant that interest-rate observations from the whole decade of the 1950's had to be excluded since investors had reason to believe that the long average rate during the preceding 10 years was, at least partly, artificial. Consequently, only postwar observations after 1961, 10 years after the Treasury–Federal Reserve Accord, were included in the tests.[18] The results are similar to those reported in Table 4-1.

We also undertook a series of tests utilizing moving averages of even shorter length. While the results were not highly sensitive to the length of the lag, we did find that shorter lags did not work as well as longer ones. For example the t-value associated with L_A

---

[18] Of course, interest-rate observations during the 1950's were used in calculating the long average rate for the 1961–1965 period.

(which was 3.83 for a 15-year lag) fell to 2.49 (1.37 after data transformation) in the case of a 5-year lag and to 2.38 (1.21 after data transformation) in the case of a 3-year lag, where λ was set equal to unity in all cases. These results suggested that investors

TABLE 4-2

REGRESSION RESULTS: DURAND DATA, 10-YEAR AVERAGES

$$S = a_0 + a_1L + a_2L_A$$

(Normal long average rate (L_A) composed of
average of Durand long rate for preceding 10 years and average historical
high and low long yields)

Data	λ	$\hat{a}_0$	$\hat{a}_1$	$\hat{a}_2$	$\hat{a}_1 + \hat{a}_2$	F	R	d'
Prewar period: 1900–1942								
Raw data	1	0.563	2.832	−2.054	0.778	0.326	.953	0.719
		(1.701)	(0.164)	(0.460)				
Transformed data	1		2.599	−1.280	1.319	0.162	.896	1.868
$(\hat{\rho} = 0.654)$			(0.245)	(0.923)				
Raw data	0.9	0.150	2.964	−1.917	1.047	0.019	.953	0.725
		(1.637)	(0.181)	(0.436)				
Transformed data	0.9		2.646	−1.143	1.503	0.627	.897	1.880
$(\hat{\rho} = 0.651)$			(0.256)	(0.776)				
Prewar and postwar periods combined: 1900–1942 and 1951–1965								
Raw data	1	−0.048	2.572	−1.715	0.857	0.080	.929	0.634
		(2.171)	(0.170)	(0.546)				
Transformed data	1		2.180	−0.540	1.640	0.370	.880	1.841
$(\hat{\rho} = 0.694)$			(0.197)	(1.099)				
Raw data	0.9	−0.971	2.720	−1.284	1.436	1.506	.928	0.616
		(1.923)	(0.188)	(0.423)				
Transformed data	0.9		2.236	−0.687	1.549	0.646	.881	1.836
$(\hat{\rho} = 0.703)$			(0.207)	(0.766)				

use a relatively long period of market history in formulating their ideas of the normal range.

4.5.c   ESTIMATION BY THE LIVIATAN TECHNIQUE

We also estimated the relationship between short rates and current and past values of the long rate using a technique developed by Nissan Liviatan for consistent estimation of equations that include a lagged dependent variable.[19] Consider the infinite-lag

[19] Nissan Liviatan, "Consistent Estimation of Distributed Lags," *International Economic Review*, 4 (January 1963), pp. 44–52.

form of equation (4-7) below:

$$S_t = \alpha L_t + \beta \sum_{i=0}^{\infty} \lambda^i L_{t-1-i} + u_t , \qquad (4\text{-}7a)$$

which can be reduced to

$$S_t = \alpha L_t + (\beta - \lambda\alpha)L_{t-1} + \lambda S_{t-1} + w_t . \qquad (4\text{-}7b)$$

Here we treat λ as a third unknown to be estimated along with α and $(\beta - \lambda\alpha)$. The method of estimation proceeded as follows. First, we replaced S_{t-1} in (4-7b) with S'_{t+1}. The latter was the calculated value of S_{t-1} from a least-squares regression of S_{t-1} on current and lagged values of the long rate. Then we performed a "second-stage" regression of S_t on L_t, L_{t-1}, and S'_{t-1} and obtained the following results:

$$S_t = \begin{array}{cccc} 0.926 & + 2.545L_t & - 2.096L_{t-1} & + 0.754S'_{t-1} \\ (2.522) & (0.394) & (0.732) & (0.360) \end{array} \; ; \; (4\text{-}7c)$$
$$R = 0.976, \qquad d' = 2.126 .$$

We note that the coefficient of the long rate is approximately equal to the value obtained in earlier tests. The estimated value of λ was 0.754. This is also consistent with the findings reported above for the finite-lag case where the best results were obtained when λ was allowed to take on relatively high values.

4.5.d   SENSITIVITY WITH RESPECT TO THE SET OF DATA CHOSEN

Table 4-3 presents some further results using U.S. Treasury yields and Grant's time series of interest rates for British government bonds. Seven-year moving averages were used in conjunction with the historic high and low yields for the respective time series.[20] The shorter time period was chosen in order to obtain enough observations to permit a test using U.S. Treasury yields. As we indicated in Chapter 1, a long-run series of comparable U.S. Treasury yields by term to maturity does not exist. Moreover, for the reasons stated above, we did not wish to include Treasury yields during the period of interest-rate pegging. Consequently, our time series (listed in Table 4-4) starts in 1951.

Results are reported for sample values of λ that produced the

[20] To obtain quotations of long-term British Treasury yields prior to 1924, we used Sidney Homer's average of long-term British government yields. See Sidney Homer, *A History of Interest Rates* (New Brunswick: Rutgers University Press, 1963), p. 409. Estimates of U.S. Treasury long-term yields prior to 1951 were obtained from the same source, p. 352.

TABLE 4-3
REGRESSION RESULTS: 7-YEAR AVERAGES
$$S = a_0 + a_1 L + a_2 L_A$$
(Normal long average rate (L_A) composed of
average long rate for preceding 7 years and average historical high and
low long yields)

Data	λ	$\hat{a}_0$	$\hat{a}_1$	$\hat{a}_2$	$\hat{a}_1 + \hat{a}_2$	F	R	d'
Durand corporate yields (annually, 1900–1965)[a]								
Raw data	1	−1.424	2.687	−1.442	1.245	0.472	.905	0.397
		(0.149)	(0.201)	(0.438)				
Transformed data	1		2.549	−1.334	1.215	0.080	.873	2.149
($\hat{\rho} = 0.810$)			(0.220)	(0.831)				
Raw data	0.82	−1.011	2.842	−1.700	1.142	0.158	.909	0.409
		(1.507)	(0.220)	(0.479)				
Transformed data	0.82		2.608	−1.493	1.115	0.027	.876	2.179
($\hat{\rho} = 0.804$)			(0.225)	(0.792)				
Grant British government yields (quarterly, Dec. 1924–Sept. 1962)[a]								
Raw data	1	−0.913	1.337	−0.514	0.823	3.644	.971	1.321
		(0.391)	(0.058)	(0.127)				
Transformed data	1		1.316	−0.560	0.756	4.584	.951	1.463
($\hat{\rho} = 0.344$)			(0.075)	(0.157)				
Raw data	0.95	−1.225	1.390	−0.498	0.892	2.059	.971	1.350
		(0.315)	(0.066)	(0.118)				
Transformed data	0.95		1.364	−0.523	0.841	2.901	.953	1.474
($\hat{\rho} = 0.330$)			(0.083)	(0.145)				
U.S. Treasury yields (quarterly, Apr. 1951–Apr. 1965)								
Raw data	1	0.007	2.071	−1.397	0.674	0.786	.744	0.462
		(1.355)	(0.327)	(0.520)				
Transformed data	1		2.514	−0.135	2.379	1.610	.827	2.217
($\hat{\rho} = 0.783$)			(0.298)	(1.161)				
Raw data	0.95	0.737	2.260	−1.792	0.468	2.283	.778	0.502
		(1.310)	(0.320)	(0.515)				
Transformed data	0.95		2.511	−0.432	2.079	1.002	.826	2.182
($\hat{\rho} = 0.762$)			(0.298)	(1.146)				

[a] Omitting 1942 through 1950 observations for Durand corporate yields and Sept. 1939–Sept. 1951 observations for Grant British Government yields.

most satisfactory results.[21] To serve as a basis for comparison, Table 4-3 also presents regression results for the Durand data on the basis of seven-year moving averages.

[21] The particular λ's reported were such that the most recent observation entering the moving average had about four times the weight of the most remote interest rate.

TABLE 4-4

YIELDS ON U.S. TREASURY SECURITIES MATURING IN 1 AND 20 YEARS:
QUARTERLY DATA, JANUARY 1951–APRIL 1965

Date mid-month	Years to maturity		Date mid-month	Years to maturity	
	1	20		1	20
Jan. 1950	1.14%	2.26%	Jan. 1958	2.56%	3.18%
April	1.21	2.36	April	1.66	3.16
July	1.23	2.43	July	1.49	3.40
October	1.44	2.44	October	3.02	3.74
Jan. 1951	1.53	2.44	Jan. 1959	3.15	3.84
April	1.75	2.64	April	3.50	3.99
July	1.70	2.67	July	3.90	4.19
October	1.70	2.65	October	4.71	4.33
Jan. 1952	1.87	2.75	Jan. 1960	4.91	4.55
April	1.66	2.70	April	3.53	4.09
July	1.89	2.63	July	3.09	4.03
October	1.99	2.76	October	2.88	3.86
Jan. 1953	2.11	2.79	Jan. 1961	2.69	3.86
April	2.11	2.91	April	2.85	3.84
July	2.23	2.99	July	2.87	3.89
October	1.83	2.85	October	2.99	3.97
Jan. 1954	1.33	2.72	Jan. 1962	3.15	4.10
April	1.12	2.52	April	3.00	3.97
July	0.76	2.50	July	3.11	4.01
October	1.00	2.54	October	2.91	4.00
Jan. 1955	1.40	2.69	Jan. 1963	3.05	3.93
April	1.90	2.79	April	3.05	4.02
July	1.96	2.86	July	3.16	4.05
October	2.36	2.87	October	3.55	4.10
Jan. 1956	2.56	2.90	Jan. 1964	3.80	4.17
April	2.96	3.11	April	3.93	4.24
July	2.57	2.99	July	3.71	4.14
October	3.14	3.18	October	3.77	4.18
Jan. 1957	3.21	3.30	Jan. 1965	4.00	4.19
April	3.35	3.34	April	4.02	4.17
July	3.65	3.56			
October	3.98	3.75			

Source: Sidney Homer, *An Analytic Record of Yields and Yield Spreads* (New York: Salomon Brothers and Hutzler, 1963), and supplements.

4.6 Interpretation of Test Results

The evidence presented in this chapter strongly supports our modified expectations hypothesis. A number of plausible assumptions concerning the formulation of the normal range were examined and all were found to lend support to our hypothesis. This result can easily be explained. It simply reflects the fact that the mid-point of the normal range is not particularly sensitive to alternative methods used in its estimation. Any method that utilizes a reasonable amount of past market history produces approximately the same estimate. In addition, we found that our hypothesis is not contradicted by using alternative interest-rate time series. Tests conducted using Treasury yield series from the United States and the United Kingdom confirm the results obtained using the Durand corporate yields. The correlation coefficients obtained are uniformly high. Moreover, in no case can we reject the hypothesis that the regression coefficients add to unity. No empirical F is significant at the 5 per cent level. While the residuals from the raw data are typically autocorrelated by the Durbin-Watson test, the data transformation successfully copes with this problem.[22]

Some aspects of our results deserve further comment. A conspicuous consequence of the procedure for transforming the data was that the significance of the coefficient of the mid-point of the normal range (L_A) was typically reduced. This was especially true for the tests conducted with U.S. Treasury yield data. Such an effect is to be expected. In cases where our estimated $\hat{\rho}$ is close to unity, the transformation procedure employed is nearly equivalent to taking first differences of the time series. In a differencing operation, with $\lambda = 1$, the long average rate will change in each period by the difference between the most recent year's long rate and the long rate n years earlier (divided by n). This means that we have been able to buy the removal of serial correlation at the cost of having a less direct representation of our behavioral hypothesis. A differencing procedure is less objectionable in the case where $\lambda < 1$. All the interest rates over the past $n + 1$ years are given at least some weight in the transformed average, and more weight is given to interest-rate changes over the most recent years. It remains true, however, that the transformation procedure tends to obscure precisely the long-run influences we are attempting to isolate.

---

[22] In the case of the British data (Table 4-3), after the data transformation the Durbin-Watson statistic indicates that serial correlation of the residuals is indeterminate at the 5 per cent level but not significant at the 1 per cent level.

Additional difficulties may be introduced when we utilize the mid-point of the historic range in calculating L_A. In many periods the historic range is a constant. It varies only when a rate falls outside of the previous range. Fortunately, there was a good deal of variation in the historic range in the Durand corporate series and the Grant British government series. In the U.S. Treasury series, however, the historic range remained constant over the (brief) period covered by our test. Consequently, it is not surprising that the coefficient of L_A is least significant in the tests using U.S. Treasury yields. Of course, this makes it particularly difficult to distinguish between the modified expectations hypothesis and the naïve hypothesis that short and long rates move together.[23] We should point out, however, that our hypothesis asserts not only that movements in short and long rates will be synchronous, but also that short rates will be more volatile than long rates. The finding that the coefficient of the long rate is significantly different from unity affirms this hypothesis.

Thus far we have paid little attention to the sign of the constant term. In the original hypothesis, the constant term represented the amount by which the long rate would exceed the short rate when the long rate equaled the long average. In that situation, with the level of interest rates at the mid-point of the normal range, our hypothesis suggests that the short rate should equal the long rate. However, if liquidity premiums exist, we would expect the short rate to lie below the long rate. Consequently, the sign of the constant term can perhaps be taken as evidence of the existence of liquidity premiums. Specifically, a negative constant term implies that the yield curve will be ascending when the level of rates is at the mid-point of the normal range and that liquidity premiums exist.

Unfortunately, unless the regression coefficients add exactly to

---

[23] Other factors also contribute to make our tests using government yields the least satisfactory of the three interest-rate time series. The period of study of the short-long differential for Treasuries was very brief, encompassing only the years 1958–1965. Moreover, during much of this period Federal Reserve policy was ostensibly trying to "nudge" short yields up relative to long-term interest rates. To the extent that they were successful in changing the shape of the yield curve, the relationship we seek to measure will also be affected. Also, because of the strong trend in the time series (which is evident from an examination of Table 4-4), problems of multicollinearity arise, since the long rate is highly correlated with the long average rate calculated up to the preceding period. Finally, we should note that other empirical studies using quarterly interest-rate series for government securities suggest that our results could be improved by the addition of a second expectational variable, which measures the direction of recent changes in rates. In Section 8.6 we present these findings.

unity, this interpretation is no longer tenable under the alternative statement of the expectations hypothesis. The constant term is inversely related to the sum of the regression coefficients. For example, ordinary least-squares regression using the raw-data coefficients of Tables 4-1 through 4-3 yields

$$\hat{a}_0 = 2.113 - 2.718(\hat{a}_1 + \hat{a}_2), r = 0.842 . \qquad (4\text{-}13)$$
$$(0.528) \quad (0.503)$$

We may use (4-13), however, to estimate whether the constant term would be significantly negative when the regression coefficients add to unity. The estimated value for the constant term when $\hat{a}_1 + \hat{a}_2 = 1$ is -0.604. Forming a confidence interval[24] for the mean value of the constant term when the regression coefficients sum to unity, we obtain, at the 5 per cent level, $-0.265 \leq \hat{a}_0 \leq -0.943$. Thus, on the basis of an average relationship derived over different time periods and utilizing three different interest-rate time series, we find that the slope of the yield curve tends to be positively biased. At a level of interest rates midway between the extremes of the normal range, the yield curve has a positive rather than a zero slope.

4.7 Recapitulation

In Chapter 3, we reformulated the traditional expectations theory. Our model suggested that the spread between long and short rates $(L - S)$ should vary inversely with the distance of the long rate from the mid-point of the normal range of long rates (which we took to be some kind of average of past long rates). In the present chapter we tested this specific hypothesis.

We found evidence that a strong inverse relationship did, in fact, characterize the Durand data covering the period 1900–1942. Unfortunately, from a statistical point of view, this direct test was found to be unsatisfactory in several respects. The long rate appeared on both sides of the equation, tending to introduce bias in the regression and correlation coefficients. Moreover, significant serial correlation in the variables also weakened the test. We were therefore forced to abandon the direct hypothesis in favor of an alternative (but equivalent) formulation. The alternative relationship treated the short rate as the dependent variable, with the long rate and average of long rates as the independent variables. We

[24] The procedure for obtaining the confidence intervals may be found in Johnston, *op. cit.*, pp. 34–37.

had to deal with transformations of these variables to remove the significant degree of autocorrelation in the time series. Even after these data transformations, however, the strong relationship predicted by the theory persisted, and the residuals were well behaved.

The regression coefficients of the alternative formulation were consistent with the theory. The average coefficient of the long rate was approximately 2.5. This says that, *ceteris paribus*, a change in the long rate of 10 basis points will be associated with a 25 basis-point change in the short rate. One of the principal results of the theoretical analysis was that short rates would be more volatile than long rates. Moreover, the theory also suggested that the higher the (mid-point of the) normal range (that is, L_A), the more likely it was for the short rate to be low relative to the long rate. Hence, the negative coefficient of L_A (which averaged approximately -1.5) also supports our reformulation of the expectations theory. We conclude that the data do not contradict our hypothesis. These tests, utilizing three different sets of interest-rate time series and several alternative time periods, offer independent evidence corroborating the findings of Meiselman that expectations play a major role in determining the rate structure. Finally, we noted that our empirical results indirectly suggest that the slope of the yield curve may be positively biased, substantiating the recent results of Kessel and others.

CHAPTER 5

Transactions Costs and the Term Structure
of Interest Rates

DESPITE the fact that we have found strong empirical evidence supporting our modified expectations hypothesis, it is by no means safe to conclude that expectations can, by themselves, provide a complete explanation of the rate structure. For one thing, the portion of the yield curve relating to the shortest maturities has typically been positively sloped even when later segments descended sharply. This tendency was noted by Meiselman, although, as we saw, it is obscured by the broad maturity categories of the Durand data.[1] Humps have also existed in the intermediate-maturities portion of the yield curve, a phenomenon for which the expectations theory can offer only a clumsy explanation. That theory does little better in accounting for the apparently "normal relationship" in which, according to the empirical information pertaining to recent history, short rates lie below long rates.[2] In any event one expects that any theoretical model will ultimately require emendation. Accordingly the remainder of this study is devoted largely to a number of modifications of the basic model, which, I believe, transform it into a richer analytic structure. The amendments involve the introduction of transactions costs and the analysis of diverse expectations and institutional maturity preferences. Each modification is justified empirically and then incorporated into a formal model based on expectations. The analysis culminates with a reconciliation of the expectations hypothesis and the institutional hypothesis. The amendments proposed in the succeeding chapters will be applied to the traditional formulation of the expectations theory. Since we have demonstrated that with our alternative formulation of an expectations model we could generate a set of interest-rate relationships with properties identical to those of the traditional analysis, we feel confident that the more familiar Hicks-Lutz analytic structure may properly serve as the foundation upon which we may build a more comprehensive theory of the term structure.

[1] David Meiselman, *The Term Structure of Interest Rates* (Englewood Cliffs: Prentice-Hall, 1962), p. 47.

[2] See, for example, Reuben Kessel, *The Cyclical Behavior of the Term Structure of Interest Rates*, Occasional Paper 91 (New York: National Bureau of Economic Research, 1965).

5.1 *Introduction of Transactions Costs*

Our first emendation concerns the introduction of transactions costs.[3] In our previous discussion, we abstracted entirely from transactions costs. It was assumed that both the purchase and sale of each security were free of brokerage charges, dealer spreads, and all other investment and disinvestment costs. In this chapter, we consider what happens when this assumption is relaxed. It will be seen that rather than constituting a minor emendation, transactions costs impart to the term structure some of its more interesting characteristics, just as friction causes the physical world to behave in the manner we are used to.

In Chapter 2 we recalled that a fundamental postulate of the traditional expectations theory of the term structure of interest rates was that holding-period yields for all securities, regardless of term, would be equal. An investor who possessed funds that he wished to employ in the bond market for a period of one year would compare one-year-holding-period yields for all securities and combinations of securities. He could buy a succession of four 90-day bills, or a one-year bond, or a four-year bond which he would sell at the end of one year, etc. If such individuals switched to those maturities initially offering the greatest yields, market forces would produce the equalized holding-period yields called for by the theory. In a situation where all participants in the market believed that future interest rates would not change, a flat yield curve would result. Moreover, the slope of the curve would be unaffected by the relative supplies of debt instruments. For if, say, there were a superabundance of six-year relative to one-

[3] Transactions costs have enjoyed an intimate affair with monetary economics for at least a generation. As early as 1935 J. R. Hicks, in "A Suggestion for Simplifying the Theory of Money," *Economica* 2 (1935), pp. 1–19, reprinted in AEA, *Readings in Monetary Theory* (Homewood, Irwin, 1951), pp. 13–32, argued that transactions charges play a crucial role in understanding the demand for money. More recently, William J. Baumol, in "The Transactions Demand for Cash: an Inventory Theoretic Approach," *The Quarterly Journal of Economics* 66 (November 1952), pp. 545–556, and James Tobin, in "The Interest Elasticity of Transactions Demand for Cash," *Review of Economics and Statistics* 38 (August 1956), pp. 241–247, have assigned a critical role to transactions costs. Thus, it was to be expected that transactions costs could shed light on a discussion of the term structure of interest rates. Indeed, the idea that transactions costs may influence the yield curve is not new. Friedrich A. Lutz, in his original article, "The Structure of Interest Rates," *Quarterly Journal of Economics* 55 (November 1940), pp. 504–510, suggested that transactions costs would tend to make the long rate on funds available to investors higher than the short rate. Recently, Kessel, *op. cit.*, has arrived independently at several of the points described in this chapter.

year securities in the market, then investors whose expected holding period was one year would gladly hold more six-year issues with the expectation of selling them after one year. This follows from the fact that, in equilibrium, an investor (whatever his holding period) is indifferent among all maturities at the going structure of market yields. Consequently, with identical expectations and zero transactions costs, changes in the relative supply of debt instruments of different maturities leave the term structure unaffected.

In this chapter it is argued that the introduction of transactions costs affects the conclusions of the traditional analysis in several important respects. If a one-year issue is bought and held to maturity, one transaction cost is incurred: the cost of buying the issue. If, on the other hand, a six-year issue is purchased and then sold at the end of one year, two transactions costs are incurred: the costs of both buying and selling the issue. Thus, with holding-period yields otherwise the same, which security the investor holds may no longer be a matter of indifference. We begin by examining the nature of these transactions costs and providing quantitative data on the relationship of transactions costs and term to maturity of the issue traded. Then we present an analytic framework within which we may determine the effect of these costs on the term structure. As our frame of reference, we utilize the traditional model of Section 2.1. In a case where the traditional theory would produce a flat yield curve, we shall find that after the introduction of transactions costs, the yield curve may have a positive slope. That the existence of transactions costs (broadly defined) imparts a positive bias to the slope of the term structure is the major conclusion of this chapter.

5.2 *Description and Classification of Transactions Costs*

Our analysis treats two major types of transactions charges: new-issue costs and trading costs. New-issue costs consist of once-and-for-all charges incurred by the borrower at the time of the new offering. They include underwriting fees (the compensation of the investment bankers who market the issue); the costs of preparing offering circulars (prospectuses); accounting, legal, and trustees fees; printing and engraving fees. We shall examine these costs in detail in Section 5.8. For the present, however, we shall note that new-issue costs tend to be large relative to trading costs. Initially, our analysis will be confined solely to trading costs, with the relative supplies of debt instruments treated as given.

Trading costs constitute the sum of all charges associated with the purchase and sale of outstanding debt securities. They include state (and formerly federal) transfer taxes, SEC fees (payable on transactions made on any registered exchange), registration fees (if the securities are to be registered in the name of the owner), brokerage charges, and the administrative costs of executing and clearing the transactions. In the analysis that follows, we shall treat only those charges that are in the nature of brokerage costs. These are by far the largest element of the total trading cost and are the most easily quantifiable. We shall also concentrate our discussion on the government-securities market, where the volume of trading is largest and transactions costs smallest compared with the markets for other debt securities. Nevertheless, the direction in which the larger transactions costs associated with the markets for corporate and municipal securities can be expected to influence the yield curve will be analyzed.

Brokerage charges, as such, are seldom paid by large transactors in the government-securities market. This is so because the relationship of the government-bond dealer to the transacting institution is typically that of a dealer rather than a broker.[4] Transactors buy directly from or sell directly to the dealer. At stated prices, the dealers stand ready to buy and sell for their "own account and risk." No brokerage charges are added. This does not mean that transactions directly with the dealer are free of transactions charges. On the contrary, the charge is simply included in the price at which the transaction is consummated. The charge may be measured by the difference between the bid price (the price at which the dealer stands ready to buy normal-sized lots of the security offered to him) and the asked price (the price at which the dealer will sell the same security). Thus, if the dealer quotes a Treasury bond "$98\frac{30}{32}$ bid–$99\frac{2}{32}$ asked," this means that he will purchase bonds from sellers at $98\frac{30}{32}$ and sell to purchasers at $99\frac{2}{32}$. The difference between the bid and asked is the dealer's spread and represents the cost of a turnaround (purchase and sale) in the issue. In our example, it costs $1.25 ($\frac{1}{8}$ of 1 point) per $1,000.00 of par value simultaneously to purchase and to sell the same security. Alternatively, we could consider the "true" price of the security to be 99 and the one-way transactions cost to be $0.625 per $1,000.00 bond.[5]

---

[4] In contrast, when an investor (even a large institutional investor) wishes to purchase equity securities listed on the New York Stock Exchange, the order is usually executed by a member firm acting as broker (that is, as agent), and a standard brokerage charge is applied.

[5] In the case of Treasury bills, quotes are typically made in terms of yield, not price. Thus, a dealer may quote a 30-day Treasury bill as "3.50 per cent

We shall begin our analysis by introducing trading costs into the perfect-certainty analysis. Trading charges are assumed to reflect only the resource costs actually incurred by the dealers in arranging for swaps of securities between buyers and sellers. Since, on an a priori basis, one would expect trading costs to be the same whichever maturity is exchanged, we shall assume that the dollar costs of trading one bond are constant regardless of maturity.[6] Moreover, we shall adopt a convention that takes the average of the bid and asked yields to represent the actual market rate of interest. We assume that one-half the full turnaround charge is applicable to each purchase and sale that is consummated. Qualifications for uncertainty and market imperfections will be made only after a relatively "pure" case has been examined.

5.3 *The Mathematics of Trading Costs*

We are now prepared to examine the influence of trading costs on the rate structure. As already indicated, initially we anchor our analysis to the perfect-certainty, traditional expectations model where all future (short) rates are expected to be identical with today's (short) rate. Moreover, we posit that no impediments to mobility exist, and hence, in equilibrium, no profitable opportunities for arbitrage can remain. Therefore, *sans* trading costs, the yield curve would have a zero slope throughout and remain constant over time. Holding-period yields would be identical for all conceivable holding periods (and whatever the combination of maturities purchased). In all the demonstrations in this section the level yield curve will serve as a convenient standard of comparison.

We now proceed to alter only one assumption of the traditional model: trading costs will now be taken to be present. Referring to Chapter 2, the concept of the holding-period yield is defined as follows:

---

bid–3.45 per cent asked." (Note that, because bond prices and yields move inversely, bid yields will always exceed asked yields.) In this case, the dealer spread is said to be 5 basis points. Alternatively, the bill could have been quoted "99.70833 bid–99.71250 asked." We then find that the transaction cost in dollars for a turnaround in 30-day bills is $0.0417 per $1,000.00 of par value.

[6] This is not to deny that there may be economies of scale present. The cost per bond of executing a very large order is undoubtedly much less than for a small order. Thus, trading costs are not likely to be identical for all investors. Later in this chapter we examine the implications of trading costs that rise with maturity. We shall see that one explanation of the trading-cost structure is the size distribution of issues with respect to maturity. In Chapter 7 we consider the implications of trading costs that differ among investors.

Holding-period yield

$$= \frac{\text{coupon interest received} + \text{capital gain (loss)}}{\text{purchase price}} . \quad (5\text{-}1)$$

In order to perform certain numerical calculations that we will need later, it is necessary to restate this condition algebraically. To do so, we introduce the following notation:

P_p = Price of a bond when purchased (not including trading costs)

P_s = Price of a bond when sold (before deducting trading costs)

i_p = Yield to maturity of a bond when purchased

i_s = Yield to maturity of a bond when sold

H = The holding period, i.e., the number of days the bond is held

T = The dollar trading cost of a turnaround

C = The (annual) coupon payment

y = The (annual) holding-period yield

N = The maturity of the issue purchased

F = The face or maturity value of the issue

Employing these symbols, adding trading costs,[7] and making the appropriate adjustments to annualize the interest rate, we may write the holding-period yield as:

$$\frac{H}{365} y = \frac{(P_s - P_p) + (H/365)C - T}{P_p + \frac{1}{2}T} . \quad (5\text{-}2)$$

Alternatively, (5-2) can be restated in more familiar form.

$$P_p + \tfrac{1}{2}T = \frac{P_s + (H/365)C - \frac{1}{2}T}{[1 + (H/365)y]} . \quad (5\text{-}3)$$

Solving for y, the holding-period yield, we obtain

$$y = \frac{-(P_p + T - P_s)365 + CH}{(P_p + \frac{1}{2}T)H} . \quad (5\text{-}4)$$

It should be noted that (5-2), (5-3), and (5-4) apply only in the case where the maturity of the issue purchased (N) is greater than the holding period (H). If $N = H$, only one transactions charge is incurred. In this case, we must rewrite (5-2) as

$$\frac{H}{365} y = \frac{(F - P_p) + (H/365)C - \frac{1}{2}T}{P_p + \frac{1}{2}T} , \quad (5\text{-}5)$$

[7] We assume that one-half the turnaround trading charge is *added* to the purchase price and the other half *subtracted* from the sale price.

and (5-4) becomes

$$y = \frac{-(P_p + \frac{1}{2}T - F)365 + CH}{(P_p + \frac{1}{2}T)H} . \tag{5-6}$$

Finally, a third formula is needed to treat the situation where a series of issues is purchased whose maturities individually are shorter than the investor's holding period. Here (5-2) becomes

$$\frac{H}{365}y = \frac{(F - P_p) + (H/365)C - (TH/2N)}{P_p + \frac{1}{2}T} , \tag{5-7}$$

and

$$y = \frac{-(P_p + (TH/2N) - F)365 + CH}{(P_p + \frac{1}{2}T)H} . \tag{5-8}$$

Having laid out the algebra we need, we shall first demonstrate one preliminary (and well-known) relationship before turning to some numerical calculations to illustrate the effect of trading costs on the term structure. We assert that, given a horizontal yield curve, it always pays an investor to chose a bond whose maturity coincides exactly with his holding period. If he purchases an issue (or series of issues) whose maturity is either longer or shorter than his holding period, his holding-period yield will inevitably decline.

PROOF: The statement requires that equation

$$(5\text{-}4) < (5\text{-}6) > (5\text{-}8) .$$

This holds since

$$T > T/2 < TH/2N ,$$

where $H > N$ on the right-hand side of the inequality by assumption.

Though important, this result is intuitively obvious. If an investor buys an issue longer than his holding period he incurs two trading costs—the cost of buying and the cost of selling. And if, on the other hand, he buys a succession of shorter maturities, he incurs continuous reinvestment costs. Consequently, an interest-rate differential is always required to induce investors to purchase maturities other than those exactly corresponding to their holding periods.

This leads immediately to our first substantive result. A fundamental theorem of the traditional expectations theory was that, in equilibrium, holding-period yields would be equalized regardless of the maturity of the issue purchased and the holding period of the investor. Indeed, this provided the basis of the argument that relative supplies of debt instruments must be irrelevant. In a world with transactions costs, this theorem can no longer hold. The constellation of yields which makes investors indifferent among maturities will now vary with the holding period of the individual investor. Moreover, each individual investor will, *ceteris paribus*, prefer to invest in a maturity equal to his holding period. Thus with a variety of holding periods, no rate structure can make every investor indifferent among maturities irrespective of his holding period. In the sections which follow, we demonstrate this proposition specifically.

5.4   *Transactions Costs and the Demand for Different Maturities—Case 1: Trading Costs Equal for All Maturities*

Building on the analysis of Section 5.3, we now illustrate the precise magnitude of the effect of transactions costs on the demand schedule for bonds of different maturities. To do so, we introduce the construct of "indifference yield curves." An indifference yield curve is the locus of interest rates for securities of different maturities that makes investors indifferent among maturities. For each class of investors with a particular holding period, we can draw a yield curve that would make its members indifferent among alternative maturities. We obtain a family of these curves, one for each possible holding period. In this section, we show how the holding-period yield curves may be constructed. We assume, initially, a perfect-certainty environment where all future (short-term) rates of interest are expected to equal today's (short) rate. As we have seen, were transactions costs irrelevant, the yield curve would be flat throughout. We continue this assumption throughout most of the chapter only because the level yield curve is such a convenient standard of comparison. Into this environment trading costs that are assumed to be equal for all maturities are introduced. Our goal is to examine the effect such trading costs have on the indifference yield curves for investors with differing holding periods.

Let us first treat the case of the investor who has funds to invest for 30 days. We assume that the 30-day rate (based on the offering yield) is fixed at 3.50 per cent. Our 30-day investor can then obtain a net yield of 3.50 per cent by purchasing a 30-day bill. We assume further that turnaround trading costs are $0.15 per $1,000.00 of par value.[8] In Section 5.2, we suggested that it would be more convenient to deal with a single yield figure than with both bid and asked yields for the same issue. As our measure of this single yield, we adopt

---

[8] This figure, approximately the current turnaround trading cost for long bills, was chosen arbitrarily for illustrative purposes only.

the convention that considers the "true" yield to be the mid-point between the bid and asked (offering) yields. Consequently, the "true" 30-day yield is 3.59 per cent, not the 3.50 per cent offering yield.[9] This fixes the first point on our indifference yield curve.

We now demonstrate how the second point on the curve is found. We seek to determine what yield (to maturity) must be obtained

TABLE 5-1

INDIFFERENCE YIELD STRUCTURE (IN PER CENT) TO GIVE 3.50 PER CENT RETURN OVER SPECIFIC HOLD-
ING PERIODS

(Assuming that dollar trading costs are the same for each maturity)

Term to maturity of issue	Holding period		
	30 days	90 days	40 yrs.
30 days	3.59	3.59	3.59
60 days	3.64	3.55	3.55
90 days	3.66	3.53	3.53
180 days	3.68	3.56	3.52
1 year	3.69	3.58	3.51
5 years	3.69	3.58	3.50
10 years	3.69	3.58	3.50
25 years	3.69	3.58	3.50
40 years	3.69	3.58	3.50

on a 60-day bill in order to make the 30-day investor indifferent between 30-day and 60-day bills. We know that such an investor will be indifferent between the two if he can earn a 3.50 per cent holding-period yield by purchasing a 60-day bill and selling it after

[9] Of the total $0.15 turnaround trading charge, we shall assume that $0.075 is applicable to the buying and the other half to the selling transaction. Therefore, the asked price (which gives a 3.50 per cent yield) equals the "true" price plus 0.075. We can then find the "true" price by using (5-3) where we substitute $F = 1000$ for $(P - \frac{1}{2}T)$ and where $C = 0$ since Treasury bills do not carry coupons. This gives

$$P + 0.075 = \frac{1000}{[1 + 0.035(30/365)]} ,$$

that is,

$$P = 997.06 .$$

To convert to the "true" yield we utilize the standard bond-price formula (3-2), where the C term is again omitted and the i term is adjusted to annualize the yield to maturity.

$$997.06 = \frac{1000}{[1 + i(30/365)]} , i = 3.59 \text{ per cent} .$$

30 days. It can be shown that the appropriate 60-day yield that does the trick is 3.64 per cent.[10] In a similar fashion, points can be found for 90-day yields, 180-day yields, and so forth. Column 1 of Table 5-1 presents the constellation of yields to maturity that makes a 30-day holder indifferent among all maturities. Columns 2 and 3 present similar calculations for a 90-day and a 40-year investor. The figures are rounded to the nearest basis point. The corresponding curves are depicted in Figure 5-1. We note that for investors with long holding periods the curve descends because of the continu-

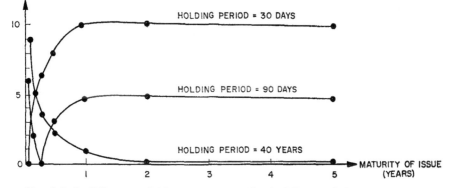

FIG. 5-1. Indifference yield curves to equalize holding-period returns, assuming trading costs equal for all maturities. Each curve represents the equalizing yield differentials for an investor with the holding period indicated.

ous reinvestment costs incurred if a succession of shorts is purchased. It is assumed that the investor with a 40-year holding period who chooses to buy 30-day bills must successively invest in 480 of these

[10] We know the 30-day yield is fixed at 3.59 per cent. Since the holding-period yield must be 3.50 per cent by assumption, we can write, by (5-2),

$$\frac{30}{365} \, 0.035 = \frac{P_s(i_s = 3.59\%) - P_p(i_p = ?) - 0.15}{P_p + 0.075} \, ,$$

where the ? stands for the yield to be found. Since a bill with 30 days remaining to maturity must command a price P_s of 997.06 (see note 9), we can solve for P_p. This gives $P_p = 994.05$. Utilizing the standard bond formula (3-2), we find that the yield to maturity of a 60-day bill priced at 994.05 is 3.64 per cent, the figure in the text.

111

bills. For investors with very short holding periods the curve ascends. If the holding period is somewhat longer, the curve first descends and then ascends.

Although we reserve for a later section an analysis of the transactions costs of bond issues and their effect on the supply functions of bonds of different maturities, we can at least indicate at this point the direction in which these preliminary results take us. Assume that the supply of debt instruments is fixed exogenously, so that equal quantities of the nine maturities (listed on Table 5-1) are supplied, irrespective of the term structure. Given this assumption, the rate structure may under certain circumstances be readily determined. For example, assume that all bond demanders have funds at their disposal for only 30 days. In this case the term structure will be that shown in Column 1 of Table 5-1; the yield curve must be positively sloped in order to induce these investors to hold longer maturities. On the other hand, if all bond demanders have holding periods of 40 years, the term structure will be that given in Column 3 of Table 5-1; investors must be paid a premium to invest in short issues. We see that the resulting term structure depends entirely on the relationship between the distribution of holding periods of investors and the maturity distribution of the supply of debt instruments. While there is no firm presumption regarding the direction in which trading costs will influence the rate structure, we do find that the yield curve will tend to be positively sloped to the extent that investors with relatively short holding periods must be induced to hold longer issues.

5.5   *A Further Look at Trading Costs*

In practice, trading costs in the markets for government and corporate bonds are not equal for all maturities. Because of features inherent in the market structure of the government-security dealers industry, we can expect that trading charges will increase with the maturity of the issue purchased or sold. Moreover, when we introduce the factor of risk aversion on the part of bond dealers and account for some characteristics of the trading markets for the different maturities of debt instruments, further arguments are adduced to explain the empirical observation that dollar trading costs increase with maturity. In this section we examine these rationalizations, leaving until the next section the question of the direction in which this pattern of transactions costs can be expected to influence the term structure.

The government-bond market is characterized by the existence of a small number of large firms that dominate the trading in Treasury securities.[11] Under these circumstances, it is easy to imagine that some form of convention for setting prices establishes itself in the market. We suggest that one such practice that has continued to affect the pricing of dealer services is price discrimination. Because the same dollar trading costs are more burdensome, in terms of yield, for short-term issues, it is probable that the elasticity of demand for shorts with respect to trading charges in much greater than for longs. In such a situation, profit-maximizing dealers will want to charge a higher dollar trading cost for dealing in longs. Given the structure of the industry, such a pricing convention can easily be maintained. Trading charges which are equal for all maturities will not maximize profits for the industry.

Uncertainty provides a further reason for expecting trading charges to increase with maturity. Dealers operate on an extremely low ratio of capital to assets. It is difficult to measure the amount of capital committed to dealer operations because some firms are engaged in several other activities (e.g., commercial banking, investment banking, etc.). For a sample of government-bond dealers I interviewed, the capital-to-net-positions[12] ratio was under 2 per cent. Moreover, the dealers are largely financed with short-term credit.

Under such circumstances, one would expect the dealers to be more afraid of *principal uncertainty* than of yield uncertainty; i.e., they constitute classic Hicksian risk averters. A large loss implies financial ruin. Consequently, in establishing a schedule of trading charges, one would expect the dealer to charge more to "take a position" in a long security, where the danger of loss of principal is relatively great, than in a short issue. The expression "taking a position" means that dealers add to their inventories (take a long position or reduce a short position) whenever a customer sells a security to them, or reduce their inventories (or go short the issue) whenever a customer buys a security. In either case the transaction is consummated for the dealer's "own account and risk." Thus, a trading charge is, to some extent, a charge for risk-taking. Since the prices of long-term securities are characteristically more volatile than the prices of short issues, long-

---

[11] For a good discussion of the workings of the government securities market see A. Meltzer and G. von der Linde, *A Study of the Dealer Market for Federal Government Securities* (Washington: Government Printing Office, 1960), and Ira O. Scott, Jr., *Government Securities Market* (New York: McGraw-Hill, 1965).

[12] The dealer's net position is defined as gross long position (securities held for the dealer's own account and risk) minus the aggregate value of securities sold short.

term issues are inherently more risky capital investments. It follows that Hicksian risk-averting dealers will charge more to take positions in long-term securities than in short issues.

Certain characteristics of the supply side of the market also influence the trading-cost structure. The maturity distribution of outstanding government securities is characterized by a concentration of issues in the early maturities.[13] Not only are there fewer securities in the over-10-year maturity category, but these securities are distributed in several individual bond issues spread out over a maturity spectrum comprising 25 years.

Such a maturity distribution has important implications for the government-bond dealer. The level of trading activity tends to be lower in the longer maturities, thereby increasing the dealer's average turnover period, that is, the time period it takes him to liquidate his position. Consequently, the dealer's profit on each turnaround (which, abstracting from price changes, equals the spread between the bid and asked prices) would have to be larger in order to give him a profit per unit of time which is equivalent to that obtained from dealing in shorts. Moreover, as mentioned earlier, the size of the typical trade on longer issues is much smaller than for short-term securities. Since there is a large fixed-cost element in the execution of each transaction, the cost per bond in executing a small order is considerably higher than for larger lots. Thus, the maturity distribution of the outstanding debt also plays a part in determining the trading-cost structure since it affects both the level of trading activity and the size of trade.[14]

[13] On February 28, 1965, the maturity distribution of the marketable government debt was as follows:

	Total marketable debt	Securities maturing in			
		Under 1 yr.	1 to 5 yrs.	5 to 10 yrs.	Over 10 yrs.
Billions of dollars	214.8	89.8	59.7	39 5	25.8
Per cent	100.0	41.8	27.8	18.4	12.0

Source: *Federal Reserve Bulletin* April, 1965.

[14] It is, of course, possible to imagine that the volume of total trading activity and the size of each individual trade in the 30-year (long) market could be the same as in the 1-year (short) market even if the volume of outstanding long securities were somewhat lower. Nevertheless, such a possibility would be unlikely if the volume of outstanding securities in the two markets were highly disparate. In the latter case, equal total trading volume would imply that the percentage

Investigation of the actual schedule of trading charges confirms that trading costs are not equal for all maturities. Table 5-2 presents transactions cost data relevant to the government securities market. The data are averages of bid-asked spreads in the "inside" market over the 1959–1965 period.[15]

The striking fact demonstrated by the table is that dollar transactions costs increase with the maturity of the issue traded. It should be noted, however, that while the dollar costs of dealing in Treasury securities increase with term to maturity, such is not the case for

TABLE 5-2

AVERAGE TRANSACTIONS COSTS OF DEALING IN UNITED STATES
TREASURY SECURITIES

Term to maturity	Dollar cost of turnaround per $1,000.00 of par value	Equivalent yield spread[a] (per cent)
1 day	$0.0005	0.18
30 days	0.0375	0.045
60 days	0.05	0.03
90 days	0.0625	0.025
180 days	0.125	0.025
1 year	0.3125	0.03
5 years	0.625	0.015
10 years	0.875	0.01
25 years	1.25	0.0075
40 years	1.25	0.005

[a] Computed by converting dollar costs of column 2 into basis-point values.

yield spreads. Column 3 of Table 5-2 converts the dollar spreads into equivalent yield spreads. Taking one-half the spread (turnaround

---

turnover of securities would be far higher in the long market, and there is no a priori reason why this should be so. If trading activity were lower, investors would be wary of accumulating a large block of securities (perhaps representing a significant portion of the available supply) since this would expose them to the risk of severe marketing difficulties should they wish to dispose of their holdings.

[15] The spreads listed in the dealer quote sheets or the daily newspapers are typically much wider than those in Table 5-2. Most transactions take place well within the stated limits, and few transactions are made outside of these limits. In arriving at the data for the table, several government-bond dealers were interviewed and asked to adjust the averages of stated spreads that were first calculated. The spreads reflect the consensus of their estimates of trading charges for an average-sized trade on actively traded issues. The averages obtained from the interviews were then checked against the results of a questionnaire on trading costs sent to the major government-bond dealers.

cost) as the cost of buying a new issue, we find that, in terms of yield sacrifice, the cost of buying longs is insignificant. This is, of course, the result of the fact that a once-and-for-all transactions cost when spread over the life of an N-year security becomes an insignificant cost per year if N is sufficiently large. But note that the calculation of Column 3 assumes that the issue is held to maturity. We shall see that the situation is quite different if an investor plans to sell the issue prior to maturity.[16]

The literature has also stressed the importance of Hicksian risk aversion for government-bond dealers as the most important explanation of the trading-cost structure. For example, the Commission on Money and Credit attributes the increased transactions costs for longs to the greater risks incurred by dealers in making markets in long-term issues.[17] Meltzer and von der Linde find that the greater costs of dealing in longs may partly be explained by the greater margin that must be put up by security dealers in carrying long-term bonds in their inventories.[18] Of course, the margin requirements are a direct function of the risk exposure of the lender. More recently, Reuben Kessel has emphasized the importance of risk aversion in determining both the trading-cost structure and the general upward slope of the yield curve.[19]

At this point it would be well to emphasize that in an attempt to explain why trading costs rise with maturity, we have had to stray from the perfect-certainty assumption of the traditional expectations theory. Moreover, we argued that the particular maturity distribution of the government debt at the present time plays an important role in influencing the trading-cost structure. Consequently, in using the actual current trading-cost structure to explain, in part, the slope of the yield curve, we must be careful to keep in mind that much

[16] Dollar spreads were converted into equivalent yield spreads by using the standard bond-price formula (3-2), where C, the coupon payment was assumed to be \$35.00, and F the face value of the bond, \$1,000.00. By solving the above equation for i using both par (\$1,000.00) and par minus the relevant turnaround transactions costs as the relevant P (purchase price), an interest-rate spread can readily be calculated.

[17] The Commission on Money and Credit, *Money and Credit* (Englewood Cliffs: Prentice-Hall, 1962), p. 118.

[18] Dealer margin requirements for bills average one-quarter of one per cent. Minimum requirements for certificates are one-half of one per cent; for bonds maturing in less than five years, one per cent; for bonds maturing between five and ten years, two per cent; and for maturities over ten years, three per cent margin must be deposited. Meltzer and von der Linde, *op. cit.*, p. 92.

[19] Reuben Kessel, *op. cit.*, pp. 44ff.

more than transactions costs, per se, are involved. Supply conditions and risk aversion are crucial in determining the structure of trading charges.

Ideally, we would like to disentangle the different determinants of trading charges in order to understand more clearly the effects of these different elements on the term structure. We suggest that one useful method of analyzing trading charges is to compare the present schedule of charges with that which existed during the Second World War. Two reasons dictate the choice of the war period for comparison. First, both the absolute and relative supply of long-term Treasury securities was considerably larger than at the present time.[20] The market in long issues could be described as possessing more fully all the desirable characteristics of the now famous trinity—"breadth, depth, and resiliency." Secondly, the Federal Reserve pursued a policy of pegging long rates at $2\frac{1}{2}$ per cent, thus reducing the possibility of significant price declines and making long-term issues a closer substitute for short-term securities in terms of liquidity. Thus, our second and third explanations of the present trading-cost structure were to a considerable extent absent during the war. As we might expect, there was a significant difference in the structure of trading charges. The cost of dealing in longs was about one-half of what it is at present,[21] while dealer spreads in the short market were only slightly lower than present spreads. But the trading charges still rose with maturity, suggesting that our first explanation (in terms of price discrimination, and independent of risk and supply considerations) is sufficient to produce an ascending-trading-cost structure.[22]

In the next section, we proceed to examine the effects of a rising

---

[20] For example, on June 30, 1945, the maturity distribution of the federal debt was as follows:

	Total marketable debt	Securities maturing in			
		Under 1 yr.	1 to 5 yrs.	5 to 10 yrs.	Over 10 yrs.
Billions of dollars	181.3	60.6	34.8	41.5	44.4
Per cent	100.0	33.4	19.2	22.9	24.5

[21] A similar observation has been made by Reuben Kessel, *op. cit.*, p. 46n.

[22] Of course, the risk factor was not completely absent. To the extent that market yields fell below $2\frac{1}{2}$ per cent, some risk of price decline still existed. Moreover, there was always the possibility that the peg would be removed.

schedule of trading charges on the indifference yield curves. To illustrate these effects, we employ the actual structure of costs listed in Table 5-2. Repeating the caveat above, we can no longer interpret the results as representing the effect of transactions costs per se. We do assert, however, that the results are indicative of the qualitative effects of pure trading costs, for it would appear that an ascending-trading-cost structure would occur to some extent even in the absence of risk and supply differences.

5.6 Trading Costs and the Demand for Different Maturities—Case 2: Trading Costs Increase with Maturity

Before illustrating the effect on the indifference yield curves of trading costs which increase with maturity, let us review the particular assumption upon which our analysis rests. We admit uncertainty and assume that government-bond dealers are both Hicksian risk averters and price-discriminating oligopolists. Of course, once uncertainty is introduced, bond buyers may display some kind of risk aversion as well. For the present, however, we assume that all bond investors have utility functions that are linear in money gains.[23] We still assume that all investors believe (uniformly) that no future rates will change and act in accordance with all the other assumptions of the traditional expectations theory. We only need add the word "expected" or "anticipated" before the phrase "future (short) interest rates" in the standard expectational analysis.

We may now illustrate the precise magnitude of the effect of trading costs that rise with maturity on the demand schedule for bonds of different maturities. Table 5-3 presents the indifference yield structure for each holding period based on a 30-day-bill yield of 3.52 per cent, where 3.52 per cent represents the yield midway between the bid and asked yields on 30-day securities. With the sechedule of trading charges set forth in Table 5-2, this would provide the investor in 30-day bills with a net yield of 3.50 per cent.

Reading down Column 1 of Table 5-3, we find the yields that must be obtained by an investor who has funds at his disposal for

---

[23] In subsequent chapters we shall introduce into the analysis different types of risk aversion on the part of bond investors. At this time, however, it will be useful to separate out these influences. Only in this way can we show that there may be a positive bias to the slope of the yield curve in the absence of risk aversion on the part of anyone but the government-bond dealers. We are also assuming that each investor knows his holding period with certainty. In practice the holding periods for many investors are not known with certainty, and a probabilistic calculation would be required.

only 30 days so that he earns a 3.50 per cent holding-period return irrespective of the security he purchases. The corresponding curve slopes more steeply than before, lying below the former curve in the short maturities. To obtain a 30-day-holding-period yield of 3.50 per

TABLE 5-3

INDIFFERENCE YIELD STRUCTURE (IN PER CENT) TO GIVE 3.50 PER
CENT RETURN OVER SPECIFIC HOLDING PERIODS

(Assuming that dollar trading costs rise with maturity as indicated
in Table 5-2)

Term to maturity of issue	(1) 30 days	(2) 60 days	(3) 90 days	(4) 180 days	(5) 1 yr.	(6) 5 yrs.	(7) 10 yrs.	(8) 25 yrs.	(9) 40 yrs.
					Holding period				
30 days	3.52	3.52	3.52	3.52	3.52	3.52	3.52	3.52	3.52
60 days	3.55	3.52	3.52	3.52	3.52	3.52	3.52	3.52	3.52
90 days	3.56	3.53	3.51	3.51	3.51	3.51	3.51	3.51	3.51
180 days	3.62	3.56	3.54	3.51	3.51	3.51	3.51	3.51	3.51
1 year	3.73	3.62	3.59	3.53	3.51	3.51	3.51	3.51	3.51
5 years	3.98	3.79	3.67	3.59	3.54	3.51	3.51	3.51	3.51
10 years	4.20	3.87	3.74	3.62	3.55	3.51	3.50	3.50	3.50
25 years	4.61	4.06	3.88	3.68	3.58	3.52	3.51	3.50	3.50
40 years	4.80	4.14	3.95	3.71	3.60	3.52	3.51	3.50	3.50

cent, he must earn a yield to maturity of 3.55 per cent on a 60-day bill. This 60-day yield just offsets the turnaround cost of buying the security and selling it after 30 days.[24] If the investor buys a one-year

---

[24] For the convenience of market traders, Treasury bills are typically quoted on a discount rather than a yield-to-maturity basis. Thus, a one-year bill to yield 4.00 per cent (discount) would be priced at 96 (per cent of par). The yield to maturity is, of course, higher than the quoted discount yield since the investor must put up only $960 for a bill of $1,000.00 face value. His effective return is actually 4.17 per cent. Moreover, bill yields are figured on a 360- rather than a 365-day year. 180 days is considered one-half a year, and a 4.00 per cent (discount) bill would then be priced at $980. Thus, the investor receives $20 at maturity, but has actually held his issue less than one-half a year ($\frac{180}{365}$). Hence *a fortiori*, his effective interest-rate return calculated on the basis of a full year will be higher. Thus, quoted bill yields understate true yields. The understatement is larger the longer the term to maturity. For the following bills, each priced on a 3.50 per cent discount basis, the true yields are: 30 days, 3.56 per cent; 60 days, 3.57 per cent; 90 days, 3.58 per cent; and 180 days, 3.61 per cent. In all calculations performed herein, we have calculated bill yields on a yield-to-maturity basis. It seems natural to assume that investors act on the basis of true holding-period yields rather than stated yields.

issue and sells it after 30 days, he must obtain a yield to maturity of 3.73 per cent to cover the (now larger) transactions costs of a turnaround. The remaining columns of Table 5-3 present similar calculations for alternative holding periods.

While the method of computation is similar to that described in Section 5.4, it may be useful to illustrate these calculations with another numerical example. For example, we shall show that if a 60-day bill is purchased to yield (i_p) 3.55 per cent to maturity and sold after 30 days at a yield (i_s) of 3.52 per cent, the holding-period yield net of transactions costs will equal 3.50 per cent. This follows from (5-2).

$$\tfrac{30}{365}\, 0.035 = \frac{P_s(i_s = 3.52) - P_p(i_p = ?) - (\tfrac{1}{2}T_s + \tfrac{1}{2}T_p)}{P_p + \tfrac{1}{2}T_p}\,.$$

We know by assumption that the holding-period yield must be 3.50 per cent and the 30-day yield next month must be 3.52 per cent.[25] Therefore, knowing i_s, we can calculate P_s from the standard bond formula (3-2). P_s will be $997.115 30 days from now. From Table 5-2 we find that the relevant trading costs ($\tfrac{1}{2}T_s$) for selling a 30-day issue are $0.01875 and the trading costs ($\tfrac{1}{2}T_p$) for purchasing a 60-day issue are $0.025 per $1,000.00 of par value. Solving for P_p we obtain $994.194. Then again utilizing the standard bond formula where P_p is known we find that i_p equals 3.55 per cent.[26]

---

[25] Since the market is assumed to be able to form specific (uniform) expectations concerning all future interest rates, the investor is always able to predict the price at which he can sell his security. Moreover, since no future (short) interest rates will ever change in the future, we assume that the 30-day holder has no reason to believe that any derived yield will change over time. If there were only 30-day holders, their demand schedule would determine the rate structure, and the term structure would conform to that derived in Column 1 (see 5.7). But this derived structure is an equilibrium term structure, not only for this period, but for all following periods. Consequently, if an investor buys a 90-day bill he expects that he can sell it in 30 days at a price to yield the *current* 60-day rate, 3.55 per cent (less turnaround transactions costs).

[26] Perhaps one additional example will be helpful. This time let us take a one-year-holding-period calculation (Column 5). If an investor buys a one-year security to yield 3.51 per cent and holds the issue until maturity, his holding-period yield (after trading charges) is 3.50 per cent. What yield must he receive on a 25-year issue to give him a 3.50 per cent return for one year net of transactions costs? It turns out that 3.58 per cent is the required yield to maturity. Assume we have already calculated that the 10-year yield must be 3.55 per cent. The first step is to determine what the 24-year yield will be next year. By note 25 this is the same yield as the 24-year yield today. We find by interpolation between the calculated 10-year yield (3.55 per cent) and 3.58 per cent, the proposed solution for the 25-year yield, that the 24-year yield is 3.578 per

The striking feature of Table 5-3 is that the effect of transactions costs all but disappears as the holding period grows longer. To put the matter somewhat differently, the yield spreads that must be offered to induce investors to hold issues with maturities longer than their holding periods are always greater for bond purchasers whose holding periods are shorter. This phenomenon is easily explained. It is intuitively obvious that the per-period effect of a fixed trading cost is smaller, the larger the number of periods over which it can be amortized.[27]

Figure 5-2 presents graphically the yield spreads over the 30-day rate which make investors just willing to hold bonds of a longer maturity. We note that it always takes a larger yield inducement to make a (say) 60-day holding period investor purchase a 10-year bond than is necessary to induce a one-year investor to extend his "natural" maturity. In this sense securities with short maturities are "more val-

---

cent. By the standard bond-price formula we find:

$$P_s(3\tfrac{1}{2}\% \text{ coupon, 24-year bond, } i_s = 3.578) = 987.52$$
$$P_p(3\tfrac{1}{2}\% \text{ coupon, 25-year bond, } i_p = 3.58) = 986.87 .$$

Utilizing (5-2) we have:

$$y = \frac{0.85 + 35.00 - 1.25}{986.87 + 0.625} \approx 0.035 .$$

Therefore, our proposed solution is the appropriate 25-year yield.

Actually, the holding-period yield is 3.504 per cent, slightly above 3.50 per cent. The appropriate 25-year yield is slightly below 3.58 per cent. Our tables round to the nearest basis point. Because of these rounding errors and also because most calculations in Table 5-3 were performed by interpolation between two proposed solutions, these data should be taken only as approximations. Note that in all calculations we assume that the bond carries that coupon (divisible by quarters) that is closest to its yield to maturity.

[27] A second reason for this phenomenon is somewhat more subtle. To the extent that transactions costs imply that the yield curve will be positively sloped, then investors can take advantage of "riding the yield curve." This terminology became popular during the period of market pegging in the 1940's. It referred to the practice of buying, say, a two-year issue with the expectation of selling it after one year, taking advantage of the fact that one-year issues were pegged at generally lower rates (higher prices). Thus, investors rode down the curve to lower yields and, hence, capital appreciation through higher prices. Returning to our own calculations, where trading costs impart a positive slope to the yield curve, opportunities for curve riding are presented. The longer is the holding period, then the longer can be the ride down the yield curve and the greater the capital appreciation from this source. This tends to counteract the effect of the larger transactions costs incurred by extending maturity beyond the investor's holding period. Then for both reasons, the longer is the holding period, the smaller will be the calculated yield spreads.

121

uable" to investors who have very short investment periods. This finding plays an important role in the work that follows.

An interesting and perhaps surprising result of our calculations is an apparent asymmetry in the effects of trading costs. Despite their existence, a 40-year investor is essentially indifferent among all maturities that sell at the same yield. This would appear puzzling, because if the 40-year investor kept reinvesting in 30-day bills, he would continually incur the transactions charges associated with the

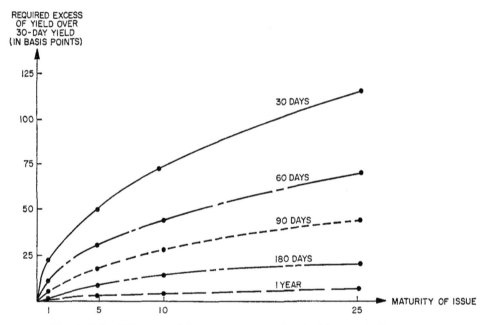

Fig. 5-2. Indifference yield curves to equalize holding-period returns, assuming trading costs increase with maturity. Each curve represents the equalizing yield differentials for an investor with the holding period indicated.

purchase of these bills.[28] On the other hand, if he bought a 40-year bond he would incur only the initial purchase cost. The answer, of course, lies in the trading-cost structure. Because the trading costs of purchasing 30-day bills are so small, it takes very little yield inducement to move a 40-year investor into 30-day bills. Conversely, an investor with a 30-day holding period requires a very large yield differential to induce him to purchase 40-year bonds. This is so because the large 40-year trading costs must be amortized over a 30-day

[28] We assume away the fact that bills of 90 days are continuously offered by the Treasury at zero transactions costs to the buyer.

period. While it is true that these large trading costs are lost in the rounding errors for an investor who purchases a 40-year bond with the expectation of holding it to maturity, this is not the case for an investor who anticipates selling the security in the near future.[29]

Hence, the current schedule of trading costs affects security buyers asymmetrically. The long-holding-period investor (given a level yield curve) is roughly indifferent as between buying a series of successive shorts or a single long issue. If he continuously reinvests in shorts, dollar transactions costs per purchase are very low, and the ability to compound interest more rapidly largely makes up for the additional number of transactions. On the other hand, if the yield curve were level, the short investor would be forced to buy only those maturities equal to or less than his natural maturity.

5.7 Two Blades of the Scissors

Having developed the determinants of the demand schedules for bonds for investors with different holding periods, we now add to the analysis hypothetical bond-supply schedules. Initially we treat these supply schedules as perfectly inelastic and exogenously given. Later we will examine the implications that transactions costs have for the determination of these supply schedules. The experiments we perform are as follows: Starting from an economy without bonds, we assume that borrowers wish to issue a certain number of new bonds of different maturities.[30] We posit that the level of rates (the

---

[29] If we introduce an additional market imperfection, the asymmetry becomes still more pronounced. By convention and tradition bond interest is payable semi-annually and the yield to maturity is always calculated on the assumption of semi-annual compounding. But the investor who continuously reinvests in 30-day bills obtains an advantage not shared by the bond holder. The bill holder is able to compound his interest monthly. The effect of monthly compounding is to add to the effective rate of interest. The 30-day bill holder who continuously reinvests at 3.50 per cent for six months earns an effective yield of almost 3.53 per cent. For the investor buying a succession of three 60-day bills, the effective yield is 3.52 per cent (approximately). Thus the yield to maturity for short bills is not strictly comparable to the yield to maturity for a 6-month bond. The yield to maturity for short bills understates the true (effective) rate that can be earned by an investor who continuously reinvests in bills, and the understatement is greater the shorter the term to maturity of the bill. To put the matter another way, in a world of no transactions costs a 3.49 per cent yield on a 30-day bill is just as good as a 3.52 per cent yield figured on a semi-annual basis. Thus, a 40-year investor would actually need no positive yield inducement on 30-day bills to make him indifferent between short- and long-term securities.

[30] The point of starting from an economy without bonds is to avoid the possibility that the initial distribution of bonds will influence the equilibrium term structure.

short rate) has already been determined in the general-equilibrium system and that the number of bonds demanded equals the number supplied. However, we do not presume that the investment periods of demanders is such that all demanders can find bonds which correspond to or are shorter than these holding periods. The question we ask is as follows: Given the maturity distribution of bonds supplied, what is the effect, on the term structure, of alternative distributions of the holding periods of bond demanders?

Inevitably, we introduce several simplifying assumptions. We assume that only nine discrete maturities are available for investment (the maturities of Table 5-3) and that every investor has a holding period which corresponds exactly to one of the nine maturities. We further posit that 900 bonds are supplied and that these bonds are evenly distributed by maturity class (i.e., 100 30-day bills are supplied, 100 60-day bills, etc.). In accordance with our assumption that the level of rates is an equilibrium one, we take it that investors possess sufficient funds so that 900 bonds are demanded. Finally, we assume that the equilibrium short rate of interest (which we shall call the net offering yield on 30-day bills) is 3.50 per cent. Thus, the yield curve will be firmly anchored to the 3.50 per cent short rate, which represents a mid-point yield of 3.52 per cent.

We begin with the two polar cases treated in Section 5.4. First, we examine the case where the supply is evenly distributed but where all bond demanders have a holding period of 30 days. Here, the equilibrium term structure of rates is that shown in Column 1 of Table 5-3 (reproduced as Column 2 of Table 5-4). Only with this term structure will investors hold all of the nine maturities offered. This is so because, as demonstrated earlier, with this term structure the 30-day holding-period yield net of transactions costs is identical no matter which of the nine maturities is purchased.[31]

Next, we consider the opposite polar case where all investors have the longest holding period, 40 years. In this case, the equilibrium term structure will be that shown by Column 9 of Table 5-3 (reproduced as Column 3 of Table 5-4). Forty-year investors will receive the same return by buying successive shorter-term issues as by purchasing one 40-year bond and holding it to maturity. An examination of these polar cases immediately reveals that transactions costs on

---

[31] Again we must remind the reader that the schedule of trading charges is not independent of the maturity distribution of the debt supplied. Indeed, by the argument of Section 5.5 we would expect that trading charges would not increase quite as much with maturity if the supply were evenly distributed as is assumed here.

the buyers' (lenders') side of the market may impart a positive bias to the slope of the yield curve. If all investors have a short holding period, the yield curve will have a steep positive slope. If all investors have a long holding period, the yield curve will be approximately flat, as it would be in the absence of transactions charges.[32] This follows from the asymmetrical effect of transactions costs which we noted earlier.

Let us now treat the case where both the supply of (900) bonds and the holding periods of the (900) demanders is evenly distributed. In this case the level yield curve indicated in Column 1 of Table 5-4 would obtain. Each demander would hold an issue whose maturity

TABLE 5-4

DERIVED TERM STRUCTURE ASSUMING SUPPLY EVENLY DISTRIBUTED
(PER CENT)

Maturity of issue	(1) Holders evenly distributed	(2) All holders have 30-day holding period	(3) All holders have 40-year holding period	(4) Holders as distributed in Table 5-5
30 days	3.52	3.52	3.52	3.52
60 days	3.52	3.55	3.52	3.55
90 days	3.51	3.56	3.51	3.56
180 days	3.51	3.62	3.51	3.59
1 year	3.51	3.73	3.51	3.63
5 years	3.51	3.98	3.51	3.70
10 years	3.50	4.20	3.50	3.72
25 years	3.50	4.61	3.50	3.74
40 years	3.50	4.80	3.50	3.74

corresponds to his holding period and each would receive a net hold-ing-period return of 3.50 per cent. While it is true that the 40-year holder is indifferent among all maturities, he has no reason to bid away the earlier maturities from those investors who would eschew the 40-year bond.

The complicated case is that where investors have various holding periods that do not correspond with the maturity distribution of the supply of debt instruments. Table 5-5 presents one hypothetical distribution of investors skewed toward short holding periods. For convenience, we assume that 900 investors exist, each demanding one bond; 200 investors have a holding period of 30 days; there

[32] Indeed, if we allow for the effects of monthly compounding even the slight negative slope of Column 3, Table 5-4, will disappear.

are 167 investors with a 60-day holding period; and so forth as detailed in the bottom row of Table 5-5. The supply of bonds is still assumed to be evenly distributed.

We must now ascertain which investors will hold which maturities. In Table 5-5, we distribute the maturities so that each investor holds those maturities as close to his natural maturity as possible. The 200 30-day investors hold only 30- and 60-day bills. The 60-day investors hold 90- and 180-day bills. The question arises why 60-day investors would not prefer 60-day bills. *Ceteris paribus,* of course, they would, but utilizing our finding in Section 5.6 we know that 60-day bills

TABLE 5-5

HYPOTHETICAL DISTRIBUTION OF INVESTORS SKEWED TOWARD SHORT HOLDING PERIODS

	Term to maturity of issue	Holding period								
		30 days	60 days	90 days	180 days	1 yr.	5 yrs.	10 yrs.	25 yrs.	40 yrs.
S*										
100	30 days	100								
100	60 days	100								
100	90 days		100							
100	180 days		67	33						
100	1 year			100						
100	5 years				100					
100	10 years					100				
100	25 years						67	33		
100	40 years							34	33	33
	D†	200	167	133	100	100	67	67	33	33

* Supply of bonds.

† Number of investors (each demanding one bond) who have funds to invest for each holding period.

are relatively *more valuable* to the 30-day holders. Recall that we noted in connection with our discussion of Figure 5-2 that it always takes a larger yield differential to induce a short holder to extend his maturity than is required for a longer holder. To put this another way, short holders will always be willing to pay a higher relative price for short issues than will a longer holder. Thus, we have distributed the shortest maturities available to the shortest holders. The 60-day holders get the shortest maturities available *after* the 30-day holders are taken care of, etc. Later we shall demonstrate that this procedure produces a term structure which meets three conditions: (1) All the debt is held. (2) Suppliers pay the lowest interest bill consistent with the total debt being held. (3) No bond buyer could be better off by purchasing any other maturity.

Let us now follow through Table 5-5 to determine what term structure is consistent with such a distribution of holders and suppliers. The 30-day rate is, of course, fixed at 3.52 per cent to give a net offering yield of 3.50 per cent. Since 100 30-day investors must be induced to hold 60-day bills, from Table 5-3 we know that the 60-day rate must be 3.55 per cent.[33] Next we must take care of the 60-day holders. But now the computations contained in Table 5-3 cease to be relevant. With such a disparity between desired holding periods and the maturity distribution of debt instruments, all holding-period yields can no longer be 3.50 per cent. The net yield obtainable accruing to the 60-day holders must be at least 3.53 per cent (the net offering yield on 60-day bills); otherwise the 60-day investors would bid the 60-day bills away from 30-day holders. Consequently, the 90-day bill rate must allow 60-day investors to earn 3.53 per cent by buying 90-day bills and selling them after 60 days. Utilizing (5-2) we find that the appropriate 90-day rate is 3.56 per cent. This provides a third point on the yield curve. But from Table 5-5 we see that 60-day holders must also be induced to hold 67 180-day bills. Utilizing (5-2) once more, we find that to obtain a 3.53 per cent return from buying a 180-day (and selling it as a 120-day) bill, its yield to maturity must be 3.59 per cent.

We shall describe one more such set of calculations since it will illustrate one additional pertinent principle. In Table 5-5 we note that 180-day holders must be induced to hold 5-year issues. What holding-period yield must they obtain? Since the 180-day rate is 3.59 per cent (giving a net offering yield of 3.58 per cent), we know they must earn at least 3.58 per cent. Otherwise they would bid 180-day issues away from the 60- and 90-day holders. It turns out that their yield must be even greater. Calculating the implicit holding-period yield which could be obtained by buying a 1-year issue (at 3.63 per cent) and selling a 180-day issue (at 3.59 per cent) we find that a 3.63 per cent return (net of trading costs) is obtained.[34] Thus 180-day holders must earn at least 3.63 per cent, or else they will bid the 1-year issues away from the 90-day holders.

---

[33] Recall that this rate produces a 3.50 per cent holding-period yield for 30-day investors who buy a 60-day security and sell it after 30 days.

[34] We must remember that every investor is free to purchase any maturity or combination of maturities he wishes. Thus we must make sure the yield on the security he holds is at least as great as that on the highest-yielding alternative.

This holding-period yield determines the 5-year rate at 3.70 per cent. Rates are determined in the same manner for all remaining maturities. The derived structure of rates is presented in Column 4 of Table 5-4.

The derived term structure satisfies the three desiderata noted above. The total debt is held at minimum expense to bond issuers. This is so because the term structure was constructed by paying each purchaser only the minimum interest-rate spread necessary to induce him to extend the maturity of his holding beyond his natural maturity. Moreover, no bond purchaser can obtain a higher yield by buying any other maturity. The 30-day holder earns a net return of 3.50 per cent on the 30- and 60-day bills. But since the spreads over the rest of the curve are smaller than those necessary to induce him to extend his maturities (cf. Column 4, Table 5-4, with Column 1, Table 5-2) he has no desire to hold any other maturity. Similarly, while the 40-year holder earns 3.74 per cent by buying a 40-year bond, it is impossible for him to earn as much buying any combination of shorter maturities. Our method of distribution and rate determination works because the necessary yield differentials of Figure 5-2 are so well behaved. For each maturity the yield spreads are always larger the smaller the holding period. Therefore, no short holder can ever find a larger holding-period return in a longer section of the yield curve[35] and since the yield curve is positively sloped, no long holder is ever induced to buy a succession of shorts.

We thus see how the two blades of the scissors may interact to determine the term structure. At this point we can make the following generalizations: Existing trading costs affect the yield curve asymmetrically.[36] If the maturity distribution of the supply of debt instruments tends to be longer than the holding-period distribution of demanders, the yield curve will be ascending. In a case somewhere between the polar extremes treated earlier (that is, in a case where demanders have holding periods scattered throughout the maturity spectrum), the effect of transactions costs will be felt mainly in the early maturi-

---

[35] This explanation while intuitively satisfying is not precisely correct. The yield spreads of Figure 5-2 assume that all holders receive a 3.50 per cent net holding-period return. In our case, investors with longer holding periods receive a *larger* return. Thus, in order to verify this proposition it was necessary actually to calculate for each holding-period a net yield obtainable from every conceivable method of investing.

[36] Even if the maturity distribution of the supply is predominantly short relative to the holding periods of bond demanders, the asymmetry described above implies that the yield curve will be approximately level.

ties. The yield curve will tend to rise sharply at first (to induce the short holding-period investors to extend the maturity of their holdings) and will then level off (since the yield spreads necessary to make long-holding-period investors extend the maturity of their bond purchases is very small).

5.8 *An Analysis of New-Issue Costs*

We have shown that if the holding periods of bond buyers tend to be shorter than the maturities of debt instruments available an ascending yield curve will result. But it is also necessary to examine the workings of the supply side of the market. Even if bond demanders can be in equilibrium in the presence of a positively sloped yield curve, one may well wonder whether bond suppliers (issuers) would upset such a relationship simply by shifting their offerings from the long to the short market. In this way suppliers could take advantage of the lower yields available on short loans, thereby eliminating any yield differentials that might otherwise exist. What we must show, therefore, is that a positively sloped yield curve can still constitute an equilibrium term structure when we allow shifting by bond issuers.

It should be noted at the outset that an individual supplier cannot simply issue securities at a net interest cost equal to the bid yield for similar debt securities. Rather, before he can bring his securities to market, he must incur a whole series of expenses, including underwriting fees, cost of preparing offering circulars or prospectuses, lawyers and accountants fees, and so forth. For convenience, we have subsumed these various categories under the heading "new-issue costs."

Unfortunately, it is not as easy to ascertain the exact magnitude of the transactions costs of bond issuers as it was for bond traders. While there is much published information from which we can infer the existence of these costs, the determination of their magnitude cannot be as precise as was our measurement of trading costs. Moreover, other factors, both psychological and economic, may play an even more important role than transactions costs in limiting the supply of short-term debt instruments. Such influences are particularly important in Treasury debt management.

The most complete data available concern the transactions costs of corporate long-term bond issuers. Table 5-6 presents relevant results of an exhaustive SEC study on the magnitude of flotation costs. The cost of underwriter compensation most nearly corresponds to the brokerage charges included in our analysis of the transactions costs of bond buyers. Since the additional expenses associated with new long-term issues are relatively large, however, they are also included in a separate column. We note that total percentage flotation costs decrease with the size of issue. For the median-sized issue, however, total new-issue costs were about $1\frac{1}{2}$ per cent of gross proceeds.

TABLE 5-6

Transactions Costs of Bond Issues as a Percentage
of Gross Proceeds

(Securities offered to the public in selected years: 1951,
1953, 1955)

Size of issue (in millions of dollars)	Compensation of investment banker	Other expenses[a]	Total costs
2.0–4.9	2.37	1.41	3.18
5.0–9 9	1.01	0.82	1.83
10.0–19.9	0.88	0.64	1.52
20.0–49.9	0.85	0.48	1.33
50.0 and over	0.88	0.32	1.19

[a] These include printing and engraving costs, Federal stamp taxes, state taxes, trustee's fees, etc., accounting, legal fees, etc.

Source: Securities and Exchange Commission, *Costs of Flotation of Corporate Securities, 1951–1955* (Washington, D.C.: U.S. Government Printing Office, June 1957).

The new-issue costs involved in utilizing alternative short-term sources of funds are less easy to determine. Here, we shall treat the two major sources: commercial paper and bank loans. The flotation costs incurred by (nonfinancial) corporations in issuing commercial paper are readily found. The standard charge ranges from $\frac{1}{4}$ of 1 per cent per annum for large companies to $\frac{1}{2}$ of 1 per cent for smaller firms.[37]

However, the strict transactions cost of issuing commercial paper understates considerably the full cost over and above the interest rate paid. This is so because commercial-paper buyers require that issuers have open (unused) lines of credit with commercial banks to cover a significant fraction of outstandings. On these open lines, a compensating-balance requirement of at least 10 per cent is required. Thus, the company that increases its outstanding commercial paper must increase its compensating balances *pari passu*, and the cost of

[37] Large sales-finance companies issue their own commercial paper. In these cases the transactions costs would have to be measured by the average cost (per dollar of paper issued) of maintaining a commercial-paper department. Presumably, these costs are somewhat lower than the charges made by brokers.

these balances must be added to the total interest plus transactions costs applicable to the paper itself.[38]

The following calculation represents a rough estimate of the total costs involved in issuing commercial paper. Assume that three-fourths of commercial-paper borrowings must be secured by an open line of credit and 10 per cent of the line must be covered by compensating balances which must be borrowed at a cost to the firm of 5 per cent.[39] This implies that an extra $7\frac{1}{2}$ cents out of every dollar of paper borrowings must be borrowed at a 5 per cent rate, an amount equivalent to an extra cost of $37\frac{1}{2}$ basis points per annum. Adding this to the average issue costs ($\frac{3}{8}$ of 1 per cent) we obtain a total cost for the issue of paper of $\frac{3}{4}$ of 1 per cent per annum, not including any other incidental expenses that are already taken into account in the estimation of the costs of long-term borrowing.

It is even more difficult to ascertain the transactions costs of bank borrowing. This is so because transactions charges are already included in the gross interest rate charged. To obtain some sort of rough evaluation of the magnitude of these charges, I have computed the average differentials between the following interest-rate time series: (1) the spread between the prime rate (the rate on short-term loans to prime borrowers) adjusted for compensating-balance requirements[40] and the rate on 9- to 12-month Treasury bills, and (2) the interest-rate spread between an average of (Moody's) Baa-rated industrials and long-term governments. Assuming that the average prime-rate borrower has a Baa rating, the interest-rate *risk* differential vis-à-vis governments should be roughly equal for each pair of rate series. The most important difference in the two constructed series is that transactions charges are included in the bank rate, while the Baa market rate is, of course, net of these charges. Thus, the differential between the adjusted prime

[38] Of course, the benefits of maintaining compensating-balance requirements may exceed mere support of new issues. Nevertheless, such requirements serve to explain that the real (fixed-dollar) cost incurred by a corporation in issuing paper far exceeds the apparent cost as measured by the commercial-paper rate.

[39] Unused lines of credit are maintained covering *at least* 75 per cent of total commercial paper outstanding for 78 per cent of commercial-paper issues, according to a questionnaire survey. See Nevins D. Baxter, *The Commercial-Paper Market* (Princeton: Econometric Research Program Research Memorandum No. 69, October 1964), p. 91. The 10 per cent compensating-balance requirement on these unused lines of credit is based on additional survey results reported in Nevins D. Baxter and Harold T. Shapiro, "Compensating-Balance Requirements: The Results of a Survey," *Journal of Finance* 19 (September 1964), pp. 483–496. See especially p. 487.

[40] The compensating-balance requirements used in the adjustment were taken from Baxter and Shapiro, *op. cit.*, p. 487.

rate and the 9- to 12-month Treasury rate has been much larger than the differential between the long (Baa) corporate and government rates. The size of this differential suggests that transactions charges associated with bank loans tend to be even higher on an annual basis than is the cost of issuing commercial paper. The differential has averaged almost $1\frac{1}{2}$ per cent per annum. We conclude that, as a rough rule, the *annual* transactions costs associated with the issuance of short-term debt instruments (composed of a bundle of commercial-paper and bank borrowing) are nearly equal to the *total* (underwriting) charges involved in the issue of long-term debt.

We could now introduce the notion of a "corporate issue period" (the period over which the corporation needs the funds) and develop the yield curves that would make the corporation indifferent as to what maturity it issued. For corporations that need funds over a long period of time the curve would slope upward. The corporation would be indifferent between continuously offering short-term securities and issuing a long-term security whose maturity exactly matched the corporation's needs only if the short rate were lower than the long rate. Of course, in a situation where the need for funds is expected to be temporary, transactions costs would produce a steep negatively sloped indifference curve. The cost of issuing long-term debt and then calling the issue (or buying it up on the open market) soon thereafter would be substantially larger than meeting a temporary need for funds through short-term borrowing.[41]

If our rough estimates of new-issue costs are anywhere near the mark, however, such an analysis will not be necessary. It appears

---

[41] We must not, however, confuse temporary needs for funds with the maturity of the asset to be financed. For example, by an argument akin to the commercial-loan theory, it is often suggested that short-term assets are appropriately financed with short-term debt. We must be careful to note the fallacy in such a facile explanation. For even taking that class of firms whose assets are entirely short-term in character (the sales-finance companies), there is still reason to believe that the predominant form of financing will be long-term. This is so because the total amount of consumer credit outstanding in the United States in the post-war period has not been subject to sharp declines. While the sales-finance companies may expect significant seasonal and cyclical variation, they have been able to count on the continuance of bulk of their receivables from year to year. See "The Behavior of Consumer Credit," *Monthly Review,* Federal Reserve Bank of New York (March 1960), pp. 50–54. In other words, the short-term maturity of these contracts belies the fact that they are essentially permanent assets of the company. Given that the bulk of funds to be raised is for the permanent capital of the company, it is then not surprising, for the reasons given above, to discover the maturity composition of the debt of the sales-finance companies has been predominantly long-term.

that the cost of changing maturity for bond issuers through the issue of a maturity which does not correspond to the period over which the corporation needs funds is much higher than the cost of maturity conversion for bond buyers through the secondary market. If this is so, we would expect to get a supply of debt instruments which accommodates the issuers' preferences. *New-issue costs are so large relative to trading costs that the differentials which are likely to arise from the effects of trading costs are not likely to be sufficient to induce movement of bond issuers from their preferred maturity area.*

We can readily illustrate this point. Consider a firm that needs funds for 25 years. Assume new issue costs are 1 per cent of the gross proceeds if 25-year bonds are issued (0.04 per cent per annum over the life of the issue) and 1 per cent per annum if a succession of short-term securities are issued. In this situation, the firm would be indifferent between the short and long markets (if interest rates were expected to remain unchanged) when the short rate was 96 basis points below the 25-year rate. But our previous analysis suggested that the magnitude of differentials likely to be caused by trading costs are considerably smaller than this. For example, we note in Column 4 of Table 5-4 that, under some reasonable assumptions concerning the distribution of holding periods, we generated a differential of only 22 basis points. It is, of course, possible to generate larger spreads. Nevertheless, not until we (unrealistically) assume that *all* investors have 30-day holding periods do we get a differential from the 30-day to 25-year yield which is (barely) enough to induce our illustrative firm to borrow at short term.

We must conclude that, over the relevant range of trading-cost-induced differentials, issuers needing long-term funds will not be induced to shift the composition of their borrowing from long to short term.[42] If the periods over which bond issuers need funds tend to be longer than the holding periods of bond buyers, then the equilibrium yield curve will tend to be positively sloped. Despite this slope, the business firm in need of long-term capital will not wish to issue successive short-term issues in lieu of long-term bonds.

In addition, many other factors militate against repetitive borrow-

---

[42] This provides an answer for Meiselman's query why borrowers do not simply turn to the cheaper source of funds and thereby eliminate the interest-rate spread. David Meiselman, "Discussion: Econometric Studies in Money Markets: II" (a paper presented to the Econometric Society, Pittsburgh, December 1962). It can also be shown that a corporation with a temporary need for funds will not be induced to sell a long-term bond with the expectation of redeeming the security prior to its maturity.

ing on short term. The bother of continuous negotiation is very costly in terms of manpower and, in the case of a non-financial corporation, tends to divert operating officials from their basic functions. Moreover, the corporation that owes a large demand debt is perpetually at the "mercy of the market." During times of credit restraint, refinancing difficulties may become particularly acute. A group of lenders may at such times be able to force the corporation into very unfavorable terms. Thus, there are reasons to suppose the existence of a strong a priori case in favor of funding which would tend to bias the distribution of corporate debt toward longer maturities.[43] We hasten to point out, however, that this case for funding in no way rules out the possibility of anticipatory or delayed funding. The *timing* of long-term debt issues may still conform to the behavior suggested by the expectations theory.[44]

The case relating to the funding of the Treasury's debt is less clear. Presumably there are significant economies of scale which result from the large size of Treasury operations. Consequently, transactions-cost differentials between short and long issues are undoubtedly smaller, though they certainly work in the same direction as they do for corporate issues. But even if short-term issues are less costly, minimization of total interest and transactions costs is only one objective of Treasury debt management. There are reasons to expect that the Treasury is limited in its willingness to put out a large quantity of short-term issues irrespective of cost considerations that might favor such a debt-management policy.

One must always keep in mind that the reason the Treasury issues interest-bearing debt in the first place is to pay people for not spending. This purchase of nonspending or illiquidity serves to avoid the inflationary spending which would result if the debt were monetized.[45] A debt which consisted only of very short-term liquid instruments might well produce results similar to turning the total debt into

[43] Interviews with executives of the leading sales-finance companies indicate that the men responsible for borrowing operations display a lively horror of too large a floating debt. Putting out new 4- to 6-month paper only to find themselves continuously confronted by maturing debt which must be paid off, they see their position much like that of Sisyphus.

[44] As we shall note in Chapter 6, empirical evidence strongly suggests that the timing of long-term issues does indeed respond to expectations. The larger transactions costs on short issues could easily be made up over the life of the loan if a delay in long-term financing enables a corporation to float bonds at significantly lower interest rates.

[45] The view that the crux of debt policy is the purchase of illiquidity is held by Richard A. Musgrave, *The Theory of Public Finance* (New York: McGraw-Hill, 1959), p. 582, and Earl R. Rolph, "Principles of Debt Management," *American Economic Review* 47 (June 1957), pp. 302–320.

money. Moreover, several other arguments also suggest that the Treasury is limited in the volume of short-term claims which it is willing to issue. A large short-term debt requiring continuous refinancing raises a number of marketing problems even for the Treasury and tends as well to interfere with Federal Reserve open-market operations.[46] Thus, it would appear that considerations other than transactions costs may also tend to make the supply of debt instruments longer in maturity than the holding period of bond demanders. This implies, in accord with the analysis of Section 5.6, that the yield curve would "normally" be positively sloped (even in the absence of risk aversion on the part of bond buyers).[47]

5.9 Transactions Costs and Financial Intermediaries[48]

The role financial intermediaries play in the process of determining the distribution of holding periods of bond demanders deserves to be mentioned. These intermediaries, in addition to their other functions, convert short maturities into longer ones.[49] The assets owned by these intermediaries are typically much longer than the term of their liabilities. This is true not only of the banking system in general but of life insurance companies and bond dealers as well.[50] Thus, intermediaries as a group are able to increase the average holding period of bond demanders. Their activity tends to reduce the interest-rate spread between short and long maturities. They are, in Kessel's terminology, essentially speculators. They are long on long-term bonds and short on short-term funds. Their economic viability is a function of the interest-rate spread between their short liabilities and long assets.[51]

[46] On the other hand, a debt which has a reasonably balanced maturity distribution tends to facilitate monetary policy by providing a vehicle whereby stringency in one sector of the market may be transmitted throughout the maturity spectrum. See Winfield Riefler, "Open Market Operations in Long-term Securities," *Federal Reserve Bulletin* 44 (November 1958), pp. 1260–1274.

[47] Indeed, the development of the secondary market is to some extent proof that the maturity distribution of the debt is longer than the holding periods of bond investors. This is not to deny, however, during other periods of history and for other societies that, for example, seasonal influences may predominate to such an extent as to suggest that a preponderance of debt with short maturities would be issued. This may partially explain why, during the period 1880–1920, there is no evidence suggesting that short rates were normally lower.

[48] This discussion relies heavily on the reasoning of Reuben Kessel, *op. cit.*, pp. 51–58.

[49] A discussion of the "arbitraging" function of financial intermediaries may be found in John G. Gurley and Edward S. Shaw, *Money in a Theory of Finance* (Washington: The Brookings Institution, 1960), pp. 121–126.

[50] Notable exceptions, however, are sales-finance and small-loan companies.

[51] Kessel, *op. cit.*, p. 52.

Why then do not these "speculators" eliminate any yield differential between short and long maturities? The answer once again is, in part, transactions costs: speculative activity has positive costs of operation. For example, consider the speculative activities of bond dealers. They borrow on short term in order to finance their inventories of securities, whose average term to maturity is considerably longer than their liabilities. To accomplish this, the dealers "scour" the country arranging repurchase agreements, and they also borrow from banks. But, needless to say, neither these nor other speculative activities of bond dealers are free of transactions costs.[52] Similarly, other intermediaries are faced with significant costs in acquiring short-term resources to finance their long-term holdings. The empirical evidence is consistent with the existence of such positive costs of operation. Experience over the past century reveals that the average level of short rates has been substantially below the average of long rates despite the "speculative" activities of almost the entire financial community. This differential can persist, in part, because these institutions must first offset their transactions costs in the very broadest sense of the term.[53]

5.10   *Some Cross-Sectional Empirical Evidence*

It is difficult to find empirical evidence that can isolate the effect of transactions costs on the term structure. Kessel and others have found that, at least during periods of recent history, short rates have been considerably below long rates on average. Of course, such findings do not, in themselves, establish that transactions costs have been important in influencing the rate structure. It could be, for example, that bond investors with Hicksian risk aversion predominate and the average yield curve would have a positive slope even in a zero-transactions-cost world. An approach which may help to shed some light on the problem, however, is a cross-sectional study of yield curves for securities that are essentially similar in all respects except their marketability. If the transactions costs for one group of issues is found to be substantially larger than for the other, then we shall argue

---

[52] Moreover, we shall show later that there are several institutional impediments which severely limit the volume of these transactions.

[53] Of course those institutions that convert short maturities into longs may also demand risk premiums for engaging in such speculative activity. Indeed, as we shall see in Chapter 6, there is direct evidence to suggest that this is so. Our aim in this chapter, however, is simply to discuss the role that transactions costs by themselves play in explaining a part of the upward bias to the slope of the yield curve.

that it is proper to infer that differences in the characteristic slopes of the yield curves may be attributed to transactions-cost differentials.

Unhappily, it is impossible to find classes of issues that differ *only* with respect to transactions costs. Corporate bonds, where transactions costs are larger than for governments, are not free of default risk.[54] One comparison which may help untangle the role of transactions costs involves juxtaposing the yield curves of Treasury securities and yield curves of obligations of the Public Housing Authority (PHA's). Default risk may be considered equivalent for the two securities, since the latter are indirect obligations of the federal government. PHA's are secured by a pledge of annual contributions by the Public Housing

TABLE 5-7

AVERAGE TRADING COSTS OF DEALING IN OBLIGATIONS OF THE
PUBLIC HOUSING AUTHORITY

Term to maturity	Dollar cost of turnaround per $1,000.00 of par value	Equivalent yield spread[a] (per cent)
90 days	$ 0.3125	0.125
180 days	0.5625	0.1125
1 year	1.35	0.135
2 years	3.00	0.155
5 years	5.25	0.11
20 years	11.50	0.065

[a] Computed by converting dollar costs of column two into basis-point values.

Administration, and the *"full faith and credit of the United States* is pledged to the payment of all amounts agreed to be paid by the Authority. . . ."[55]

The total amount of PHA obligations outstanding is relatively small, however, and is divided into a myriad of small issues which are direct obligations of several local public agencies. As a result, the markets for these issues tend to be "thin" in comparison with the government-securities market, and trading costs are very large. Table 5-7 presents estimates of the average trading costs of dealing in PHA obligations. These data are comparable to the trading costs

[54] Even the Durand data are probably not completely free of default risk. Moreover, as we indicated in Chapter 1, the Durand yield curves are not well delineated in the important early maturities where transactions costs are likely to exhibit their greatest effect.

[55] The quotation is from an opinion, dated May 15, 1953, of the Attorney General of the United States, to the President of the United States.

for government securities reported in Table 5-2, and the method of collection of the two sets of estimates is identical. We find that trading costs for PHA's are about five times as large as for governments in the short end of the maturity spectrum and almost ten times as large for longer maturities.

We can now repeat the analysis of Section 5.6 to demonstrate the effects of the PHA trading-cost structure on the indifference yield

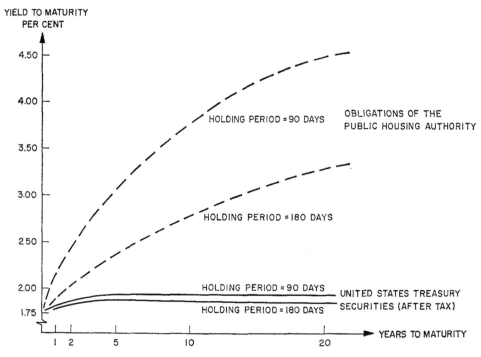

FIG. 5-3. Indifference yield curves for Public Housing Authority and Treasury securities compared.

curves of bond investors. A few illustrations will be sufficient to demonstrate the main conclusion. Figure 5-3 presents comparisons of the indifference yield curves for governments and PHA's for investors with 90- and 180-day holding periods.[56] We note that the indifference yield curves for PHA's are considerably steeper than those for governments. To the extent that investors with short holding periods must

[56] The indifference (mid-point) yield curves were constructed so that the investor receives a net after-tax yield of 1.75 per cent whichever security he purchases. Government yield curves are plotted on an after-tax basis assuming a 50 per cent tax rate. PHA securities are tax exempt.

be induced to hold longer securities, the yield spreads that must be offered on PHA issues must be substantially larger than those on Treasury securities. Consequently, in a situation where bond investors have short holding periods and the supply is evenly distributed among maturities, the slope of the actual yield curve for PHA's would be considerably steeper than that for governments. If these assumptions approximately describe actual market conditions, this should actually be the case.

The data support this qualitative contention. Figure 5-4 shows the

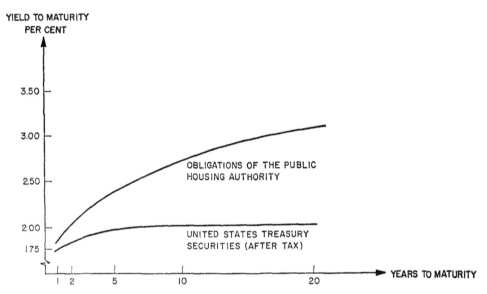

Fig. 5-4. Average yield curves for Treasury and Public Housing Authority securities, December 1960 through March 1965.

average yield curve for Treasury and PHA securities during the period December 1960 through March 1965.[57] We note that the average PHA yield curve starts slightly higher than the Treasury curve, and the after-tax yield spread continuously widens with maturity. This is consistent with the hypothesis that commercial banks (whose earnings are taxed at a corporate tax rate) with short holding periods

[57] The PHA yield curves were constructed by averaging the offering yield curves of each new PHA issue during the period indicated. Since PHA obligations are issued serially (i.e., a new issue consists of a series of bonds maturing in yearly installments), it is possible to draw a yield curve for each new issue. An after-tax Treasury yield curve was then calculated on each PHA offering date (assuming a corporate tax rate), and the average of all observations for each maturity was found. The yield curves start with a maturity of one year.

must be paid an increasing differential premium over Treasury securities in order to be induced to extend the maturity of their holdings.[58] These data provide independent evidence suggesting that transactions costs may significantly influence the term structure of interest rates.[59]

5.11 *Conclusion*

In a setting of the traditional expectations model, our analysis has revealed that the structure of transactions costs presently observed in debt markets imparts a positive bias to the slope of the yield curve. The asymmetrical effects of trading costs on the demand side of the market imply that investors with long holding periods are essentially indifferent between shorts and longs at the same yield. Short-holding-period investors, on the other hand, always prefer short to long issues. Transactions costs do not have the same effect on bond suppliers. Suppliers who need funds over prolonged periods prefer long to short issues, since the transactions costs per unit of time are lower the longer the issue. Our analysis suggests that as long as the holding periods of demanders tend to be shorter than the issue periods of bond suppliers, the yield curve will first rise sharply and then level off. Thus

[58] According to bond dealers I have interviewed, commercial banks (and other short-holding-period investors who pay corporate tax rates) are the major participants in the market for PHA and Treasury securities up to a maturity of about 10 years. However, there still remains the question, why investors with long holding periods do not switch from governments to PHA's and thereby eliminate the yield differential in the long end of the market. To some extent, they do. The yield differentials that remain in the long PHA maturity spectrum are not sufficient to attract investors with short holding periods. The reason that the differential is not completely eliminated is that the marginal switcher from long governments to long PHA securities does not pay a corporate tax rate. Many major participants in bond markets either pay no tax (as in the case of pension funds and elymosynary institutions) or pay taxes at a reduced rate (as in the case of life insurance companies).

[59] Some bond-market experts have suggested to me that two additional factors may also influence the shape of the PHA yield curve. These are (1) a possibility that the tax-exemption privilege may be removed from municipals in the future and (2) a possibility of changes in future tax rates. It is argued that the likelihood of lower future taxes and the possible removal of the tax-exemption privilege could make municipals worth less in the future. Consequently, it is suggested that one reason for the steeper municipal yield curves is the risk of future capital losses on long-term municipals that would accompany either of these occurrences. What this argument overlooks, however, is the prevalent view that were the tax exemption to be removed, it would most likely be removed from *new issues* of municipals and not from already outstanding securities. Hence, outstanding tax-exempt issues would be worth more owing to the suspension of new issues. Thus, the net effect on the yield curve from these considerations would appear to be indeterminate.

we found that the effect of transactions charges will be felt mainly in the very early maturities. Finally, we noted that transactions costs (in the very broadest sense of the term) in part prevent the operations of financial intermediaries, as "speculators," from eliminating this differential. Cross-sectional empirical evidence was adduced in support of our hypothesis.

The differential effect of transactions costs on the slope of various segments of the yield curve is even more clearly seen if we take a case where the market expects lower interest rates in the future. Suppose that all investors uniformly expect that 30-day rates (currently at 4.00 per cent) will fall 2.5 basis points each month until

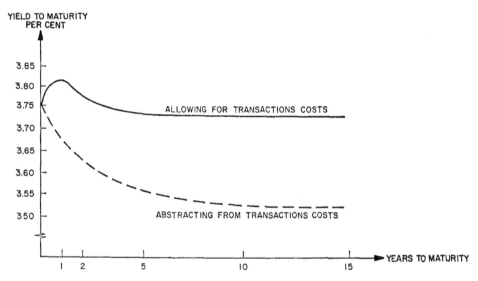

Fig. 5-5. Effect of transactions costs on the term structure.

they reach 3.50 per cent. In *all* subsequent periods 30-day rates are expected to be 3.50 per cent. Figure 5-5 depicts the yield curves that would result, both allowing for and abstracting from transactions costs. Abstracting from transactions charges we have a monotonically descending yield curve consistent with expectations of lower interest rates (higher bond prices). When the effect of transactions charges is introduced, however, the yield curve presents a "humped" appearance, with a peak within the first year.[60] Thus, we see that in a

[60] The yield curve allowing for transactions costs was calculated by adding yield differentials derived from Table 5-4, Column 4, to the values of the yield curve as given by the pure expectations theory. Thus we implicitly assume that

case where rates are expected to fall, the yield curve will not necessarily be monotonically descending. Because the effect of transactions costs is strongest in the early maturity areas, the yield curve is likely to be ascending, at least throughout most of the Treasury bill area. The empirical evidence seems to support this contention. The slope of the yield curve for Treasury securities has typically been positive through the very early maturities even when later segments of the curve were negatively sloped.[61]

The introduction of transactions costs also affords insights into one cyclical peculiarity of the term structure which was noted by Kessel. Kessel found that the amount by which implicit short rates tended to overestimate future short rates was not constant over the cycle. He found that these "liquidity premia," as he called them, tended to be larger when interest rates were high and lower during periods of low rates.[62] This finding is entirely consistent with a theory of the term structure where no bond investors are assumed to be Hicksian risk averters. The existence of dealer risk aversion will, by itself, tend to produce this result. Trading costs are not constant over the interest-rate cycle. They tend to be higher during periods of high interest rates and lower during periods of easy credit. Table 5-8 presents estimates of the cyclical variability of trading costs.[63] Consequently, the upward bias imparted to the slope of the yield curve will tend to be greater during periods of high rates. Thus trading costs and their determinants offer a simple and appealing explanation for many of the "irregularities" of the term structure which have been discussed by recent empirical investigators.

---

the distribution of holding periods relative to the maturity of the outstanding debt is the same as in our example described in 5.6. This calculation must be considered only an approximation, however. This is so because Table 5-4 assumed that yields would remain unchanged from period to period. In the present case, 30-day yields are expected to fall in subsequent periods. Therefore, the shape of the yield curve must also change (until two years have passed and all future short rates are then expected to remain unchanged). Consequently, the appropriate yield differentials due to transactions costs are only approximately correct.

[61] This has been noted by David Meiselman, *The Term Structure of Interest Rates*, p. 47.

[62] Kessel, *op. cit.*, pp. 25–27.

[63] These estimates were obtained by a questionnaire survey of the leading bond dealers. "Good" market conditions were specified to refer to periods of general credit ease. Respondents were asked to consider "unsettled" conditions to be those of "active" credit restraint such as occurred during the end of 1959. Of course, the increase in trading costs during times of unsettled market conditions is a direct reflection of the increase in risk perceived by the dealers.

TABLE 5-8
DEALER SPREADS UNDER ALTERNATIVE MARKET CONDITIONS
(in basis points)

Maturity	Governments Market conditions		PHA obligations Market conditions	
	"Good"	"Unsettled"	"Good"	"Unsettled"
3 months	2.0	4.0	10.3	20.5
6 months	2.0	3.7	8.4	18.2
1 year	2.1	5.3	10.2	18.6
2 years	2.4	5.3	13.6	21.0
5 years	1.5	2.2	9.2	15.8
20 years	0.8	1.6	5.6	10.0

In conclusion, we must again warn the reader that our results cannot be attributed wholly to pure transactions costs. The present pattern of trading costs that rise with maturity, upon which many of our results depend, could be explained fully only by introducing elements of risk aversion on the part of the government-bond dealer and by calling attention to specific supply conditions prevailing in particular markets. To the extent that Hicksian risk aversion influences the trading-cost structure, we must recognize that transactions costs are simply the vehicle whereby such attitudes toward risk alter the shape of the yield curve. While we were unable to obtain a precise empirical measure of the extent to which various components determine the structure of trading costs, such a decomposition must be effected (at least conceptually) if we are to increase our understanding of the determinants of market yield differentials. And even if we assign the most important role to risk aversion, it is important to realize that risk aversion on the part of the bond dealers alone is sufficient to provide a characteristically positive slope to the yield curve.

CHAPTER 6

Modifications for Institutional Preferences and
Diverse Expectations: Some Empirical
Evidence on Behavior Patterns

IN THE PRECEDING CHAPTER, we began our construction of an over-all theory of the term structure with the introduction of transactions costs into the traditional expectations model. In the course of this exercise we were forced to abandon the assumption of perfect certainty and to introduce risk aversion on the part of the government-bond dealers, who establish the structure of trading charges. Nevertheless, we continued to make two important assumptions: that individual investors held uniform expectations concerning all future short-term rates of interest and that their utility functions were linear in money gains. Since no risk aversion of any kind existed on the part of investors, arbitrage between maturities would continue until no interest-rate differentials remained other than those either justified by expectations or accountable to transactions charges. In this and the following chapter, we shall relax these assumptions and focus on the important question of how individual investors actually behave.

6.1 The Expectations versus the Hedging-Pressure (or Institutional) Hypothesis

Before undertaking a study of the behavior of investment managers, it will be useful to review briefly the kinds of assumptions about portfolio practices that have been offered in the literature. As we indicated in Chapter 2, beliefs about individual behavior encompass the full range of possibilities. On the one hand, some theorists hold that expectations alone determine the rate structure, while at the other extreme there are institutionalists who insist that the short- and long-term markets are essentially segmented. The former argue that, unless expectations of future rates are influenced, the term structure is insensitive to changes in the maturity distribution of a fixed supply of debt instruments, since, at the margin, individuals freely substitute among maturities in response to any interest-rate differentials over and above those justified by their expectations. Investigators of the latter persuasion come close to suggesting that interest rates in each market are determined solely by internal supply and demand interactions, as neither borrowers nor lenders shift between markets in response to interest-rate differentials.

J. M. Culbertson, the leading protagonist of the institutional or hedging-pressure hypothesis, alleges that many market participants cannot or will not change the maturity composition of their portfolios to take advantage of expected profitable investment opportunities. Culbertson claims that financial institutions select a maturity structure suited to their needs and hold to that structure regardless of expected future interest-rate changes.[1] Expectations-induced changes in the maturity composition of the portfolio play no role in his theory. The hedging-pressure argument stresses that different groups of institutions tend to confine their security purchases to the specific maturity sectors of the market that match the maturity composition of their liabilities. Thus, life insurance companies are characterized as exclusively long-term investors, while nonfinancial corporations tend to confine their financial investments to short-term bonds. Commercial banks, while operating over wider maturity sectors than corporations, are also considered to be primarily short-term investors. As we mentioned in Chapter 2, an implacable type of risk aversion could provide the theoretical grounds for such hedging behavior.

Similarly, on the borrowing side of the market, the maturity composition of debt issues is said to be related to the period of time for which the funds are needed or to the type of physical assets to be purchased with the funds. A business that finances plant construction by short-term borrowing will "impair its liquidity position."[2] In consequence, the institutionalists hold that on both the borrowing and lending sides of the market movement among maturities is severely inhibited. They conclude that changes in the maturity structure of the supply of debt instruments (largely associated with shifts in the importance of activities characteristically financed by different types of credit), combined with changes in the cyclical flow of funds to various maturity-specialized investing institutions, fully explain cyclical differences in the behavior of the term structure. Expectations are dismissed as an insignificant element in the process of rate-structure determination. Carried to its extreme, the institutional view would imply that the short- and long-term markets are essentially independent.[3]

[1] J. M. Culbertson, "The Term Structure of Interest Rates," *Quarterly Journal of Economics* 71 (November 1957), p. 499.

[2] *Ibid.*, p. 494.

[3] The above view of the market must also implicitly assume that speculators,

At the other end of the spectrum, there are modern writers who accept the pure expectations hypothesis as a full explanation of the term structure. Meiselman, while agreeing that some investors may be rigidly committed to specific maturity sectors, argues that market excess-demand schedules for securities of each maturity tend to be infinitely elastic at rates consistent with expectations of future short rates.[4] This occurs because, so long as speculators are both indifferent to uncertainty and adequately financed, they will adjust the quantities of securities they take from or supply to the market so as to maintain a structure of rates consistent with their mathematical expectations. Meiselman concludes that the traditional expectations theory can provide a complete description of the behavior of default-free yields over the current century.[5]

There is, of course, a variety of positions intermediate between these two extremes. Nevertheless, these polar models of the term structure, and the assumptions about investor behavior patterns that they contain, may usefully serve as background for the following two chapters of our study. They focus our attention on the type of investor response to interest-rate differentials that is the crucially important assumption in the theory of the term structure. A priori arguments cannot settle the matter; it is a question which ultimately must rest on the evidence. In this chapter we shall examine some empirical evidence on the microeconomic level which bears on the competing assumptions just described. From a careful study of the portfolio practices of major institutional investors and an examination of the actual workings of the government-securities market, we shall seek to determine what evidence supports either of the extreme positions. On the basis of this study of the facts, we shall proceed, in Chapter 7, to construct a model which synthesizes elements of these two contradictory views.

---

operating to take advantage of differences between holding-period yields for longs and shorts, are either absent or that their operations are too insignificant to alter the rate structure.

[4] David Meiselman, *The Term Structure of Interest Rates* (Englewood Cliffs: Prentice-Hall, 1962), p. 57.

[5] While Meiselman is prepared, in principle, to admit that transactions costs might be important, his view is that ". . . in the market for Treasury securities transactions costs are extremely small, so small that they would appear to get lost in the rounding errors for all but the very shortest issues." See his "Discussion: Econometric Studies in Money Markets II" (a paper presented to the Econometric Society, Pittsburgh, December 1962).

6.2 Some Aggregate, Cross-Sectional Evidence

6.2.a AN ANALYSIS OF THE TREASURY SURVEY OF OWNERSHIP

The Treasury Survey of Ownership of Government Securities provides one easily accessible source of data on institutional holdings
of securities of different maturities.[6] The Survey provides a maturity
breakdown of the aggregate portfolios of Treasury securities of financial institutions by class. Data are provided for commercial banks,
life insurance companies, mutual savings banks, and several other
classes of institution. Through an examination of these data, we should
at least be able to obtain some insights concerning the portfolio behavior of these institutions. Specifically, if financial institutions simply
matched the maturity of their assets to the maturity of their liabilities,
we would find that, unless the maturity of their liabilities changed,
these investors would be rigidly committed to particular maturity sectors. Thus, if we calculated, for each class of institution, the shares
of the total (government) portfolio held in various maturity
categories, we would expect these shares to be stable over time. For
example, under the institutional hypothesis, we would expect that
life insurance companies, whose claims are mainly long-term, would
be invested largely in long-term (over 10 years in maturity) bonds
and that the share of long-term securities in their portfolios would
be relatively constant. On the other hand, the expectations hypothesis
implies quite a different type of behavior. As the relative supply of
bonds changed or as particular institutions altered their expectations,
we would anticipate that investors would alter the proportion of their
investments in each maturity sector. Consequently, the portfolio shares
allocated to the different maturity sectors would vary over time.[7]

In order to determine whether an analysis of institutional holdings
of governments lends any credibility to the institutional theory of

[6] U.S. Treasury Department, *Treasury Bulletins,* 1952–1965.
[7] We should point out in advance that there are serious limitations to this
analysis. Even if our assumption that there was no change in the composition
of the liabilities of the institutions surveyed were correct, there would still be
a problem in looking at only one type of asset, namely Treasury securities.
The maturity composition of an institution's *total* portfolio of marketable securities
might remain constant if shifts in the maturity composition of the government
securities held were balanced by opposite shifts in the remainder of the portfolio.
The results of more satisfactory microeconomic empirical investigation will be
reported later. A look at these aggregate data should, however, at least help
us to focus on the relevant issues.

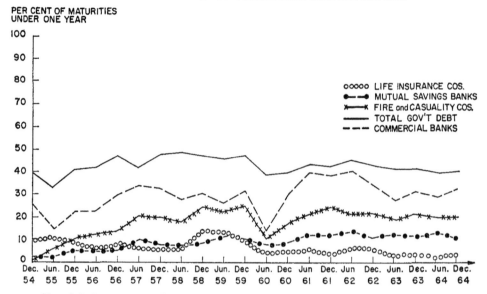

FIG. 6-1. Percentage of government-bond portfolios of financial institutions maturing within 1 year.

the term structure, data on aggregate portfolio holdings of government bonds for each class of institution were first converted into percentages (shares) by maturity category. Figures 6-1 through 6-4 juxtapose the time series of these shares, by maturity sector, for each class of institution with the share of the total marketable government debt,

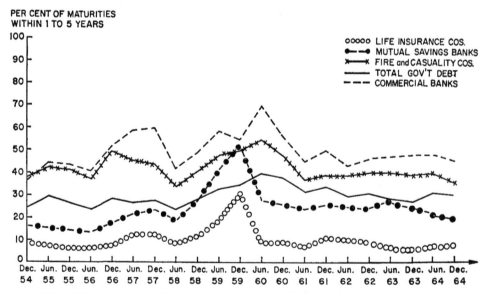

FIG. 6-2. Percentage of government-bond portfolios of financial institutions maturing within 1 to 5 years.

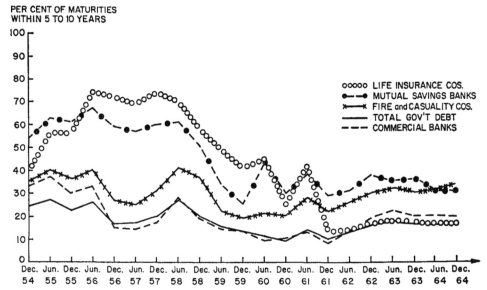

FIG. 6-3. Percentage of government-bond portfolios of financial institutions maturing within 5 to 10 years.

as a standard of reference. Figures 6-5 and 6-6 present the relative shares of total debt outstanding and total commercial-bank portfolios from a different perspective. Even a cursory examination of these figures reveals that the maturity composition of institutional portfolios has been remarkably variable. This immediately casts doubt on at

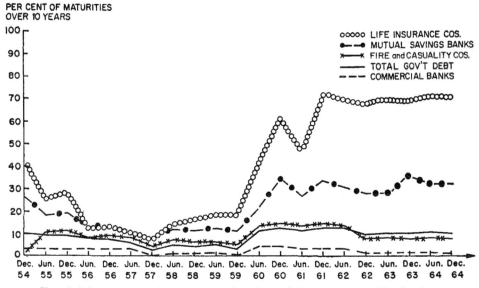

FIG. 6-4. Percentage of government-bond portfolios of financial institutions maturing in over 10 years.

PER CENT

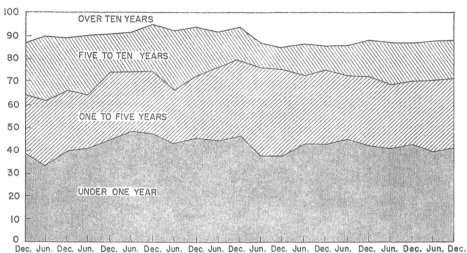

FIG. 6-5. Maturity distribution of total marketable government debt.

least the extreme form of the hedging-pressure hypothesis. Portfolio shares, by maturity category, for the institutions represented have tended to be considerably more variable than the relative shares of various maturities in the total government debt.

Examples from recent bond-market history tend to highlight this

PER CENT

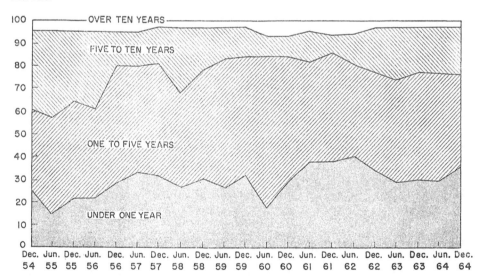

FIG. 6-6. Maturity distribution of commercial-bank holdings of governments.

150

finding. From June 1958 through June 1960 the total amount outstanding of Treasury securities with maturities from 1 to 5 years increased from $39.4 billion (*23.6 per cent of the total*) to $72.8 billion (39.6 per cent).[8] Figure 6-2 depicts this change (see the solid line). All financial institutions tended to increase their relative shares of 1- to 5-year issues during this period. What is remarkable is the extent to which life insurance companies (classically long-term investors) increased their holdings in this maturity sector. Similarly, mutual savings banks and fire and casualty companies bought significant quantities of these issues. This offers *prima facie* evidence that certain classes of financial institution not only can but do make substantial shifts in the maturity composition of their portfolios. Table 6-1 presents data on the maturity distribution of the aggregate portfolios of nonfinancial corporations covered by the Treasury Survey of Ownership. Unfortunately the Treasury did not report maturity breakdowns prior to 1960. Nevertheless, it appears that corporations (supposedly short investors unwilling to stray from the Treasury-bill market) were at times induced to purchase significant quantities of intermediate-term issues. Finally, note in Figure 6-4 the substantial shifts out of and into the long-term market by the institutions depicted. Figure 6-7 indicates that government-bond dealers have also made substantial changes in the maturity composition of their inventories of governments.

These aggregate cross-sectional data appear to be patently inconsistent with the extreme institutional hypothesis. It is ironic that an argument presumably based on institutional considerations can be so at variance with the apparent facts of institutional portfolio behavior. This conclusion would be even more strikingly demonstrated were we to deal with portfolio flows rather than stocks. Aggregate portfolio flows reveal that a large degree of flexibility appears to characterize the behavior of portfolio managers. Only in one respect do these data support the arguments of the institutional school. We do find that certain institutions maintain portfolios that have a relatively short average maturity while other institutions tend to hold portfolios composed primarily of long-term bonds. For example, we note (from Table 6-1) that corporations tend to hold an insignificant proportion of their portfolio in bonds maturing in over 5 years. Similarly, we find that life insurance companies tend to keep the bulk of their

---

[8] Throughout most of this period the Treasury was prohibited from selling securities with maturities over 5 years, because the level of (long) rates was higher than the $4\frac{1}{4}$ per cent interest ceiling on these issues.

TABLE 6-1

MATURITY DISTRIBUTION OF PORTFOLIOS OF NONFINANCIAL CORPORATIONS COVERED BY TREASURY SURVEY OF OWNERSHIP

	June 30, 1960	Dec. 31, 1960	June 30, 1961	Dec. 31, 1961	June 30, 1962	Dec. 31, 1962	June 30, 1963	Dec. 31, 1963	June 30, 1964	Dec. 31, 1964
Per cent of port-folio maturing in										
Less than 1 year	73.62	77.89	83.48	82.51	84.27	84.31	77.38	73.57	75.34	73.86
1 to 5 years	25.00	20.88	15.00	16.53	13.93	14.18	18.68	22.99	20.36	21.90
5 to 10 years	0.74	0.54	1.13	0.68	1.40	1.39	3.73	2.78	3.12	2.98
Over 10 years	0.65	0.67	0.39	0.28	0.40	0.13	0.21	0.66	1.18	1.26

securities in longer-term maturities. Moreover, while all classes of institutions appear to make broad substitutions into adjacent maturities, we do not find evidence of significant substitutions from very short (under 1 year) into very long (over 10 years) maturities. In Section 6.4 we shall interpret these findings.

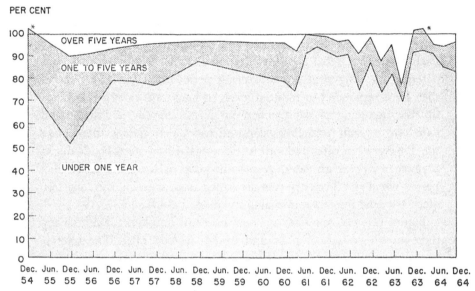

FIG. 6-7. Maturity composition of bond dealers' government portfolios.

* Dealers has a net short position in securities maturing in over 5 years.

6.2.b THE FLEXIBILITY OF BOND SUPPLIERS

In examining data for the supply side of the market, we focused not on the specific arguments of the institutional school, but rather on an important consideration which its members have inexplicably overlooked. Institutionalists are correct in asserting that, within the relevant range of rate differentials, private- and municipal-bond issuers do not appear to have been induced to make *long-run* changes in the maturity composition of their debt. But what these writers overlook is the degree of flexibility available to issuers in adjusting the timing of long-term bond issues. As we indicated in the preceding chapter, while transactions costs may prevent issuers who need funds over a long period from borrowing perpetually at short term, these costs will not prevent *some* borrowing at short term for a limited period until conditions become more favorable for the flotation of long-term claims.

The empirical evidence is consistent with the hypothesis that long-term borrowing and refunding are to an important extent postponable, thus allowing expectations to exert considerable influence. There is a tendency for a high level of interest rates to restrict the supply of new long-term issues. Many corporations have refrained from floating long-term bonds during periods of relatively high long-term interest rates. They may postpone coming to the market and may meet their immediate needs by drawing down their liquid assets or by short-term borrowings from commercial banks and other lenders. Similarly, state and local governments have found it advisable to avoid entering the long-term market during periods of high rates, whereas they have responded to reduced levels of long-term rates by accelerating the financing of construction programs. Finally, although motivated by several (sometimes contradictory) debt-management goals, the Treasury has often reduced its offerings of long-term bonds during periods of very high rates. A case in point is the 1959–early 1960 period when the Treasury was prevented from entering the long-term market by the interest-rate ceiling mentioned above.

Figure 6-8 presents data on new issues of long-term bonds during three-month periods of peak and trough interest rates. The interest-rate figure below each date gives the average long-term government rate during the quarter,[9] which provides an indication of the level of long-term rates in general. We note that, at least for the periods of maximum credit restraint and ease, the data are consistent with the hypothesis suggested above. Total long-term issues during the second quarter of 1958 (when interest rates reached their trough and bank reserves were ample) were more than double the total issues during the first quarter of 1960 (when interest rates reached their peak and long-term markets were disorganized). Qualitatively, all groups of issuers responded similarly.

With respect to municipal-bond issuers, several studies have concluded that issuers possess a great deal of flexibility in the timing of new issues of long-term bonds. For example, Roland Robinson finds considerable evidence of deferral of issues during periods of "credit tension" and acceleration of financing during periods of credit

---

[9] The long-term government rate was calculated from monthly averages reported in the *Federal Reserve Bulletin*. Again, we warn the reader that these data must be interpreted with great caution. It is one thing to suggest that long-term borrowing is interest-elastic and quite another matter to show that this borrowing was shifted to the short-term market. The latter contention is the crucially important one for the expectations theory, and, except as indicated below, sufficiently refined data are not available to test it.

ease.[10] "They [the state and local issuers] try to delay financing when conditions appear unfavorable but then hurry to the market when conditions improve."[11]

Frank Morris also finds evidence that a significant volume of municipal-bond sales was shifted from the final stages of the boom when interest rates were relatively high to the recession and recovery period

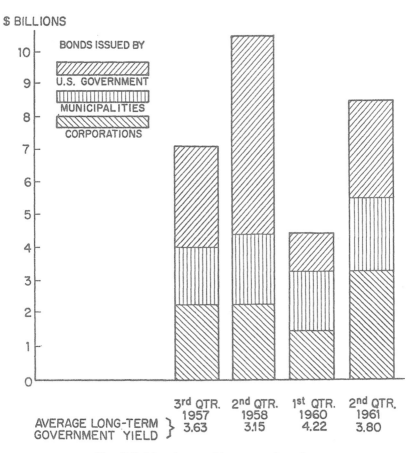

FIG. 6-8. New issues of long-term bonds.

when rates were relatively low.[12] Table 6-2 presents his results in terms of percentage deviations from the 1952–1958 trend line. A

[10] Roland I. Robinson, *Postwar Market for State and Local Government Securities* (Princeton: National Bureau of Economic Research, Princeton University Press, 1960).

[11] *Ibid.,* p. 56.

[12] Frank E. Morris, "The Impact of Monetary Policy on State and Local Government: An Empirical Study," *Journal of Finance* 15 (May 1960), pp. 232–249.

pronounced countercyclical response of bond issuers is clearly evident. Especially interesting is Morris' finding that bond sales vary more than "contracts awarded" and "construction put in place." Morris explains that when bond sales are postponed the construction is financed by utilizing current revenues, *drawing down short-term asset holdings,* and by *borrowing at short term* with the hope of funding the debt at lower interest rates at some future time. Other studies have marshalled evidence of postponement of bond sales during periods when interest rates have risen sharply by comparing planned bond sales as inferred from reports in the financial press with the subsequent actual new issues.[13] We conclude that, even if the long-run

TABLE 6-2

PERCENTAGE DEVIATIONS OF STATE AND LOCAL GOVERNMENT BOND SALES, CONSTRUCTION CONTRACT AWARDS, AND CONSTRUCTION PUT IN PLACE, FROM 1952–58 REGRESSION LINES[a]

	12 Months ending with July 1953, peak	12 Months centered around August 1954, trough	12 Months ending with July 1957, peak	12 Months centered around April 1958, trough
Bond sales	−10.7	+26.6	−13.5	+11.4
Contract awards	− 4.8	+ 2.1	− 3.5	+ 3.4
Construction put in place	− 5.3	+ 3.6	− 1.1	− 1.6

[a] Source: Frank E. Morris, "The Impact of Monetary Policy on State and Local Governments: An Empirical Study," *Journal of Finance* 15 (May 1960), p. 240.

maturity composition of outstanding debt is determined by institutional considerations, the data on municipal-bond issues are not inconsistent with the hypothesis that expectations play an important role in determining the timing of borrowings of the various maturities.

[13] See Richard C. Pickering, "Effects of Credit and Monetary Policy Since Mid-1952 on State and Local Government Financing and Construction Activity," unpublished manuscript which reflects the personal views of the author and not necessarily those of the Board of Governors of the Federal Reserve System, with which he was then associated, April 1955; Frank E. Morris, "A Study of Municipal Bond Sales Postponed During the Past Nine Months," *IBA Statistical Bulletin,* No. 3 (April 1957); and John A. Cochran, "Postponement of Corporate and Municipal Bond Issues, 1955–1957," unpublished manuscript which reflects the personal views of the author and not necessarily those of the Federal Reserve Bank of New York, with which he was then associated, August 1957.

These studies have been summarized in Charlotte Demonte Phelps, "The Impact of Monetary Policy on State and Local Government Expenditures in the United States," in *Impacts of Monetary Policy,* a series of Research Studies prepared for the Commission on Money and Credit (Englewood Cliffs: Prentice-Hall, 1963), pp. 621–647.

6.3   *Some Microeconomic Evidence*

Suggestive as these results may be, there are serious drawbacks to such an aggregative approach. Looking at the data on the demand side, we find several difficulties. In the first place, the changing composition of reporting institutions and the lack of detailed institutional breakdowns in the early periods mar the usefulness of the Survey for long-run comparisons. Moreover, since the Survey covers only government securities and since comprehensive data on changes in the composition of liabilities of the reporting institutions are not available, any inferences from such data must be treated with considerable caution. For example, a commercial bank might increase the maturity of its government holdings solely because it had fewer long-term loans in its portfolio. We would be misled into the conclusion that the bank had lengthened the maturity of its investments, whereas the average maturity of the total portfolio of loans and investments might well have remained constant. Similarly, a bank might lengthen its portfolio in response to an influx of savings deposits (that is, a lengthening of the maturity of its liabilities). These shifts in the maturity composition of the bank's government portfolio would be quite consistent with an extreme institutional view. Finally, we should note that only *movement* among maturities can be measured by our statistics, whereas *mobility* is all that is required by the expectations theory. While mobility can always be inferred from movement, absence of movement does not imply a lack of mobility. Even with perfect mobility, there will be no actual movement if the rate structure already reflects investors' evaluation of the appropriate yield relationships.

Analogous objections can be leveled against our inferences from the supply data. All we have really suggested is that the demand for long-term funds may be responsive to long-term interest rates. Even ignoring the identification problem involved, except in the case of municipal issues, our data do not justify fully the inference that there was a spillover of (some of) this demand to the short-term market during periods of credit restraint, a condition necessary for the supply side of the market to behave in conformity with the expectations analysis. Our findings are therefore consistent with other hypotheses as well. In addition, the data presented are extremely crude. For example, municipal issues are all classified as long-term if the maturity is longer than one year, hardly a satisfactory dividing line for analytic purposes. Insofar as corporations are concerned, we have no adequate data on the maturity composition of bank borrowings. The available data include only public offerings and private placements. Thus it would appear that the evidence so far assembled is insufficient to support any definitive conclusions concerning the relevance of the competing hypotheses. For these reasons it was necessary to investigate the portfolio behavior of financial institutions and the financial policies of bond issuers on the microeconomic level.

For the demand side of the market, interviews were conducted with officers of several money-market banks, with portfolio managers of a sample of other financial institutions who are important participants in the debt markets, and with a number of government-bond dealers and investment advisors. Each institution's portfolio behavior during the past decade was reviewed with reference to the composition of its assets and liabilities and its responses to changes in expectations. The bond dealers were particularly helpful not only in explaining their own operations but also in providing concrete evidence regarding the portfolio behavior of their customers. A similar microeconomic investigation was made of individual institutions on the supply side of the market. The results of these investigations do not lend themselves easily to quantification or statistical testing, and thus they may fail to engender much confidence. In many cases, the reader will be forced to rely on the objectivity of the investigator. I would emphasize, however, the care that was exerted to render a conscientious and unbiased account. "Soft" as these data may be, they do add significantly to our store of knowledge concerning portfolio behavior patterns and, at the very least, suggest improvements in the formulation of the over-all theory of the determination of the rate structure.

6.3.a AN ANALYSIS OF THE PORTFOLIO BEHAVIOR OF COMMERCIAL BANKS

In the following section we report on a series of interviews conducted during 1963 and 1964 with the portfolio managers of ten commercial banks. Included in the sample were seven large New York City commercial banks with deposits of over $1 billion, one large city bank outside New York with deposits of approximately $500 million, and two country banks with deposits of between $100 and $200 million. Each interview consisted of a number of broad questions concerning the general *modus operandi* of the portfolio manager and then a detailed analysis of portfolio transactions during the past ten years. As a result of these interviews, the banks were categorized into three groups depending upon the extent to which expectational considerations influenced the management of the banks' portfolios.

The criteria used to distinguish between expectations-induced and hedging portfolio behavior were based on the motives behind the individual transactions. Portfolio behavior was classified as hedging if the motives for the transaction conformed to assumptions of the institutional school, as described in Section 6.1 above. Thus, responses such as "We always place new investable funds in the long market," "We lengthened our government portfolio because we had fewer opportunities to invest in term loans," or "We invested in longs that year because we had a large inflow of savings deposits" were all taken to indicate hedging portfolio behavior. Portfolio behavior was classified as expectations-induced if the motive for the transaction was primarily that of trying to anticipate future interest-rate (price) movements. Responses such as "The '4¼'s' looked very attractive for capital appreciation," "We placed all new funds in the bill market to await better buying opportunities in long-term bonds," or "The 'Magic Fives' looked out of line with prevailing yields" were taken to indicate expectational motives. While information on specific portfolio transactions cannot be revealed, quotations from those interviewed were included wherever possible.

GROUP 1: Portfolio activities not influenced significantly by expectational considerations

Bank Number 1

"The maturity of our government-bond portfolio responds passively to loan demand. During periods of easy money when it is hard to find good loans we expand the maturity of our portfolio of governments and move more aggressively into municipal bonds. During periods of tight money we sell intermediate-term bonds and thus allow our portfolio to shorten in maturity."

A review of portfolio activity over the past decade revealed that an insignificant number of transactions were influenced by expectations.

Bank Number 2

"The maximum maturity of any bond in our government portfolio is five years.[14] Our portfolio of government securities is heavily concentrated in securities maturing within one year. Thus, we are always able to liquidate securities for loan expansion without significant capital losses. Only when short-term holdings have been reduced below a specified minimum level would we ever liquidate intermediate-term holdings.

---

[14] Savings deposits represented an insignificant percentage of total deposits for this bank.

When credit conditions then shift from tightness to ease, short-term holdings are restored to previous levels before we buy any securities with longer maturities."

A review of portfolio activity over the past decade indicated that expectational considerations were insignificant in influencing changes in the maturity composition of the portfolio.

Bank Number 3

"We try to keep an evenly spaced maturity distribution of securities up to 8–10 years in our portfolio, with a somewhat greater concentration of short-term issues. Additions to the portfolio are usually spread throughout the maturities we hold, except that we often buy substantial blocks of long-term issues to compensate for the passage of time shortening existing holdings."

The maturity distribution of the bank's portfolio changed during the past decade for two primary reasons. (1) When loan demand was particularly heavy, the bank allowed its short-term portfolio to become depleted. (2) After January 1962, when the interest-rate ceiling was raised on savings and time deposits, the bank experienced a substantial inflow of saving deposits. In response, the maturity of the portfolio of marketable securities was increased. While the bank moved heavily into "Magic Fives" during late 1959, because they "looked attractive for capital gains," expectations-induced changes in the maturity of the portfolio were not significant throughout most of the period.

GROUP 2: Portfolio activities influenced significantly by expectational considerations

Bank Number 4

During the first five of the ten years under review, investment policy was subordinated to loan policy. When loans increased, the amount of risk that the bank managers wished to take in the investment portfolio decreased. In consequence, there was a conscious attempt to shorten the maturity of the portfolio of marketable securities. On the other hand, when loans decreased the managers felt it was possible to take on more risk in the investment portfolio, and the average maturity of the portfolio lengthened.

"We feel that this was a period of quite unsuccessful management of our government portfolio. We shortened our portfolio just before substantial rallies in the bond market and therefore lost opportunities for significant capital appreciation. Alternatively, when loan demand was off and we bought long-term securities, we suffered severe capital losses during the ensuing market decline. As the business recovery got up steam, interest rates rose, and we had to sell our long- and intermediate-term securities at a discount in order to meet rising loan demand. We have finally learned that reaching out for longs during a period of slack loan demand can turn out to be a very foolish investment policy.

"Now we have completely changed course. We have moved away from the idea of just buying bonds and holding them to maturity. We now realize that we can make sizable portfolio profits by re-shuffling the maturity composition of our marketable securities. Our portfolio moves during the past five years have been dictated by expected loan demand in future periods and by expected movements in market interest rates. In this connection, we have also increased the maximum maturity that we now buy for our portfolio from ten to twenty years."

Examination of specific portfolio transactions revealed that changes in the maturity composition of the portfolio were mainly expectations-induced during the second five-year period.

Bank Number 5

"Our primary aim is to make loans. We try to keep the average maturity of the government-bond portfolio fairly short so that we can easily accommodate increased loan demand without taking capital losses. Our directors view capital losses as a sign of bad portfolio management. This has tended to limit my freedom in shifting among maturities.

"At times, however, when I felt that extraordinarily good opportunities for capital gains existed, I did take the risk of buying some blocks of longer maturities. In late 1959, for example, rates were at their highest levels in 40 years. I didn't see much danger of capital loss by extending the maturity of the portfolio, and intermediate-term issues were yielding more than short-term securities. The opportunity to buy intermediates on a 5 per cent (yield) basis was well worth the slight risk."

Bank Number 6

Examination of portfolio activity over the past decade indicated that changes in the composition of the bank's assets and liabilities played an important role in explaining changes in the maturity composition of the portfolio. Many changes in the maturity composition of the portfolio, however, were induced by expectations of changes in interest rates. There were several examples of sizable positions taken in long-term issues (over ten years) with the expectation of holding these issues for a period of only one year and reselling them for expected capital gains. There was also evidence of expectations-induced shifts between governments and municipals. This bank limited the maturity of bonds purchased to 15 years.

161

Bank Number 7

The directors of this bank felt that a policy of prudence required that the *average* maturity of their government portfolio be kept under five years. Nevertheless, when there were "good prospects for capital appreciation," the bank at times committed more than one third of its portfolio to securities maturing in five years or more. While some portfolio changes were to be explained by nonexpectational factors such as changes in the loan-deposit ratio, there was every evidence that expectations played a major role in determining changes in the average maturity of the bank's portfolio.

Bank Number 8

"Our investment committee limits me [the portfolio manager] to a maximum maturity of seven years. They intend this restraint to be flexibly applied, however. More than once I have been able to convince them that longer-term securities were sufficiently attractive, in terms of capital appreciation expected over the next year, to justify a large commitment of funds in securities maturing in from ten to twenty years. We have been very fortunate in correctly forecasting which way the market would go. These portfolio switches have proved an excellent device to boost our investment earnings."

GROUP 3: Portfolio activities influenced primarily by expectational considerations

Bank Number 9

"We follow a conscious program of trying to 'arbitrage the interest-rate cycle.' In practice this comes down to trying to guess what is going to happen to the economy and to the bond market. Based on these predictions, we try to judge the comparative opportunity and comparative risk associated with various government securities.[15] We then select

---

[15] Calculations of comparative price opportunities and price risks for various Treasury securities have been used by Sidney Homer, of the government-security firm, Salomon Brothers and Hutzler, in his advice to portfolio managers. Homer proceeds by arbitrarily assuming a certain high level and a certain low level of market interest rates one year hence. He then calculates the probable price performance of each individual issue if interest rates move to those levels. This gives the investor some indication of the relative opportunity for capital gain and risk of capital loss for each Treasury issue. The reader will note how similar this type of calculation used by market practitioners is to the formal model that we presented in Chapter 3. See Sidney Homer, "Comparative Price Opportunity and Price Risk from Various Issues of Long-Term United States Government Bonds," Memorandum to Portfolio Managers from Salomon Brothers and Hutzler, June 2, 1965.

those issues for large commitments which we believe will enjoy the best price performance in the year ahead. We limit our commitments in these issues or maturity sectors only insofar as we are concerned with limiting our risk exposure. If the opportunities are sufficiently attractive, however, we will go way out on a limb in taking on risk."

Examination of portfolio activity over the past decade revealed that expectations-induced purchases and sales were the dominant influence in determining changes in the maturity composition of the portfolio.

Bank Number 10

A review of portfolio activity for this bank revealed substantial portfolio shifts induced by expectations. For example, during one period over two-thirds of the securities in the bank's portfolio were to mature within one year. A year later, the composition of the portfolio had been changed so that almost two-thirds of the securities had maturities longer than one year, with a significant portion of these maturing in from three to five years. The shift was explained entirely by a change in expectations.

This bank has been so successful with its aggressive portfolio policy that during some periods the bank's average rate of return on (default-free) United States government obligations actually *exceeded* its average rate of return on customer loans.

This examination indicated that the conclusions suggested by the aggregate, cross-sectional data do not overstate the degree of flexibility characterizing the practices of commercial-bank portfolio managers. In fact, repeated examples were found of expectations-induced shifts in portfolio composition of a greater magnitude than appeared in the aggregate data. It is also important to note that two of the three banks in the group where expectational considerations were insignificant in influencing portfolio behavior were smaller banks outside of New York City. There was every evidence that expectational elements played a major role in determining changes in the maturity composition of the portfolios of marketable securities for the large New York City banks. Even when risk aversion or other considerations led to the adoption of conventional sanctions prohibiting the purchase of certain maturities, they did not prevent substitution over broad maturity ranges of the yield curve.

We conclude from this investigation that profit-motivated speculative movement between maturities seems to be quite prevalent among commercial-bank portfolio managers. However, the possibility that some institutionalists may have overstated their case should not obscure the important kernel of truth in their position. Portfolio managers for commercial banks do have maturity preferences. This was stressed repeatedly during the interviews. Most commercial bankers did set up a maximum maturity limit for the portfolio. The putatively reasonable limits of prudence varied among particular institutions as well as with the objective opportunities presented by the market. Nevertheless, it was clear from these interviews that hedging objectives also influenced portfolio behavior. Bankers are well aware that they assume increased risk whenever they lengthen the average maturity of their portfolios. In many cases, they admitted freely that such lengthening would be accomplished only if, in their judgment, such lengthening promised extraordinary opportunities for capital gain. In summary, my interviews support the Hicksian liquidity-premium model, which accords well with the risk-averting behavior displayed by these commercial bankers. On the other hand, this evidence suggests that the degree of risk aversion varies considerably from bank to bank.

6.3.b AN ANALYSIS OF THE BEHAVIOR OF LONG-TERM INVESTORS

Interviews were also conducted with the managers of institutions that are normally considered long-term investors. I interviewed the portfolio managers of three life insurance companies and three mutual savings banks and reviewed their portfolio activity for the past decade. In addition, through their account records with government-bond dealers, I studied the activities of several other long-term investors. Through this indirect route, I was able to expand my sample by three mutual savings banks and seven life insurance companies. I was able also to examine the portfolio activity of five pension funds through interviews with a pension-fund investment advisor. Hence, in all, the practices of twenty-one long-term investment institutions came under review. In the case of these long-term investors, rather than reporting the results of the portfolio activity in detail, we limit ourselves to summary findings. These are presented in Table 6-3.[16]

Table 6-3 presents evidence of considerable interchangeability

[16] Our results may be slightly biased and may report somewhat more flexibility among maturities than is actually present. In reviewing the account records of the government-bond dealers, it was very difficult to pick a random sample of companies. Despite my best efforts to ensure a random selection, I suspect that the government-bond dealers in some cases selected those account cards where they were particularly proud of the portfolio performance that had been achieved.

among maturity sectors in the portfolio behavior of financial institutions normally considered to be long-term investors. Many managers of the investment portfolios of insurance companies and pension funds frequently purchased significant quantities of intermediate-term issues when they believed such action was warranted by their expectations. Savings banks and savings and loan institutions have been particularly

TABLE 6-3

PORTFOLIO PRACTICES OF 21 INVESTING INSTITUTIONS
NORMALLY CONSIDERED TO BE LONG-TERM INVESTORS

Number of cases	Description of investment behavior
	GROUP 1: No Evidence of Expectations-Induced Behavior
3	(a) Short- and intermediate-term securities are never bought. All inflows of funds are immediately invested in long-term securities, thereby achieving the benefits of "dollar averaging."
2	(b) All funds are usually invested in long-term securities. Short-term issues are purchased only to meet specific fund requirements. The timing of purchases is not influenced by expectations because of the difficulty of predicting future interest rates.
	GROUP 2: Limited Evidence of Expectations-Induced Behavior
4	(a) Purchases are usually confined to long-term bonds, but substantial quantities of intermediate-term bonds are purchased if sufficiently large yield inducements exist as, for example, during the 1959–1960 period.
7	(b) Purchases are usually confined to long-term bonds, but new funds may be temporarily placed in short- or intermediate-term issues if substantially better buying opportunities for long-term bonds are foreseen within the next year.
	GROUP 3: Extensive Evidence of Expectations-Induced Behavior
3	(a) On the basis of expectations, one-third to one-half of the bond portfolio has at times been shifted into securities maturing in under 5 years.
2	(b) Investment strategy has been dominated by an attempt to tailor the average maturity of the portfolio to "play the cycle of interest rates."
21	

aggressive in adjusting the average maturity of their portfolios in accordance with expectational considerations. While we did find several cases of segmented portfolio behavior (mainly among life insurance companies), expectations-induced shifts in the maturity composition of the portfolios of these institutions was widespread.

An inescapable conclusion from this investigation is that, except in isolated circumstances, it is unreasonable to talk of segmentation in any absolute sense. Nevertheless, all the financial institutions interviewed did exhibit clear maturity *preferences*. Commercial bankers do consider themselves to be primarily short-term investors: they will extend the maturities of their holdings only when sufficient yield inducements exist. Similarly, but at the other end of the spectrum, pension funds and life insurance companies view themselves as "ordinarily long-term investors" who should stray from their usual maturities only "under special circumstances."

In light of this evidence, we must reinterpret segmentation to mean simply that many buyers and sellers have habitual maturity preferences and require differential premiums to induce them to move from their preferred maturities. The return differentials necessary to induce investors who prefer short maturities to move to the longest maturity area may indeed be larger than the constellation of interest-rate spreads encountered in practice. Consequently, some members of these classes of financial institution may never have been induced to buy significant quantities of long-term bonds. But we must reject the idea that no differential, however large, can induce any movement. Our evidence suggests that differentials sufficient to induce most investment managers to shift the composition of their portfolios over broad ranges of maturities have frequently occurred. Even if no single institution operates in all maturities, as long as there is sufficient overlapping in the range of maturities that different investors' holdings do span, they can provide the links in a continuous chain tying together the various maturity sectors of the bond market.

6.3.c THE INFLUENCE OF EXPECTATIONS ON BOND SUPPLIERS

I conducted a parallel investigation for the supply side of the market. To study the practices and motives of bond issuers, I interviewed the financial officers of 3 sales-finance companies and examined the case histories of 11 large corporate-bond financings and 8 municipal-bond flotations. The weight of this evidence suggests that the institutionalists are correct in asserting that, within the observed range of rate differentials, private- and municipal-bond issuers have not been induced to make long-run changes in the maturity composition of their debt. Nevertheless, considerable evidence on the microeconomic level suggests that the *timing* of many long-term bond issues is strongly influenced by expectations.

Figure 6-9 presents semi-annual data on the maturity distribution of the outstanding debt of one of the largest corporate bond issuers, General Motors Acceptance Corporation (GMAC). Debt under one year includes bank loans, outstanding commercial paper and marketable bonds. Note that, while a target ratio of 40 per cent short-term, 60 per cent long-term debt appears to have been the aim of GMAC, substantial temporary shifts have been made in the maturity composition of total borrowings. Note especially how, during the easy-money period of 1958, the maturity of GMAC's debt was lengthened. During early 1960 and late 1957 (periods of peak interest rates), GMAC allowed its debt to shorten appreciably. An attempt has consistently been made to adjust the timing of long-term borrowings. With the characteristic financial acumen of its parent, GMAC has generally been quite successful in these attempts.

PER CENT

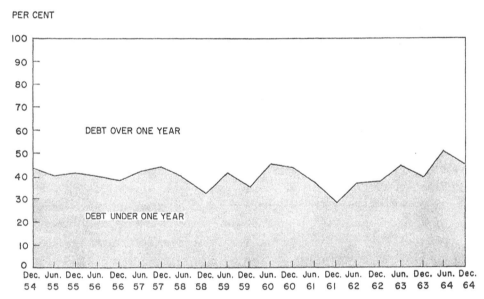

FIG. 6-9. Maturity distribution of outstanding debt of General Motors Acceptance Corporation.

Nor does this performance seem atypical. Numerous other examples can be adduced to buttress our conclusion. All the sales-finance companies interviewed provided excellent examples of expectations-induced behavior. They are continuously borrowing in all sectors of the market. At any time, they freely shift large amounts of their borrowing to maturity sectors that, on the basis of the yield curve, seem most attractive from their viewpoint. Moreover, the case studies of corporate and municipal bond financings revealed that expectations play an important role in adjusting the timing of these bond offerings. In over three-quarters of the cases studied, expectational considerations altered either the timing or the size of the bond offering. During 1958, because they felt that long-term borrowing costs were unusually low, many issuers floated particularly large offerings anticipating future fund needs and liquidating short-term indebtedness incurred when previous bond offerings were delayed. The proceeds from anticipatory bond sales were typically invested in Treasury bills. On the other hand, during late 1959 and early 1960, several prospective issues of long-term debt were cancelled, and fund requirements were temporarily met by short-term credit.

An interview study, by Pickering, of all state and local finance officers who issued municipal bonds during the first half of 1958 (a period of peak bond prices) provides additional evidence.[17] Pickering asked the finance officers when they had originally planned to sell the bond which put them in the sample. If they sold the bond later (earlier) than they had originally planned, a bond-sale postponement (acceleration) was noted. Additional questions were then asked to determine why the postponement or acceleration had been made and how the municipality had adapted to the change in plans. Pickering found that 11 per cent of all municipal-bond sales during the first half of 1958 had either been postponed during the preceding tight-money period or had been floated in anticipation of future construction programs because "interest rates were so low." In 40 per cent of the cases where postponements had occurred, the municipalities utilized short-term, temporary bank loans to prevent construction delays. Proceeds from all bond sales that were accelerated because of favorable marketing conditions were invested either in short-term Treasury bills or in time deposits.

In sum, on the microeconomic level there appears to be considerable evidence that expectations influence the maturity of bond offerings in the short run and, through this, the rate structure. When rates are expected to rise, issuers tend to increase the supply of long-term bonds and to invest in short-term securities the proceeds not immediately needed. When rates are expected to fall, issuers reduce the supply of long-term bonds but increase the supply of short-term debt by new borrowings and by portfolio sales. As we suggested in Chapter 3, this is precisely the mechanism by which the expectations of suppliers help to account for the characteristic slopes of the yield curve.

---

[17] Richard C. Pickering, "State and Local Government Bond Financing During the First Half of 1958," unpublished manuscript which reflects the views of the author and not necessarily those of the Board of Governors of the Federal Reserve System, May 1959, as reported in Phelps, *op. cit.,* pp. 634–635.

6.4 *Modifications for Diverse Expectations and the Role of the Professional Speculator*

While the results of our empirical investigation conflict with an unqualified version of the institutional theory of the rate structure, they suggest that the pure expectations model is equally unrealistic. In particular, Meiselman's reconciliation, described in Section 6.1, was found to be inapplicable in two respects. For relevance, it must rely either on (a) uniformity of expectations and absence of risk aversion among market participants on either the demand or supply side of the market, or on (b) the existence of a group of adequately financed speculators who render the excess-demand schedules for securities of different maturities infinitely elastic at rates consistent with their (uniform) expectations.[18] Empirical investigation into the actual workings of the market suggest that neither of these assumptions holds.

6.4.a TESTS FOR DIVERSITY OF EXPECTATIONS

In the first place, we have already noted that maturity preferences do affect the behavior of participants on both sides of the market. Moreover, an attempt at direct examination of expectations suggests a more Keynesian view concerning the distribution of expectations among investors. Keynes, in the *Treatise,* characterized uncertainty as the existence of a dispersion of opinions constituting the full range of "bull-bear" positions.[19] The variety of opinions can, as a matter of fact, serve as a measure of the degree of uncertainty in the market as a whole. In any situation in which there is imperfect knowledge of the future, a dispersion of expectations would seem to be a natural state of affairs.

Our first test for uniformity of the range of opinions consisted of an examination of the advisory letters of four leading bond-investment advisors over the period 1958–1965.[20] I assumed that these widely read letters, whether they simply reflect or actually form existing expectations, can serve as a surrogate for the questioning of market participants themselves.

There are, of course, enormous difficulties in interpreting information of this kind. Advisory-letter writers are unfortunately prone to

---

[18] In Chapter 7 we shall demonstrate the necessity of these conditions.

[19] J. M. Keynes, *A Treatise on Money* (London: Macmillan, 1930, and New York: Harcourt, Brace, 1930), I, Chapter 15.

[20] *Moody's Bond Survey;* Sylvia Porter, *Reporting on Governments;* T. Goldsmith, *Goldsmith's Washington Service;* and Murray Olyphant, "Government Bonds," *Banking,* Journal of the American Bankers Association.

excessive amounts of jargon and gobbledygook. Moreover, consistency of analysis and opinion is not their forte; they will sometimes take a variety of divergent views within the same letter. Consequently, the survey of these letters was necessarily impressionistic rather than rigorous. One could form judgments of the letter writers' opinions only against a background of their own previous writings and their characteristic mode of presentation. Some effort was made to reduce the scope for arbitrary judgment in the analysis. Where possible, our analysis focused on the summary paragraph of the letter, from which it was usually easy to crystallize a specific opinion. Moreover, no market letters of government-bond dealers were used in the analysis. The opinions in these letters usually reflect only the trading position of the particular dealer. We are consequently often treated to the spectacle of a firm oscillating between bullish and bearish views as the accident of their trading position dictates.

TABLE 6-4

OPINIONS OF FOUR BOND-MARKET ADVISORS DURING SELECTED PERIODS

	PORTER	GOLDSMITH	MOODY'S	OLYPHANT
June–July 1958	Bearish	Neutral turning to bearish	Bullish	Bullish
Jan.–Feb. 1960	Bearish turning to neutral	Neutral turning to bullish	Bullish	Neutral turning to bearish
May–June 1961	Bearish	Bearish	Bearish	Bearish
Jan.–Feb. 1965	Bullish	Neutral	Bearish	Neutral

Table 6-4 presents a summary of the opinions of the four experts during four two-month periods from 1958 through 1965. The first three periods represent times of interest-rate turning points. Only three classifications are used to describe each opinion. "Bullish" opinion represents a belief that bond prices would rise (that is, interest rates would fall). "Bearish" views are those anticipating lower bond prices and higher interest rates. "Neutral" advice represents a feeling that interest rates would remain essentially unchanged from present levels.

We note from Table 6-4 that during three of the four periods studied the complete range of views from bull to bear was held concurrently by these investment advisors. In mid-1961 it would appear from our admittedly oversimplified characterization of their opinions that their views were uniformly bearish. But even in this period when the letter writers concurred on the direction of rate changes, there was still wide disagreement on the likely magnitude of rate movements. Table 6-5 presents a detailed account of their opinions during this period. These statements are paraphrased from the summary sections of the letters and represent a composite opinion during the period indicated. We find that Porter was almost neutral in her views. She was classified as bearish because of the general tenor of her letters during the period, but she could just as well have been labelled "neutral." Goldsmith's statement was strongly bearish. It must be considered particularly strong since he is not usually given to hyperbole. Incidentally, note how his advice mentions explicitly the avenues through which we suggested earlier that the expectations theory would

TABLE 6-5

OPINIONS OF BOND-MARKET ADVISORS DURING
MAY AND JUNE OF 1961

PORTER: I expect easy money to continue but with a levelling out of rates. The near-term outlook for prices remains favorable, but the probability of lower rather than higher prices also remains.

GOLDSMITH: The balance-of-payments problems will be the controlling factor. I advise bond offerers to speed up their offering dates and banks to shorter the maturity of their portfolios.

MOODY'S: We expect an uptrend of interest rates to start unfolding soon, but the rise in yields should be moderate.

OLYPHANT: Under the circumstances perhaps bond prices will show little change for a while, although slight declines in the prices of longer-term obligations seem more likely than the reverse.

be affected. Bond issuers are told to "speed up" their offering plans to take advantage of transitory low rates, and bankers are exhorted to "shorten" their portfolios to protect themselves against the expected price drop. Moody's is also clearly bearish, though more moderately so than Goldsmith. Olyphant is nearer to Miss Porter, though explicitly bearish to a very mild degree. Note the similarity of the probabilistic form of his advice to the price-expectations models we presented in Chapter 3. This evidence suggests that, even during periods when general opinion is most nearly similar, the bond market is typically characterized by a considerable dispersion of opinion.

A more satisfactory test of uniformity of expectations was provided by a direct survey of the opinions of a sample of portfolio managers. On April 1, 1965, a questionnaire surveying interest-rate expectations was sent to a sample of 200 investing institutions which are important participants in the government-securities market.[21] The following two questions were included in the questionnaire:

(1) For each of the following future dates, what are your best estimates of (a) the range between which yields on 90-day Treasury bills will lie and (b) the single most likely value for the yield which will prevail?

	Range	*Most Likely Value*
July 1, 1965: Between_____% and_____%		_____%
Oct. 1, 1965: Between_____% and_____%		_____%
Jan. 1, 1966: Between_____% and_____%		_____%
Apr. 1, 1966: Between_____% and_____%		_____%
Apr. 1, 1967: Between_____% and_____%		_____%

(2) For each of the following dates, please provide the same information for 10-year government bonds.

	Range	*Most Likely Value*
April 1966: Between_____% and_____%		_____%
April 1967: Between_____% and_____%		_____%

Summary statistics calculated from the responses are presented in Table 6-6. Figures 6-10 and 6-11 depict the actual distribution of responses for the range between which the forward yields were expected to lie.[22]

These results indicate that the expectations of the major participants in the bond market are not uniform. Even when predictions of Treasury-bill rates are made only three months in advance, a wide

[21] The sample consisted of 119 banks, 16 life insurance companies (LICO's), and 65 nonfinancial corporations (NFC's). The bank sub-sample was drawn from a larger sample of 500 banks, constructed by Baxter and Shapiro. See Nevins D. Baxter and Harold T. Shapiro, "Compensating-Balance Requirements: The Results of a Survey," *Journal of Finance* 19 (September 1964), pp. 483–496, for a description of the design of the larger sample. All banks in the Baxter-Shapiro sample with 1962 deposits of over $200 million were included. This ensured that almost all of the nation's 50 largest banks were represented. Similarly, the 65 NFC's surveyed were the largest in a Baxter-Shipiro sample drawn from the "Fortune 500" and "50 Biggest" lists. Finally, the LICO's surveyed were 16 of the 40 largest in the industry. Larger institutions were deliberately overrepresented in the sample to ensure the inclusion of the most important participants in the government-securities market. A fuller description of the design of the survey and a complete report of the results may be found in Edward J. Kane and Burton G. Malkiel, "The Term Structure of Interest Rates: An Analysis of a Survey of Interest-Rate Expectations" (Princeton: February 1966), mimeographed.

[22] For purposes of display, the distributions actually plotted represent a tabulation of observations consisting of each five-basis-point interval spanned by each respondent's high and low estimates.

dispersion of opinion is evident. As the length of time to the date for which the prediction is made increases, there is also an increase in the diversity of expectations, as indicated by the standard deviations and ranges of the distributions.[23] Moreover, the number of respondents willing to make a quantitative prediction decreased as the remoteness of the prediction increased. Of the 113 respondents to the questionnaire, 89 were willing to make quantitative predictions for bill rates

TABLE 6-6

MOMENTS OF THE DISTRIBUTION OF EXPECTED INTEREST RATES

	Expected range			Most likely value			Number of respondents
	Mean	Standard deviation	Skewness	Mean	Standard deviation	Skewness	
Bill rates							
July 1, 1965	4.01	0.13	1.40	3.99	0.07	1.28	89
Oct. 1, 1965	4.05	0.18	1.54	4.01	0.11	1.77	88
Jan. 1, 1966	3.96	0.20	0.47	3.96	0.14	0.00	83
Apr. 1, 1966	3.80	0.26	−0.49	3.86	0.20	−0.79	79
Apr. 1, 1967	3.65	0.42	−0.22	3.66	0.37	−0.61	77
Bond rates							
Apr. 1, 1966	4.12	0.20	0.03	4.12	0.15	−0.55	86
Apr. 1, 1967	4.00	0.29	−1.57	3.98	0.26	−3.45	81

three months in advance, while only 77 were willing to predict rates two years in advance.[24]

[23] Since Figures 6-10 and 6-11 plot the range estimates, it is true that our figures will tend to show more variability than would similar figures constructed with point estimates. Nevertheless, a comparison of the first three moments of the range and most-likely-value predictions indicates that there is very little difference between the two distributions.

A striking lack of uniformity in past projections was also revealed. Less than 15 per cent of the respondents found both April 1965 bill rates and bond rates to be in accordance with their year-ago projections of these rates. The point is not that expectations proved incorrect, but rather that a considerable diversity in the sign of the errors was revealed. Supporting data are reported in Kane and Malkiel, *op. cit.*

[24] Some respondents who refused to make quantitative estimates of forward rates did indicate in accompanying letters that they had conscious qualitative expectations about future rate movements. These expectations were likely to be expressed as vague feelings about the market such as "Rates might fall significantly within the next 12 months," or "I expect little change in rates for the remainder of the year." It is interesting to note that more respondents were willing to predict forward bond yields than forward bill rates.

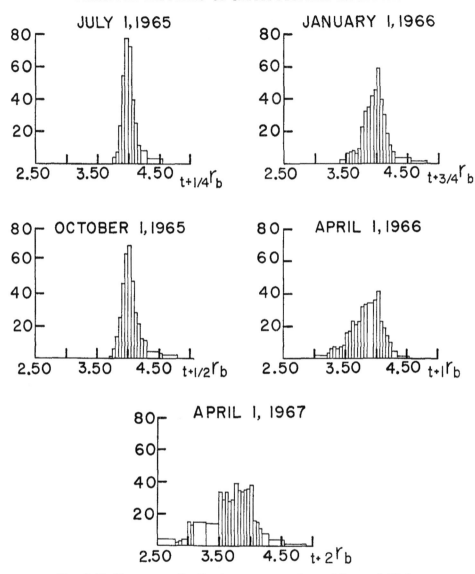

FIG. 6-10. Frequency distributions: expectations of forward 90-day
bill yields.

Thus, the weight of the evidence supports the Keynesian picture
of diverse expectations. The variety of views and the range of the
differences in quantitative estimates were surprisingly wide. One re-
calls Terence's apt comment, "Quot homines, tot sententiae." There
exist in the bond market as many opinions as there are participants
in the market.

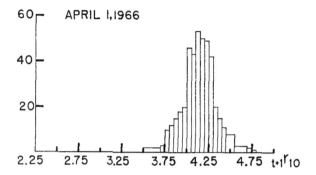

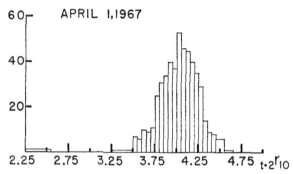

FIG. 6-11. Frequency distributions: expectations of forward 10-year bond rates.

6.4.b CONSTRAINTS ON THE ACTIVITY OF PROFESSIONAL SPECULATORS

We turn now to the role of professional speculators in the market. It will be recalled that their activity played a crucial role in Meiselman's reconciliation of hedging portfolio behavior with the pure expectations theory. We shall first distinguish between two types of speculation. If a corporation-portfolio manager, with funds to invest for six months, buys a five-year bond in anticipation of a larger holding-period yield, he is engaging in a speculative transaction. He is trading a certain six-month return for an uncertain one. This type of speculative activity is crucial for the validity of the expectations theory of the term structure. We have suggested, on the basis of our empirical evidence, that these speculative transactions are very common and are carried out by all major classes of investors. We have argued, however, that such speculation reflects both the diverse expectations of market participants and the different types and degrees of maturity preferences characterizing the market. In this section we turn to a second class of speculative activity which we shall call "professional speculation." In essence, such a transaction involves borrowing in one market (maturity range) and lending in another. Meiselman describes such activity as follows: "For example, the professional speculator may buy bonds on margin, borrowing in the call money market to finance his acquisitions. Or, he may sell bonds short and use the proceeds of the sale to make very short-term loans."[25] Thus, professional speculation can be described as the simultaneous maintenance of a long and short position in different maturities. When a government-bond dealer sells short a six-month certificate and simultaneously buys a five-year bond, this can be considered the typical professional speculative transaction.

In order to evaluate the prevalence of such behavior, this section focuses on the institutional imperfections which circumscribe the volume of this type of speculative transaction. The impediments described below have all been encountered during our investigation of the actual workings of the market. The most important of them are applicable to the operations of any potential professional speculator. We have also encountered some considerations applicable only to government-bond-dealer firms or -dealer banks. Since they are the most skilled and knowledgeable participants in the market, these institutions are the prime candidates for the role of professional speculator.

Perhaps the most important constraint limiting the volume of professional speculative transactions is the fact that it is enormously difficult to sell short significant quantities of government securities because of the complexities (and, in many cases, the impossibility) of borrowing the securities that must be delivered to fulfill the sales contract. During interviews with government-bond dealers, the most recurrent theme was the scarcity of securities available for borrowing. Many times opportunities for profitable speculation were recognized by the dealers, but they were unable to take advantage of the opportunities because they were unable to borrow the securities in question in a "block" (that is, in sufficient quantities to make the transactions worthwhile). This finding has also been stressed by two studies of the government-securities market.[26] As the Treasury-Federal Reserve

---

[25] Meiselman, *The Term Structure of Interest Rates*, pp. 7–8.

[26] *Treasury-Federal Reserve Study of the Government Securities Market* (Washington: U.S. Government Printing Office, 1959), Part I, pp. 23–24. The study reports (p. 24), "considerable comment was made to the effect that short selling

Study commented, ". . . in the absence of short selling, arbitrage of opportunities arising from yield spreads . . . becomes difficult."[27]

Even if securities are available for borrowing, there are additional obstacles limiting the volume of short selling. One important consideration is the uncertainty attached to the borrowing commitment. The lender of securities may call his loan at any time and force the dealer to cover his short position at an inopportune time.[28] In addition, there is a borrowing cost of $\frac{1}{2}$ of 1 per cent which must be paid on securities sold short. Thus, in order to maintain a short position, the speculator must not only pay out the interest during the period (that is, the coupon on the bond sold short) but also the (per annum) borrowing charge. There are also institutional and legal restraints limiting the maturity of the issues which government-bond dealers and other speculators may use to borrow short-term funds on repurchase agreements.[29] Conventional, but rigidly enforced, constraints limit the maturity of issues used to secure repurchase agreements to a maximum of two years. On its part, the Federal Reserve will undertake repurchase agreements only for government securities with a maturity under 18 months.

In addition, in the case of dealer banks, complications arise from the U.S. tax law, which encourages commercial banks to make each

---

in the present market is seriously hampered by the relatively limited facilities to borrow securities." See also A. H. Meltzer and G. von der Linde, *A Study of the Dealer Market for Federal Government Securities* (Washington: U.S. Government Printing Office, 1960), pp. 47–48.

[27] *Treasury-Federal Reserve Study of the Government Securities Market*, p. 23. In this connection, it might be useful for the Treasury to make securities from the Trust Funds available for borrowing. This would vastly improve the functioning of the market by permitting effective professional speculation to take place. It might be held, however, that such a privilege could permit an undesirable volume of destabilizing speculative transactions at certain times. In particular, it might be argued that the possibility of a large volume of short selling might exacerbate market declines and lead to "disorderly" market conditions. If such were the case, the lending activities could simply be curtailed during these periods. By varying the availability of such securities and the terms of borrowing, the administration of the privilege could add a useful countercyclical device to the policymakers' tool kit.

[28] This factor has been stressed by Ira O. Scott, Jr., *Government Securities Market* (New York: McGraw-Hill, 1965), p. 126.

[29] Repurchase agreements (RP's) are short-term arrangements between government-bond dealers and (usually) corporations for the financing of the dealers' inventory. They are often executed by making a specific sale contract covering a part of the dealer's inventory together with an agreement to "buy back" the securities at a specific price at a future date. RP's are also effected with the Federal Reserve Bank (at the initiative of the Reserve Authorities).

year either a "loss" year or a "gain" year.[30] By allowing commercial banks to treat, for tax purposes, Treasury securities other than bills as stock-in-trade when there are losses and (so long as they have been held at least six months) as capital assets when there are gains, U.S. tax law has encouraged banks to concentrate gains in one year and losses in another. This is so because net losses on security sales in any taxable year may be deducted from income in their entirety. Consequently, *realized* losses are, in effect, half made good by the U.S. Treasury. If, on the other hand, net (long-term) gains are realized, these are taxed at preferential capital-gains rates. For most banks the relevant marginal tax-rate differential is 23 per cent, that is, the 48 per cent regular corporate tax rate minus the 25 per cent maximum rate on long-term capital gains. But since only *net* losses or gains in any year receive beneficial tax treatment, it is wasteful of the tax advantage for banks to take significant gains in a loss year or losses in a gain year.

To see how this tax benefit can at times cause a dealer bank to refrain from taking otherwise profitable opportunities for professional speculation, as well as from making profitable portfolio switches, consider the following case. Assume that the dealer bank has already committed itself to making the year in question a gain year. Such decisions are typically made early in the year and, once made, are rarely reversed. Assume further that the opportunity for a profitable speculative transaction arises that would involve selling an intermediate-term issue on which a book capital loss of \$500,000 would have to be realized. This loss must be set against the bank's existing capital gains and would cancel out a potential \$115,000 tax saving: $(0.48 - 0.25) \times \$500,000$. Consequently, this transaction and many otherwise profitable ones may not be undertaken. What it is most important to note in this discussion is that these tax considerations not only militate against the sale of the issue from the portfolio of the bank (which we do not consider to be professional speculation) but also will prevent the bank *qua* dealer from selling the security short in the course of its trading and speculative activities. This is so because the Internal Revenue Service has ruled that securities "short against the box" (that is, sold short while a long position

---

[30] The two following paragraphs are largely taken from Burton G. Malkiel and Edward J. Kane, "U.S. Tax Law and the Locked-In Effect," *National Tax Journal* 16 (December 1963), pp. 389–396. See also Robert H. Parks, "Income and Tax Aspects of Commercial Bank Portfolio Operations in Treasury Securities," *National Tax Journal* 11 (March 1958), pp. 21–34.

is maintained in the bank's investment portfolio) for 30 days or longer will be considered for tax purposes as actual portfolio sales. Consequently, these tax considerations directly affect the dealer bank's trading activities.

A more fundamental reason for the absence of such speculative activity on the part of the dealers is given by Meltzer and von der Linde.[31]

> [It] reflects the dealers' view of their function in the market. Generally, they appear to be much less concerned with correcting or influencing long-term trends in the bond market than with smoothing short-run, day-to-day changes in price. Their principal concern is the servicing of customers or other dealers and the elimination of erratic short-term movements in price . . . most dealers do not take either speculative long or short positions for the purpose of making capital gains.

Interviews with bond dealers confirmed this finding. The most knowledgeable and "professional" participants in the Treasury market felt that, both by training and inclination, and because of their limited capital, they were unfitted to engage in large speculative transactions.

Finally, whatever speculative transactions are undertaken are not free of transactions costs, and, recalling our observations on dealer transactions charges, we must conclude that probably the most important group of professional speculators are known to demand Hicksian liquidity premiums. Since government-bond dealers charge additional fees to take positions in longer-term issues in the course of their regular business, it seems reasonable to expect that they would demand the same sort of risk-premium protection when they assume positions as speculators in governments. Therefore, whatever limited professional speculative activity does occur is not likely to be conducted in terms of expectations alone, and it is not structured to lead to long rates which are any simple geometric average of expected short rates.

6.5 *Recapitulation*

In this chapter we have attempted to establish the following conclusions: The bond market is not segmented in any absolute sense. Utilizing aggregate data and the results of extensive interviews, we found that most bond investors substituted broadly among securities over wide ranges of the yield curve in accordance with their expectations. We also found that the price-expectations model of Chapter 3 seemed

---

[31] Meltzer and von der Linde, *op. cit.*, p. 21.

to conform remarkably well to the behavior reported in the interviews. Moreover, many borrowers were able, at least for a limited time, to adopt a variety of financial plans to meet their financing needs.

We found, nevertheless, that investors and suppliers are not indifferent among different maturities offering the same expected holding-period yield. Strong maturity preferences are present on both sides of the market. A valid version of the segmentation hypothesis, then, asserts simply that many buyers and sellers must be paid differential premiums to induce them to move from their preferred maturities.

We also found that a "pure" expectations theory was equally unrealistic. In the first place, as has just been noted, both maturity preferences and diverse expectations typically characterize the market. After reviewing the advice given by professional market advisors and the results of a questionnaire survey, we were forced to conclude that market opinions have been widely dispersed during recent periods. Finally, we noted that several institutional factors narrowly circumscribed the volume of professional speculative activity in the government-securities market. This last observation suggests that previous attempts to reconcile the expectations and segmentation theories are not really acceptable. It is to the task of providing such a reconciliation that we turn in Chapter 7.

CHAPTER 7

A Synthesis of the Expectations
and Institutional Theories*

WE HAVE SEEN that neither a purely institutional (hedging-pressure) nor an exclusively expectational theory of the rate structure seems consistent with the relevant body of empirical knowledge. Nevertheless, such unicausal theories are aesthetically pleasing, and this may account for their popularity among some modern economists. Above all, such explanations are simple, and, in the case of the perfect-certainty formulation of the traditional expectations approach, the theory is elegant. Previous nontheoretical attempts to combine the various explanations of the interest-rate structure have been essentially impressionistic. It is therefore with considerable trepidation that we attempt to synthesize these two antithetical positions. For, whatever this union may breed, it will not be harmony. Nevertheless, we shall see that, as one frequently says of mismatched couples, "They need one another."

7.1   The Objective and Assumptions of the Analysis

Our objective in this chapter is to build an over-all model of the rate structure which synthesizes elements from opposing theories. We shall first present two polar cases which represent the extreme positions of the expectations and institutional schools. Next, we shall begin to relax the assumptions implied in these polar cases. Finally, utilizing the observations on the actual behavior patterns of the various parties in the market, which were reported in the previous chapter, we shall attempt to synthesize these cases into an over-all theoretical model where the interplay of elements taken from both extreme constructs will determine the term structure.

In the tradition of rate-structure theory, our theoretical approach utilizes the methods of partial equilibrium and comparative statics. We take as data for the model the general level of interest rates,[1]

---

* Large parts of Sections 7.4 through 7.6 of this chapter were taken from my article, "The Term Structure of Interest Rates," *American Economic Review, Papers and Proceedings* 54 (May 1964), pp. 532–543.

[1] The process whereby the level of rates is determined is by no means obvious. Under the pure expectations theory, the short rate is usually taken to represent "*the* interest rate for a given time period that is described by the general theory of interest." See

and the total demand and supply of funds. We assume that these data are all consistent with one another and represent the solution to the general equilibrium system. We can then examine the equilibrium conditions governing one part of the machinery with the aid of the assumption that the requirements of equilibrium in the other parts of the system are simultaneously satisfied. We shall then ask what interest-rate structure is consistent with different maturity distributions of the outstanding debt. In comparing full-stock equilibria, we shall consider different maturity compositions of the total debt, and we will therefore allow the proportion of outstanding debt constituted by short-term securities to vary from zero to 100 per cent of the total. Given an over-all interest-rate level that induces investors to supply precisely the amount of money required to buy all the available debt, we seek to determine the spread between the long and short rates that will make investors willing to hold some given proportion of long and short debt. This experiment is repeated with each different maturity distribution of issued debt, and the equilibria are compared. Throughout this analysis, we always assume that initial bond holdings are zero. Such an assumption allows us to abstract from any wealth effects which might arise.[2]

In order to illustrate each case by means of specific example, the discussion will assume that only two maturities are outstanding and that the shorter issue matures in one year while the maturity date on the long issue is two years hence. Both securities are taken to

---

Joseph W. Conard, *Introduction to the Theory of Interest* (Berkeley: University of California Press, 1959), Part Three, pp. 298–299. In this case, the short-holding-period yield for *all* securities would equal the short rate. Under an assumption that the debt markets are entirely segmented, this equality no longer holds, and some average of interest rates over the different maturities might possibly be taken as an index of the level of rates. But, however we define the level of interest rates, we can provide a rate structure consistent with it. This is so because we will solve for a rate structure only in terms of the spread between long and short rates. Depending upon how the level is actually defined, the absolute interest rates may be determined in terms of the magnitude of the over-all interest-rate level.

[2] When the maturity composition of the outstanding debt changes, interest rates on the different maturities may well be affected, and capital gains or losses will accrue to existing security holders. These effects are rather unpleasant to deal with and will be ignored. This practice of disregarding the influence of initial holdings follows that of Don Patinkin, *Money, Interest and Prices* (Evanston: Row, Peterson, 1956), p. 142 and *passim*. It has been justified (in an economy where only private debt exists) by an assumption of neutral distribution effects; that is, the effect of the gains of bond holders from a fall in interest rates exactly balances the effect of the losses suffered by bond issuers.

carry $3\frac{1}{2}$ per cent coupons. Bond investors are provided with the $20 million desired by security issuers. In the extreme case where expectations alone determine the rate structure, we will assume that the one-year interest rate expected in year two equals $3\frac{1}{2}$ per cent. If the current one-year rate is $3\frac{1}{2}$ per cent, then both bonds sell at par and the yield curve is horizontal. This will always be the frame of reference within which we compare yield curves derived from other assumptions specifying the nature of supply inflexibilities, maturity preferences, and diverse expectations. Again we remind the reader that a flat yield curve is posited under the pure expectations theory only to facilitate comparisons.

7.2 Case 1: Complete Segmentation

We first deal with an extreme version of the segmentation hypothesis.[3] We assume that different investing institutions with differing structures of claims against them are rigidly committed to one market or the other. Life insurance companies, for example, write annuity contracts, which in essence guarantee to the annuitan at specified earning rate over the life of the contract. Therefore, the insurance company may avert risk by investing the proceeds from the sale of such contracts in the long market to ensure them a profit regardless of what happens to interest rates over the life of the contract. Commercial banks, on the other hand, faced with a structure of liabilities where an overwhelming portion are payable upon demand or on short notice, are assumed to prefer very short maturities. In this way commercial banks protect themselves against the risks of realizing capital losses on securities sold to meet deposit drains or loan requests. The extreme hedging-pressure theory assumes that the market is dominated by investors with such absolute risk aversion that they will not shift between maturities regardless of relative interest rates. The yield structure will then be determined by the supply and demand within each segmented market.

We may illustrate this case by using the specific assumptions enumerated above. Of the $20 million provided to investors, we shall assume that $10 million of these funds is in the hands of short (one-year) investors and $10 million is held by long (two-year)

[3] *It should be noted that we do not imply that Professor Culbertson, or any other writers who have emphasized the impediments to mobility which characterize the debt markets, has ever suggested that such a world exists. We use this polar case purely for purposes of exposition.*

investors. In this limiting case of the institutional model, investing institutions simply place the funds at their disposal into one market or the other and realize whatever yield is obtainable at the time the investment is made. According to this view, life insurance companies sell annuity contracts to individuals whose demand for

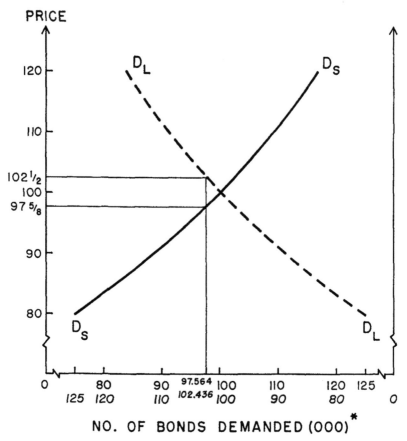

FIG. 7-1. Marshallian illustration of Case 1.

annuities is not responsive to relative interest rates on indirect securities offered by financial intermediaries.[4] The risk-averting insurance companies then place these funds in the long (two-year)

[4] We must assume, of course, that, in response to changes in relative interest rates, individual savers do not shift among financial institutions offering different types of claims. Inflexibility on the part of institutions is not sufficient, by itself, to make the short and long markets independent.

184

market no matter what the interest rate happens to be. Similarly, segmented short-term investors place all the funds at their disposal in the short market. Under these assumptions, we may draw the demand curve for each (D_LD_L, the demand curve for long bonds, and D_SD_S, the demand curve for short issues) maturity as a rectangular hyperbola, showing equal expenditures of funds ($10 million) throughout (see Figure 7-1). If 100,000 ($1000 par value) bonds are supplied in each market, then both short- and long-term bonds will sell at par, and (since both coupons are fixed at $3\frac{1}{2}$ per cent) the yield curve will be horizontal at the $3\frac{1}{2}$ per cent level.

We may now assume instead that 102,436 bonds are supplied in the short market and 97,564 bonds are supplied in the long market. The short price falls to $97\frac{5}{8}$ and the long price rises to $102\frac{1}{2}$. Since the coupons on each bond are fixed, we can then calculate the

TABLE 7-1

YIELD VOLATILITY BASED ON MATURITY OF ISSUE

| | (1) Supply of bonds = 102,436 Price = $97\frac{5}{8}$ | (2) Supply of bonds = 97,564 Price = $102\frac{1}{2}$ | (3) Range of fluctuation, Col. 1 |
Maturity of issue (years)	Yield (per cent)	Yield (per cent)	minus Col. 2, in basis points
1	5.99	0.98	501
2	4.76	2.22	254
20	3.66	3.33	33

yields to maturity in each market by the use of the standard bond-price formula (3-2). Two-year (long) issues yield 2.22 per cent and one-year securities yield 5.99 per cent. Of course, we can repeat the same experiment, this time supplying 102,436 bonds to the long market (so the long price falls to $97\frac{5}{8}$) and 97,564 bonds to the short market (so the short price rises to $102\frac{1}{2}$). In this case, the corresponding yields to maturity are 0.98 per cent for the one-year bonds and 4.76 per cent for the two-year obligations. This leads us immediately to our first result. Even under the extreme assumptions of complete market segmentation analyzed here, the mathematics of bond prices indicates that yields of short-term issues will fluctuate more than yields of long securities in response to the same changes in the supply of bonds. This point is made more dramatically if we let the long issue be a 20-year bond. Table 7-1 indicates the yield volatility of issues of various maturities on the basis of a market experiment of the sort we have just performed. Note that the longer the maturity of the issue, the smaller is the yield fluctuation for a given change in the supply of bonds outstanding.[5] Whether one holds an expectational or an institutional view, we see that the role of bond-price movements must be accorded an important place in any tableau of the determinants of the rate structure.

In order to construct a diagrammatic apparatus which can deal with other hypotheses about the rate structure, we now offer an

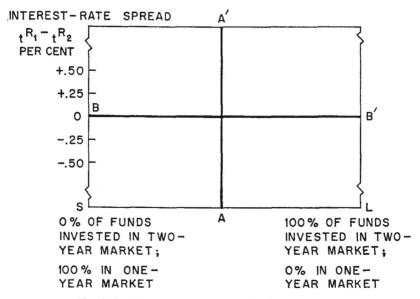

FIG. 7-2. Polar cases represented by box diagram.

alternative version of our Marshallian supply-demand graph (Figure 7-1). Figure 7-2 is a box diagram in which we measure along the abscissa the percentage of the (fixed) total stock of funds which investors chose to allocate between the two markets, and represent along the ordinate axis the difference between the two interest rates.[6] Vertical line AA′ is what we shall call a *holding curve*. It indicates what proportion of their funds investors will be willing to hold in each market at alternative interest-rate differentials. Because AA′ is vertical and A is the midpoint of SL, this holding

---

[5] This follows directly from Theorem 1 of Chapter 3.

[6] We remind the reader that we utilize the notation of Chapter 3. Capital R's represent actual rates; small r's expected rates. The prescript gives the period when the rate becomes applicable; the subscript, the duration of the loan.

curve represents the case where, irrespective of the interest-rate spread, half the available funds are allocated to the short market and half to the long market. (Line BB' is not yet relevant.) This is clearly an example of a perfectly segmented market. Here any attempt by suppliers to draw more funds from one market by offering more bonds for sale in that market must necessarily be frustrated. All that will change is the interest-rate spread between the short and long markets. The rate structure will be determined by the number of bonds suppliers attempt to sell in each market. We may generalize these observations by noting that the holding curve characterizing any case of complete segmentation will be vertical, with its abscissa given by the ratio of the funds seeking investment in the two markets.

7.3 Case 2: Complete Flexibility and Identical Expectations

The antithesis of perfect segmentation is the polar case of the pure expectations model. Here we assume that all investors antici-pate that the one-year rate of interest next year will be equal to the rate on one-year issues today (say $3\frac{1}{2}$ per cent).[7] We postulate further that there are no costs of investment and that investors' utility functions are linear in money payoffs (there is no risk aver-sion). Consequently, all investors are indifferent between the fol-lowing pairs of alternatives: (1) investing for one year either by purchasing a one-year bond or by purchasing a two-year bond and selling it at the end of one year; (2) investing for two years either by purchasing a two-year bond or by purchasing a one-year bond today and reinvesting the proceeds upon maturity in another one-year bond to mature at the end of year two.

Given these assumptions, it follows that the yield curve must be horizontal at the $3\frac{1}{2}$ per cent level. If there were any yield spread which made, say, long-term rates higher than short rates, then all investors would want to buy long-term bonds. We can illustrate this in terms of the investing institutions utilized in our previous case.

Insurance companies would now want to buy two-year bonds and expect to hold them to maturity. Commercial banks would also want to buy two-year issues even if they expected to sell them at the end of the first year to meet deposit drains or increased loan re-

---

[7] Little generality is lost by assuming that no change in the short rate is expected. The effect of an anticipated rise or fall in the short rate is readily taken into account in the determination of the term structure, as we shall show.

quests. Diagrammatically, this result is depicted by the horizontal holding curve BB' in Figure 7-2, which coincides with the horizontal axis. The line BB' shows that only a zero interest-rate spread is consistent with investors' expectations and desires. In general, the height of BB' depends upon the specific future one-year rate which is anticipated by the market. The relationship is given by the Lutz-Hicks averaging formula (2-2). If the forward rate is expected to be below the current one-year rate, the relevant line will lie above BB' (that is, one-year rates will exceed two-year rates). If the forward rate is expected to be above the current one-year rate, the relevant line will lie below BB'. The horizontal-holding-curve case is the situation that Meiselman has in mind when he says, "The expectations hypothesis implies that changes in the maturity composition of outstanding debt, when total debt is given, will have no long-run effect on the term structure . . . ."[8]

Meiselman has pointed out that even if some individual investors hedge (either long or short) on the basis of risk aversion, this need not contradict the expectational hypothesis.

> It is only necessary that one class of adequately financed transactors have an infinitely elastic excess demand schedule. . . . Speculators with given expectations adjust quantities of securities taken from or supplied to the market in order to maintain the structure of rates consistent with expectations . . . . Thus, it is not necessary that both the borrowing and lending sides of the market have infinitely elastic market schedules in order to observe the market phenomena consistent with the expectations hypothesis.[9]

It is important to emphasize, however, that the term structure will remain unaffected by changes in the maturity composition of the outstanding debt only if, through the error-learning process, these speculators tend to develop *identical* (uniform) forecasts. Thus, we find that Meiselman's reconciliation of the expectations and institutional hypothesis is not really a synthesis of the two. By postulating the presence of a group of adequately financed speculators whose utility is linear in money and whose expectations are all identical, Meiselman has in effect taken us back to the perfect-certainty formulation of the traditional expectational theory.

[8] David Meiselman, *The Term Structure of Interest Rates* (Englewood Cliffs: Prentice-Hall, 1962), p. 49.
[9] *Ibid.*, p. 57.

7.4   *Case 3: Introduction of Diverse Expectations*

We now introduce diversity of expectations and examine its consequences. In doing so we shall retain the assumptions that transactions costs are zero and that there are no maturity preferences. Hence investors will be considered to be perfectly mobile; that is, they will move their holdings from one market to the other if any interest-rate spread exists over and above that justified by their expectations as to future interest rates. Nevertheless we no longer take all expectations of future interest rates to be identical. Moreover, no professional speculators are assumed to exist.[10] Several different ways in which diverse expectations can be introduced will be considered. We shall subsequently examine the determination of the term structure when some investors have identical expectations, others have diverse expectations, and still others are rigidly committed to particular maturities. Finally, we shall introduce these considerations into the relative supply function.

7.4.a   CASE 3A: DEMANDERS HAVE DIVERSE EXPECTATIONS BUT NO MATURITY PREFERENCES—NO SUPPLY FLEXIBILITY

We begin by treating the case where all bond demanders are perfectly flexible between maturities, have no risk aversion (that is, have no maturity preferences), but have differing expectations. In this case we take the supply schedule of bonds to be completely inelastic with respect to interest-rate differentials. We first posit investors' expectations concerning future one-year rates to be uniformly distributed over a range of, say, plus or minus 100 basis points from the present one-year rate. Under these assumptions, we can then order the subjective beliefs of all owners of funds in terms of the rate they expect to apply. The rectangular density function D'D'' (in the lower half of Figure 7-3) arrays investable funds according to their owners' firm expectations of the forward one-

---

[10] We shall continue to make use of the distinction between professional speculation and portfolio speculation (flexibility), which we employed in the preceding chapter. In view of the results of our interviews however, we shall concern ourselves, in what follows, only with the second type of speculation, which we shall treat simply as port-folio flexibility. Since a very limited amount of professional speculation occurs in practice, and since we have suggested that professional speculators do not have uniform expectations and do have some degree of risk aversion, our results will not be affected by this simplification. Nevertheless, we shall indicate as we proceed how professional speculation can easily be accommodated by the model.

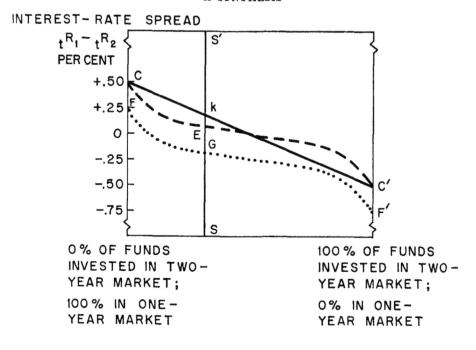

INTEREST- RATE SPREAD

$_tR_1 - _tR_2$ PER CENT

+.50
+.25
0
-.25
-.50
-.75

0% OF FUNDS INVESTED IN TWO-YEAR MARKET; 100% IN ONE-YEAR MARKET

100% OF FUNDS INVESTED IN TWO-YEAR MARKET; 0% IN ONE-YEAR MARKET

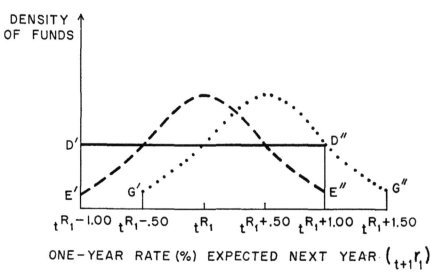

DENSITY OF FUNDS

$_tR_1 - 1.00$ $_tR_1 - .50$ $_tR_1$ $_tR_1 + .50$ $_tR_1 + 1.00$ $_tR_1 + 1.50$

ONE-YEAR RATE (%) EXPECTED NEXT YEAR $\left(_{t+1}r_1 \right)$

Fɪɢ. 7-3. Derivation of demand functions from density functions.

year rate. The area under the density function to the left of any point on the horizontal axis represents the fraction of investors who believe that the one-year rate next year will be no greater than the rate indicated at that point.

It is then an easy matter to construct the market demand curve for two-year (and hence residually for one-year) bonds as a function of the interest-rate differential between one- and two-year rates, $_tR_1 - _tR_2$. The linear holding curve CC' (in the upper half of Figure 7-3) is constructed via the standard Hicks-Lutz averaging formula from the density function D'D'', just described. For example, point C on the holding function corresponds to point D' on the density function. This is the threshold interest-rate differential at which the first dollar of funds is attracted into the two-year market. Investors who expect that the forward (one-year) rate will be 100 basis points below the current (one-year) rate (point D' above the axis in the lower figure) will enter the two-year market whenever the two-year rate is no more than (approximately) 50 basis points below the one-year rate (point C in the upper diagram).[11] At point C', corresponding to D'', the last dollar of funds enters the two-year market. Here, relative interest rates are such that all investors prefer to be invested in long maturities. At intermediate interest-rate spreads, just those investors who feel that the actual rate on two-year bonds is higher (lower) than the rate called for by their expectations purchase two-year (one-year) bonds. Thus, the abscissa in the upper diagram will always equal the cumulative area of the lower diagram. Given the actual maturity composition of the debt, we may read off the term structure directly. As drawn, point K represents the equilibrium interest-rate spread, where short rates lie above long rates.

This analysis leads us to another important result. Even if all investors are indifferent as to the maturity of their portfolios, and value securities exactly in accordance with the postulates of the pure expectational theory, we have found a case where *any* change in the maturity composition of the outstanding debt (that is, any shift in the supply function SS') will change the term structure. For example, if the relative supply of two-year issues is increased (SS'

---

[11] The diagram assumes the current one-year rate to be 3.5 per cent. By the averaging formula, unity plus the two-year rate $(1 + _tR_2)$ is the geometric mean of (unity plus) the current one-year rate (1.035) and (unity plus) the anticipated forward one-year rate, which, at point D', is 2.5 per cent. Thus we have $1 + _tR_2 = [(1.025)(1.035)]^{\frac{1}{2}} = 1.03$ (approximately). Hence the interest-rate spread $(_tR_1 - _tR_2)$ is $0.035 - 0.030 = 0.0050$, which gives us the level of C in the upper graph.

shifts to the right) the spread between one- and two-year rates will decrease (the equilibrium point K will be lowered). The expectations hypothesis need not imply that in the long run the term structure is insensitive to changes in the maturity distribution of the outstanding debt. Where investors have diverse rather than identical expectations, the rate structure cannot be determined without specific reference to the relative supplies of debt instruments. In fact, only through this kind of analysis can we find the "representative" investor whose expectations determine the rate structure in accordance with our price-behavior models of Chapter 3. Note that such a "representative" investor is not the "average" investor in the sense that his expectations conform to the mean expectations of the market. He is more properly a "marginal" investor. The expectations theory under diverse expectations does not necessarily imply that the rate structure will conform to the consensus of the judgments of the various market participants.

In order to describe explicitly the determinants of the height, slope, and curvature of the holding curve, we shall next treat several different cases of diverse expectations. Let us assume that the density function is E'E'', which is, roughly, a truncated normal distribution of expectations. In this case the holding curve becomes CEC'. The end points are the same as those of CDC', described above. Intermediate points are derived in a wholly analogous way. Take any point on the horizontal axis of the lower half of Figure 7-3. Convert the forward rate indicated into a subjectively appropriate two-year rate (and rate differential) by (2-2) as illustrated in note 11. The corresponding point on the holding curve in the upper part of the figure will have as its ordinate the rate spread so derived and as its abscissa the area to the left of that point on the density function. Note that by reducing the variance of the density function (that is, by postulating that expectations are less diverse) we have flattened the slope of the holding curve over the bulk of the relevant range. In the limiting case (Case 2) where all investors have identical expectations (and no maturity preferences), the holding curve becomes infinitely elastic. Thus, the more similar are the expectations of market participants, the less sensitive will be the rate structure to relative supply changes. Finally, we should note the effect of a change in expectations where all investors increase their forecasts of the forward rate by, say, 50 basis points. If the old density function was E'E'', the new function becomes G'G'' and the holding curve shifts downward from CDC' to FGF'. In this event, the probability that the yield curve will be positively sloped is increased.[12] This is so because now the yield curve can descend only if the relative supply of bonds is predominantly short term. For most possible relative supplies the curve will ascend.

7.4.b CASE 3B: ELEMENTS OF THE EXPECTATIONS AND
       SEGMENTATION CASES COMBINED

We have argued at length, in Chapter 6, that neither a pure expectations nor a complete segmentation approach appears to describe the behavior of bond demanders. Nevertheless, for the sake of completeness, we shall treat briefly the case where groups of investors, behaving according to the segmentation and pure

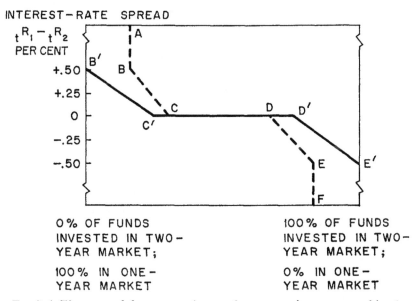

FIG. 7-4. Elements of the expectations and segmentation cases combined.

expectations theories, respectively, combine to determine the holding curve. First we shall look at the holding curve when all investors are flexible between maturities but expectations are identical for some transactors and diverse for others. Curve B'C'D'E' (Figure 7-4) assumes that half the investors (funds) have identical expectations that the future short rate will equal today's short rate and the other half have uniformly distributed expectations of next year's forward rate $(_{t+1}r_1)$ over the range, $_{t}R_1 - 1.00 \leq _{t+1}r_1 \leq _{t}R_1 + 1.00$.

---

[12] While maturity preferences will not be introduced until later, it may be useful now to point out that the shift in the density function and holding curve also illustrates the case where all investors are (Hicksian) risk averters to the same degree and add a 50 basis-point liquidity premium to the forward rate (see equation 2-9).

B'C'D'E' is obtained by horizontal addition of (one-half) curve CDC' in Figure 7-3 and (one-half) curve BB' in Figure 7-2. We note that, within segment C'D', the term structure will be insensitive to relative supply changes. Thus, if a significant number of investors hold similar expectations, it is possible that some changes in the maturity composition of the debt will have no effect despite the wide *range* of existing expectations.

Curve ABCDEF is also formed by horizontal addition. It assumes that the total funds available for investment in the market are distributed in three equal parts among the three types of investors described in Cases 1, 2, and 3 (where the density function is taken to be rectangular). Note that the horizontal segment of the curve has been reduced from C'D' to CD. The curve also contains two vertical segments, AB and EF, where attempts by suppliers to draw additional funds from the short or long market serve only to increase the interest-rate spread between the markets. We observe, as above, that the sensitivity of the rate structure to relative supply changes depends upon both the magnitude of the change and the position from which the change was made.

7.4.c FLEXIBILITY IN THE SUPPLY FUNCTION INTRODUCED.

Thus far we have been looking at the demand schedule for short (and long) debt in terms of the interest-rate spread between the two markets. We assumed that the total volume of funds was fixed, and we let the maturity distribution of the supply determine the rate structure. Thus, we did not explain why the supply was whatever it happened to be and assumed that the supply function was totally inelastic. Whatever interest structure was determined, we assumed that borrowers were not free to move between the two markets on the basis of their expectations. In this section we relax these restrictions and allow flexibility in the supply side of the market as well.[13]

---

[13] While the supply flexibility treated in this section is assumed to result where issuers modify the maturity composition of their borrowing, flexibility can be introduced in other ways. All suppliers might be perfectly inflexible, yet professional speculators could adjust the quantities of bonds available to investors in such a manner as to impart some elasticity to the supply. For example, assume that professional speculators were able and willing, at a particular interest-rate differential, to sell short some quantity of one-year bonds and simultaneously to buy the identical quantity of two-year securities. This would make the supply schedule infinitely elastic at that interest-rate spread over a range along the abscissa equal to the quantity of bonds involved. Analytically there is no difference between this case and the case where suppliers adjust the relative quantities of bonds themselves.

The building of the supply function is perfectly analogous to the construction of the holding curves (or demand functions), which we have just completed. In Figure 7-5, supply function HIJKLM reflects the following assumptions: one-half the suppliers are rigidly committed to one maturity area (that is, are "inflexible" suppliers), one-quarter to the long market, and one-quarter to the short. The other half of the suppliers are flexible. One-quarter hold the identical expectation that future short rates will remain unchanged, and the remaining quarter hold expectations uniformly distributed

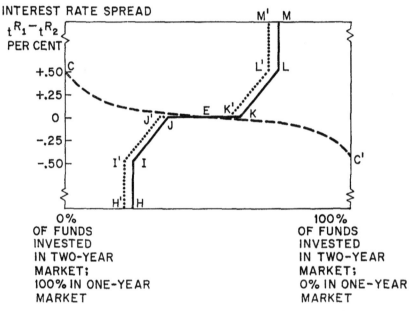

Fig. 7-5. Flexibility in the supply function introduced.

over the range of future rates we used previously in deriving the holding curves. H'I'J'K'L'M' represents the supply curve after inflexible suppliers choose to move MM' = HH' of bonds from the two-year to the one-year market. Even with a nonhorizontal holding curve such as CC' (from Figure 7-3), it now no longer follows that any change in the inflexible supply must alter the constellation of rates. Given the degree of supply flexibility postulated, the shift of the supply function depicted in the diagram will leave the rate structure unaltered. This is so because flexible suppliers who hold identical expectations that the forward rate will equal the current rate will move an amount of bonds equal to MM' from the one-year to the two-year market so as to offset the previous shift and leave the effective supply unchanged. By combining this supply function with other holding curves derived from the previous analysis, we can see clearly that supply flexibility increases the chances that the group with similar expectations will determine the interest-rate spread. In the limiting case of complete supply flexibility, zero new-issue costs, and uniform expectations among suppliers, the demand for securities is irrelevant for the determination of the rate structure. The distribution of expectations and degree of mobility of suppliers as well as demanders must be added to the model as important members of the cast of determinants of the rate structure. All further cases will assume that supply flexibility is substantial.

7.4.d CASE 3C: DIVERSE EXPECTATIONS—NO MATURITY PREFERENCES —SUPPLY FLEXIBILITY

We now treat a case identical with 3a but into which limited supply flexibility is introduced. Investors are assumed to have no preferences between maturities but to have diverse expectations. CC′ (upper part of Figure 7-6) is the curve giving the percentage of holdings demanded in the form of two-year (and hence residually, of one-year) bonds as a function of the interest-rate differential. It is constructed from the density function of investable funds, cc′ in the lower part of the figure, in the manner described in the discussion of Case 3a.

AA′ is the supply curve of bonds. We assume that the portions DA of two-year bonds and A′E of one-year issues are supplied irrespective of the interest-rate spread.[14] All remaining bond suppliers will vary their maturity with relative interest rates. The interest-elastic segment of the supply curve assumes diverse expectations on the part of suppliers, and its construction (from a density function similar to cc′) is completely analogous to that of the holding curve. As drawn, AA′ and CC′ intersect at a zero interest-rate spread that happens to be consistent with the mean expectations of suppliers and demanders. But note that any change in the quantity of bonds issued by inflexible suppliers will upset this rela-

[14] While this analysis does not include transactions costs explicitly, we have suggested in Chapter 5 that issue costs may lead to a sectoring of bond suppliers over a wide range of interest-rate differentials. This could explain the complete inelasticity of portions of the supply schedule over certain ranges of interest-rate differentials. We might also interpret the inelastic portion of the supply to be that part of the government debt where the maturity is chosen for reasons other than interest-rate differentials.

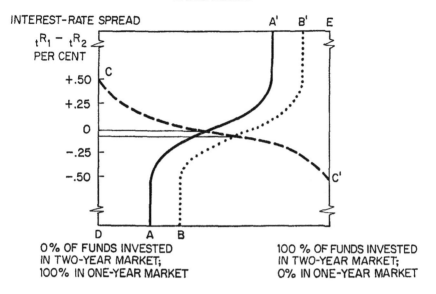

0% OF FUNDS INVESTED
IN TWO-YEAR MARKET;
100% IN ONE-YEAR MARKET

100% OF FUNDS INVESTED
IN TWO-YEAR MARKET;
0% IN ONE-YEAR MARKET

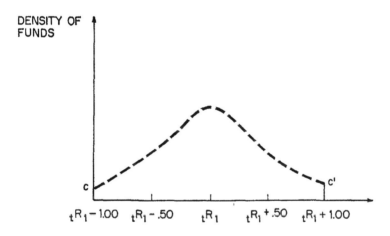

ONE-YEAR RATE (%) EXPECTED NEXT YEAR $(_{t+1}r_1)$

FIG. 7-6. Illustration of Case 3c.

tionship. For example, if inflexible suppliers choose to move $AB = A'B'$ bonds from the short to the long market, the relevant supply curve becomes BB', and the one-year rate must then lie below the two-year rate.

7.5 *Case 4: Uniform Expectations—Maturity Preferences*

We next treat a case where all market participants hold uniform expectations that the future one-year rate will equal the one-year rate of today. In this case, however, we assume that different market participants have definite preferences and must be paid if they are to shift from their preferred maturities. In Figure 7-7, the discontinuous holding function FGHF′ assumes that funds FG belong to investors who have strong preferences for income certainty (over the two-year period) and must be paid a premium of

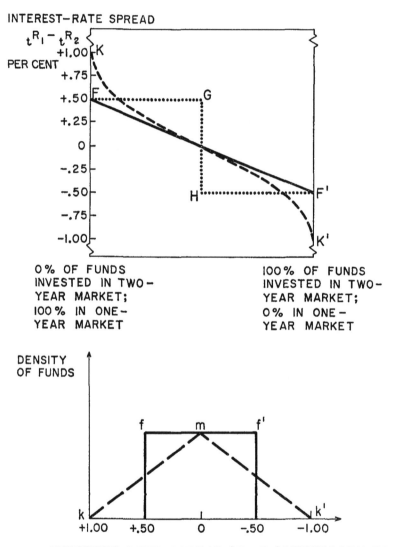

INTEREST−RATE SPREAD

$_tR_1 - {_t}R_2$

PER CENT

0% OF FUNDS
INVESTED IN TWO−
YEAR MARKET;
100% IN ONE−
YEAR MARKET

100% OF FUNDS
INVESTED IN TWO−
YEAR MARKET;
0% IN ONE−
YEAR MARKET

DENSITY
OF FUNDS

INTEREST−RATE SPREAD $({_t}R_1 - {_t}R_2)$ NECESSARY TO INDUCE INVESTORS TO HOLD TWO-YEAR ISSUES (%)

FIG. 7-7. Introduction of maturity preferences.

198

50 basis points on one-year issues to induce them to invest in these securities. Funds HF′ belong to investors who have a strong preference for principal certainty (that is, they are Hicksian risk-averters) and demand a 50-basis-point premium on two-year issues to induce them to enter the two-year market.

The alternative holding curve FF′ may be a more realistic construction in light of the indication of our interviews that the strength of such maturity preferences differs among and within classes of financial institutions. FF′ is derived from the rectangular density function ff′, which now arrays investable funds according to the interest-rate differential necessary to induce them into the two-year market. The area under the density function to the left of any point on the horizontal axis represents the fraction of investors who want to invest in two-year issues at the rate differential indicated at that point. Because the density function of Figure 7-7 already has these interest-rate differentials on the horizontal axis,[15] the construction of the holding curve is now trivial. For any rate spread along the horizontal axis of the density function and the cumulative area associated with it, the corresponding point on the holding function (upper figure) has, as its ordinate, the same rate differential and, as its abscissa, the area just described.

In general, the slope and curvature of FF′ will depend upon the distribution both of funds among different financial institutions and of the degree of risk aversion among portfolio managers. While no supply function is drawn on Figure 7-7, it is easy to derive one analogous to AA′ in Figure 7-6. The interest-elastic portion would in this case represent different maturity preferences on the part of issuers. Again we would find that the term structure was sensitive to relative supply changes despite uniformity of expectations.

7.6 Case 5: Diverse Expectations—Maturity Preferences

The most interesting, and empirically the most relevant, form of our synthesis assumes that market participants have diverse expectations and specific maturity preferences. It will be useful to treat first the simple variant (which differs only slightly from Case 3c) where all participants have diverse expectations but the same maturity preference. For example, let us add to Case 3c the assumption that all investors are to the same degree Hicksian risk averters.

---

[15] Note that the density function of Figure 7-6 had expected interest rates along its abscissa. It is immaterial, of course, which of the two quantities we use, since forward rates may readily be converted into rate differentials.

In this case, we would add a constant Hicksian liquidity premium (L_2) to the anticipated forward rate. The density function cc' would then shift to the right and the holding function CC' would shift downward (see note 12 to this chapter). This increases the probability that the yield curve will be positively sloped, that is, that backwardation will be present. Similarly, if all demanders are taken to prefer certainty of income over the long-run and, hence, longer issues, the probability of a contango is increased.

The complicated case treats both diverse preferences and expectations. Let us assume (as in Case 4) that the density function ff' characterizes the maturity preferences of the market. We assume further that an identical rectangular distribution describes the subjectively appropriate yield differentials justified by the diverse expectations of market participants.[16] Positing the two distributions to be independent, we may form the combined density function to account for the composite effects of subjectively appropriate differentials arising out of maturity preferences and diverse expectations. The combined density function for simple distributions may be found by the method of convolution.[17] In Figure 7-7, density function kmk' is found by convolving two rectangular distributions of the form ff'. The distribution kmk' arrays each dollar of funds in the market by the total interest-rate spread necessary to induce investment in the two-year issue, taking account of both expectations and maturity preferences. From the combined density function, we may then construct the holding function KK' directly. We note the range of KK' is wider and its slope is nowhere less steep than that of FF'. Thus, the presence of both diverse expectations and maturity preferences will usually increase the influence of supply changes on the term structure.

The effects of transactions costs, which we analyzed in the preceding chapter, may easily be accounted for in the present framework. To the interest-rate differentials that formerly made wealth holders indifferent between the one- and two-year markets, we would now add the transactions costs which must be covered if a security is purchased that does not correspond to the buyer's holding period. One-year holders could be induced to purchase two-year securities only if the rate differential in the market were sufficiently greater

---

[16] In terms of the density function of Figure 7-6, we assume the presence of a rectangular distribution of expectations of next year's forward rate ($_{t+1}r_1$) over the range $_tR_1 - 1.00 \leq \,_{t+1}r_1 \leq \,_tR_1 + 1.00$.

[17] The density function of the sum of two independent continuous random variables is the convolution of the density functions of the random variables. See Harold Freeman, *Introduction to Statistical Inference* (Reading: Addison-Wesley, 1963), Chapter 20.

than that attributable to expectations alone so as to overcome the holder's maturity preferences and transactions costs. This would have the effect of increasing the range of possible interest-rate spreads. Investors with short holding periods who were willing to buy two-year issues only if they had a positive yield inducement and no transactions costs would now require an even larger premium to induce them into two-year securities. *Mutatis mutandis*, the same argument applies to investors with long holding periods.[18] We should emphasize, however, that a model accounting for the influences of maturity preferences and transactions costs does not vitiate the importance of expectations. On the contrary, expectations remain a major force in the determination of the rate structure, and, as expectations at any time become more uniform, the term structure becomes less sensitive to changes in the relative supply of debt instruments.

7.7 *A Generalization to Three Maturities*

In this section and in the Appendix, we extend the preceding analysis to account for three securities: a short, an intermediate, and a long issue. This extension serves two purposes: (1) It indicates that the demand-supply apparatus of the preceding analysis can be generalized so as to determine interest rates in the multi-maturity case. (2) It allows us to isolate what sort of circumstances lead to the phenomenon of the humped yield curve. Recourse to a three-maturities model is unavoidable here. By definition, a hump means that there is an intermediate rate which exceeds both a shorter and a longer rate.

The pure expectations theory is able to offer only a very clumsy explanation of humps in the yield curve. For example, to explain some of the yield curves existing in the 1959–1960 period one must postulate the following set of expectations: First, investors must be assumed to believe that short rates will be high and rising for the next four to five years. During the subsequent two years, approximately, investors must expect short rates to decline to extraordinarily low levels. Finally, in the following period, rates must be

---

[18] The present framework can also accommodate the possibility that different transactors may not pay the same transactions costs per dollar of security traded. For example, transactors who trade in very small quantities (odd lots) usually pay somewhat larger trading costs per bond. Similarly, government-bond dealers and dealer banks trade in the market on a "wholesale" basis, while nondealers trade at "retail." This would simply mean that the yield inducements that make wealth holders indifferent between the two markets may not be the same for two investors with identical expectations and maturity preferences.

expected to rise again sharply and thereafter remain constant at a level equal to the then current long rates. The argument which attributes such a constellation of forward rates to the expectation of business-cycle turning points (many years in the future) seems implausible. Hopefully, a three-market model of the type we have been developing can account for such occurrences more convincingly.

It is, of course, quite plausible that changes in the maturity composition of the debt can have this effect. Nevertheless, a little thought indicates that the argument is most cogent in a model in which markets are not absolutely segmented. A change in relative supplies could not have any effect (in particular, it could produce no hump) in a pure expectations model. It is, therefore, important to show that our more eclectic model is one which yields results that accord readily with intuition and observation.

In our analysis of the three-security case, we shall admit both maturity preferences and diverse expectations. We posit the existence of two groups of investors. The first group will be assumed to be averse to long maturities. We assume that these "short hedgers" demand no liquidity premiums to substitute between short- and intermediate-term issues but that no investor in the group will purchase long maturities unless the long rate is higher than the rate on intermediates. The second group of investors dislike short maturities. These "long hedgers" substitute freely between longs and intermediates in accordance with their expectations, but no member of this group will purchase a short issue unless the rate on shorts is above the rate on intermediates. Both groups have diverse expectations.

As we saw in Chapter 6, available evidence suggests that partial flexibility may be a good generalization for the actual portfolio practices of many institutions. We found that throughout the postwar period commercial banks did not purchase significant quantities of longs. Similarly, we found that life insurance companies did not normally substitute between short and long securities. On the other hand, many of these institutions purchased significant quantities of intermediate-term issues. We suggested that the range of interest-rate differentials which have existed in the market has apparently not been sufficient to induce such movement. To put the matter somewhat differently, partial segmentation of the market may be the best characterization of the facts of the matter, at least over some range of interest-rate differentials.

Since our interest is only in demonstrating how a hump in the yield curve may occur, our switching restrictions need only be weak ones. We do not say, for example, that commercial banks will *not* switch to the long market if long rates are higher than intermediate rates. We posit only that no shift to a less desirable maturity will occur if the yield inducement is negative. Since a humped *yield curve implies negative yield inducements for both long* hedgers and short hedgers,[19] even this weak restriction allows us to ignore certain regions of the demand functions of the two groups of market participants: short hedgers should have no interest in long maturities, while long hedgers should similarly eschew short maturities. Of course, in applying our analysis, we must remember that this behavior may obtain only over a very limited range of rate differentials.

While a formal demonstration of the conditions under which an increase in the relative supply of intermediate term securities can produce a hump in the yield curve will be postponed to the Appendix, here we can at least indicate intuitively how such a hump might occur. Consider a situation in which equilibrium yields to maturity were equal for all three securities. Now assume that the monetary authorities exogenously increase the relative supply of intermediate-term issues. This might be accomplished by an open-market swapping operation whereby for every two new intermediate-term bonds sold to the public, the monetary authorities buy one short- and one long-term bond. Given the assumptions of our analysis, and assuming no change in expectations, a hump in the yield curve must occur.

Since expectations are diverse, short hedgers can be induced to hold more intermediate-term bonds only if they can obtain a higher yield on intermediates than on shorts. All short hedgers who believe that future interest rates will fall must already be invested in intermediate-term issues on the assumption that the former flat yield curve was an equilibrium term structure. Consequently, some

---

[19] With a humped yield curve, long hedgers would receive a lower interest on (less desirable) short-term securities than on intermediates. Short hedgers would find themselves in the same position. Long-term securities would be yielding less than more desirable intermediates. Of course, even if longs yield less than intermediates, a short hedger may still have an inducement to purchase longs if the market long rate is higher than the subjective rate consonant with his expectations. Thus we are, in effect, assuming that the liquidity (solidity) premiums demanded by short (long) hedgers to switch into the long (short) market are sufficient to overcome any yield inducements arising from expectations which differ from the rates implicit in the rate structure.

short hedgers who think that rates will rise (that is, who are less willing to extend the maturity of their holdings) must be induced to buy intermediates. This can only be accomplished if the intermediate rate lies above the short rate. But the same argument applies to the long hedgers, *mutatis mutandis*. Consequently, the intermediate rate must lie above both the short and the long rate. The greater the supply of intermediates, the more reluctant will be the marginal buyer who must be induced to hold intermediate-term securities and the greater will be the hump in the yield curve.[20]

During the 1959 and 1960 period of high interest rates, the relative supply of intermediates increased substantially. It is highly plausible that the accompanying humped yield curves are explained by precisely the mechanism that has just been described. The evidence of Chapter 6 suggests that, as the relative supply of intermediates increased, both short hedgers (e.g., commercial banks) and long hedgers (e.g., life insurance companies) shifted into these securities. But if expectations of future interest rates were not identical, additional investors could be induced into intermediates only at higher relative interest rates.

Note that we have thus far assumed that both groups substitute between their preferred maturity and intermediate-term bonds entirely in accordance with their expectations. If we posit that in addition the short hedgers demand liquidity premiums to substitute intermediate for short maturities and that the long hedgers demand solidity premiums to substitute intermediate for long maturities, it would be even more likely that a hump would occur. The yield inducement on intermediate-term securities would then also have to compensate for the differential strength of maturity preferences within classes of financial institutions. Consequently, the rate on intermediate-term securities must rise *a fortiori* if additional less-willing buyers are to be induced to shift from their preferred maturities. We shall demonstrate these propositions formally in the Appendix which follows.

APPENDIX TO CHAPTER 7

A Three-Market Model of the Term Structure

Following the intuitive discussion in the text, this Appendix presents a simple three-security model of the term structure and

---

[20] Since the long (short) rate is below the rate on intermediate securities, by assumption no short (long) hedgers will be induced to purchase any long (short) securities.

shows a plausible set of conditions under which an increase in the relative supply of intermediate-term securities will produce a hump in the yield curve.

7A.1 *The Assumptions and Notation*

We may recapitulate the assumptions of the three-market model as follows: There are two groups of investors. The first substitutes freely between short and intermediate issues, the second between intermediates and longs. Both groups have diverse expectations. The amount of money available to both groups for investment sums to the total supply of bonds. In particular, we assume: The short issue matures in one year, the intermediate issue in two years, the long security in three years. For the purpose of formulating numerical examples, we assume the short rate is fixed at $3\frac{1}{2}$ per cent. The distribution of expectations as to forward rates $(_{t+1}r_1)$ and $(_{t+2}r_1)$ are assumed to be rectangular over a range bounded by $_tR_1 + 1.00$ and $_tR_1 - 1.00$.

We utilize the following notation:

M_T^S: The total funds given to short hedgers (investors who prefer short and intermediate maturities).

M_1^S: The funds placed by the above group in the short (one-year) market.

M_2^S: The funds placed by the above group in the intermediate (two-year) market.

M_T^L: The total funds given to the long hedgers (investors who prefer long and intermediate maturities).

M_2^L: The funds placed by the above group in the intermediate (two-year) market.

M_3^L: The funds placed by the above group in the long (three-year) market.

S_i: The (inelastic) supply of i-year bonds. Thus, S_1 is the supply of one-year bonds, etc.

7A.2 *The Holding Curve for the Short Hedgers*

We begin by deriving the holding curve of two-year bonds for the group of short hedgers. Figure 7A-1 derives this function graphically from the specific assumptions noted above.[1] The bottom diagram represents the allocation of the fixed total of funds among

---

[1] Throughout this Appendix, we assume for simplicity that long rates are simple arithmetic averages of present and future short rates.

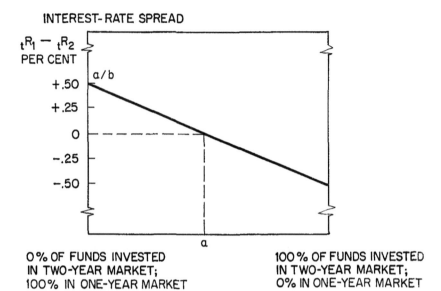

INTEREST-RATE SPREAD

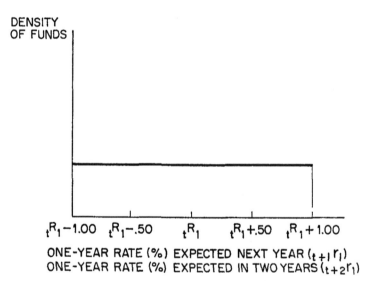

Fɪɢ. 7A-1. Demand function for short hedgers.

the short hedgers. Because the density function is rectangular, the holding curve must be linear.

Since M_2^s declines with increases in the interest-rate differential, we may write this equation as follows:

$$M_2^s/M_T^s = a - b(_tR_1 - {}_tR_2) \ . \tag{7A-1}$$

We note that a represents the fraction of funds placed in the two-year market when a zero interest-rate spread exists (between the one-year and two-year rates). a/b represents the interest-rate differential at which the first dollar of funds enters the two-year market. (In the figure, this is the y intercept.) The demand for one-year bonds emerges as the residual of (7A-1).

$$M_1^s / M_T^s = 1 - a + b(_tR_1 - _tR_2) \ . \tag{7A-2}$$

7A.3   *The Holding Curves for the Long Hedgers*

Let us now consider the class of investors who substitute between two- and three-year issues. By assumption, they have a rectangular distribution of expectations concerning the forward rate in year three $(_{t+2}r_1)$. Since their distribution has the same range as that of the short hedgers, the density function of Figure 7A-1 applies to both groups. This is indicated along the abscissa. The holding function for three-year (and hence residually for two-year issues) is analogous to (7A-1).

$$M_3^L / M_T^L = c - d(_tR_2 - _tR_3) \ . \tag{7A-3}$$

But, while the holding function for short hedgers assumed that the one-year rate $(_tR_1)$ was a constant (3.50 per cent), such an assumption for the two-year rate $(_tR_2)$ is not admissible. In this case, the two-year rate is a variable in the model. Hence, Figure 7A-2 (which

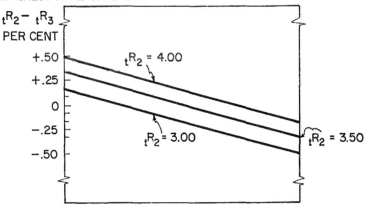

INTEREST-RATE SPREAD

$_tR_2 - _tR_3$
PER CENT

+.50 $_tR_2 = 4.00$
+.25
0
−.25 $_tR_2 = 3.00$ $_tR_2 = 3.50$
−.50

0 % OF FUNDS INVESTED
IN THREE-YEAR MARKET;
100% IN TWO-YEAR MARKET

100 % OF FUNDS INVESTED
IN THREE-YEAR MARKET;
0% IN TWO-YEAR MARKET

FIG. 7A-2. Demand functions for long hedgers.

depicts the allocation of funds by the long hedgers) shows a family of holding functions of which three sample curves are drawn. In principle, there is one for each value of $_tR_2$. Consequently, we note the dependence upon $_tR_2$ of c, the fraction of funds invested in the three-year market when a zero interest-rate spread exists, and, therefore, of the y intercept (c/d), i.e., the point where $M_3^L = 0$.[2]

Under our assumptions, the relationship between c/d and the interest-rate differential between the one- and two-year rates is linear.[3] For convenience, we may write the relationship for the specific data of our model as follows:

$$c = a - a(_tR_1 - _tR_2) \tag{7A-4}$$

[2] The (inverse of the) slope $(-d)$ is a constant, however (see note 3).

[3] To demonstrate this assertion, we first offer an intuitive interpretation of the y intercept in Figure 7A-2, (c/d), that is, the point where $M_3^L/M_T^L = 0$. This is the interest-rate differential where the *first* dollar of funds enters the three-year market. But the first investor (dollar of funds) to enter the three-year market must have the *lowest* expectation of the forward one-year rate applicable for year three, or, what is the same thing, the highest price expectation for the bond two years from now. We may then write

$$M_3^L/M_T^L = 0 \text{ when } c/d = _tR_2 - _tR_{3,\min}$$

where $_tR_{3,\min}$ is the lowest three-year rate which satisfies any investor. But, by the argument above, $_tR_{3,\min}$ is formed as the average of current and future short rates including $_{t+2}r_{1,\min}$ (the lowest one-year rate expected for year three). Consequently, writing out $_tR_2$ and $_tR_{3,\min}$ explicitly (assuming arithmetic averaging) we have

$$\frac{c}{d} = \frac{_tr_1 + _{t+1}r_1}{2} - \frac{_tr_1 + _{t+1}r_1 + _{t+2}r_{1,\min}}{3} . \tag{7A-3a}$$

Simplifying (7A-3a) we have the y intercept (c/d) depending linearly on $_tR_2$,

$$c/d = \tfrac{1}{3}_tR_2 - \tfrac{1}{3}_{t+2}r_{1,\min} . \tag{7A-3b}$$

By taking any other y value on the generalized demand function (e.g., where $M_3^L/M_T^L = 1$) we obtain a second equation such as (7A-3b), and with the aid of these two equations we can solve for the (inverse of the) slope in Figure 7A-2, $(-d)$. By an argument completely analogous with the one above we have

$$M_3^L/M_T^L = 1 \text{ when } (c - 1)/d = _tR_2 - _tR_{3,\max} . \tag{7A-3c}$$

Again writing out the long rates in terms of the relevant current and forward short rates, we have

$$\frac{c - 1}{d} = \frac{_tr_1 + _{t+1}r_1}{2} - \frac{_tr_1 + _{t+1}r_1 + _{t+2}r_{1,\max}}{3} = \tfrac{1}{3}_tR_2 - \tfrac{1}{3}_{t+2}r_{1,\max} . \tag{7A-3d}$$

We may then calculate the slope directly from (7A-3d) and (7A-3b). We find that $(-d)$ is a constant (that is, it does not depend on any of the variables of the model).

$$-d = -\frac{1}{\frac{_{t+2}r_{1,\max} - _{t+2}r_{1,\min}}{3}} = -\frac{1}{\frac{4.5 - 2.5}{3}} = -1\tfrac{1}{2} . \tag{7A-3e}$$

where a is the same constant that appeared in (7A-1) and (7A-2).[4] We may write the demand function for three-year and two-year bonds as

$$M_3^{\mathrm{L}}/M_{\mathrm{T}}^{\mathrm{L}} = a - a({}_tR_1 - {}_tR_2) - d({}_tR_2 - {}_tR_3) \qquad (7\text{A-5})$$

and

$$M_2^{\mathrm{L}}/M_{\mathrm{T}}^{\mathrm{L}} = 1 - a + a({}_tR_1 - {}_tR_2) - d({}_tR_2 - {}_tR_3) . \qquad (7\text{A-6})$$

7A.4   Equilibrium Conditions

We next present a statement of the equilibrium conditions for the model. We are given that the total amount of funds available for bond investors equals the total supply of bonds.[5]

$$M_{\mathrm{T}} \equiv M_{\mathrm{T}}^{\mathrm{S}} + M_{\mathrm{T}}^{\mathrm{L}} = S_1 + S_2 + S_3 . \qquad (7\text{A-7})$$

Moreover, we have assumed

$${}_tR_1 = {}_t\bar{R}_1 = 3.50 \text{ per cent} .[6] \qquad (7\text{A-8})$$

For equilibrium, we require the supplies and demands in each market to balance:

$$S_1 = M_1^{\mathrm{S}} = M_{\mathrm{T}}^{\mathrm{S}}[1 - a + b({}_tR_1 - {}_tR_2)] \qquad (7\text{A-9})$$

$$\begin{aligned} S_2 = M_2^{\mathrm{S}} + M_2^{\mathrm{L}} &= M_{\mathrm{T}}^{\mathrm{S}}[a - b({}_tR_1 - {}_tR_2)] \\ &+ M_{\mathrm{T}}^{\mathrm{L}}[1 - a + a({}_tR_1 - {}_tR_2) + d({}_tR_2 - {}_tR_3)] . \end{aligned} \qquad (7\text{A-10})$$

$$S_3 = M_3^{\mathrm{L}} = M_{\mathrm{T}}^{\mathrm{L}}[a - a({}_tR_1 - {}_tR_2) - d({}_tR_2 - {}_tR_3)] . \qquad (7\text{A-11})$$

7A.5   Simplification of the Model

In keeping with the symmetrical nature of our example, we continue to assume that $M_{\mathrm{T}}^{\mathrm{S}} = M_{\mathrm{T}}^{\mathrm{L}}$, that is, we build into the model no presumption concerning an asymmetry in the distribution of funds between long and short investors.[7] To express our supply figures in relative terms, we divide through by $\frac{1}{2} M_{\mathrm{T}}$, the amount of money available to each class of investors. This transforms our system of

---

[4] Utilizing (7A-3b), we can obtain (7A-4) in the following manner: We substitute the constant found in (7A-3e) for $-d$, subtract $a_t R_1$ and add $1.75 = a_t R_1$ and then rearrange in the linear form of (7A-4).

[5] We must also assume $M_{\mathrm{T}}^{\mathrm{S}} \geqq S_1$ and $M_{\mathrm{T}}^{\mathrm{L}} \geqq S_3$.

[6] In effect, we are assuming that this arbitrary value of ${}_tR_1$ ensures that the over-all bond market is in equilibrium.

[7] In the analysis which follows we shall only examine the implications of changes in the relative supply of debt instruments. Needless to say, a similar analysis can be made for changes in the relative distribution of funds. Our particular restriction is made solely for the sake of convenience of presentation. It is not a necessary one.

equations as follows:

$$
\begin{bmatrix} \dfrac{S_1}{\frac{1}{2}M_T} \\[2ex] \dfrac{S_2}{\frac{1}{2}M_T} \\[2ex] \dfrac{S_3}{\frac{1}{2}M_T} \end{bmatrix} = \begin{bmatrix} 1 - a + b(_tR_1) & -b & 0 \\[1ex] 1 + (a - b)(_tR_1) & b - a + d & -d \\[1ex] a - a(_tR_1) & a - d & +d \end{bmatrix} \begin{bmatrix} 1 \\[1ex] _tR_2 \\[1ex] _tR_3 \end{bmatrix}
$$

$$
= A \begin{bmatrix} 1 \\[1ex] _tR_2 \\[1ex] _tR_3 \end{bmatrix}. \qquad (7A\text{-}12)
$$

In (7A-12) we have two unknowns and only two independent equations.[8] To determine the unknown R's, we omit the first row of the vector of relative supplies and of the matrix of coefficients (A).

The objective of this analysis is to demonstrate how an increase in the relative supply of intermediate-term issues can produce a hump in the yield curve. Such a hump can arise in the absence of any complex supply relationships. To emphasize this and to facilitate algebraic analysis, we deal only with a very simple pattern of relative supplies. In particular, we assume that the supplies of one-year and three-year issues are always equal. Under this assumption, an increase in the relative supply of two-year bonds implies that the relative supplies of one- and three-year bonds decrease, with both decreases equal. Consequently, the relative supplies of two- and one-year (three-year) issues satisfy the following linear relationship:

$$
\frac{S_2}{\frac{1}{2}M_T} = 2 - 2\left[\frac{S_1}{\frac{1}{2}M_T}\right]. \qquad (7A\text{-}13)
$$

For further convenience, we shall identify the following shift parameter:

$$
\frac{S_1}{\frac{1}{2}M_T} = \frac{S_3}{\frac{1}{2}M_T} \equiv \alpha. \qquad (7A\text{-}14)
$$

Substituting this into (7A-13), we have

$$
\frac{S_2}{\frac{1}{2}M_T} = 2 - 2\alpha. \qquad (7A\text{-}15)
$$

[8] One of these equations is not independent, since equilibrium in two markets by (7A-7) implies equilibrium in the remaining one.

Also, let us denote the relative interest-rate differentials as follows:

$$\frac{{}_tR_2}{{}_tR_1} \equiv Z_1 . \qquad (7\text{A-}16)$$

$$\frac{{}_tR_2}{{}_tR_3} \equiv Z_2 . \qquad (7\text{A-}17)$$

7A.6 *Generation of a Humped Yield Curve*

In common-sense terms, we expect that increases in S_2 should increase these interest-rate differentials. Therefore, *starting from a situation where rates on all securities are equal*, an increase in the relative supply of intermediate-term issues should cause a hump in the yield curve. This requires that as α is reduced ($S_2/\frac{1}{2}M_T$ is increased), the two-year rate rises relative to the one-year rate (Z_1 increases), and the three-year rate (Z_2 increases). Writing these conditions in terms of derivatives, what we are undertaking to prove is that

$$\frac{\partial Z_1}{\partial \alpha} < 0 \qquad (7\text{A-}18)$$

and

$$\frac{\partial Z_2}{\partial \alpha} < 0 . \qquad (7\text{A-}19)$$

We first perform certain elementary operations on (7A-12). Omitting the first row of the vectors and the matrix A, incorporating the definitions (7A-14) through (7A-17), and transposing the first column of A to the left-hand side of (7A-12), we have

$$\begin{bmatrix} 2 - 2\alpha - 1 - (a - b)({}_tR_1) \\ \alpha - a + a({}_tR_1) \end{bmatrix}$$

$$= \begin{bmatrix} b - a + d & -d \\ a - d & d \end{bmatrix} \begin{bmatrix} {}_tR_1 Z_1 \\ {}_tR_1 Z_1 \\ Z_2 \end{bmatrix} = B \begin{bmatrix} {}_tR_1 Z_1 \\ {}_tR_1 Z_1 \\ Z_2 \end{bmatrix} . \qquad (7\text{A-}20)$$

Note that, writing out the determinant $|B|$ we have $|B| = bd$. Solving (7A-20) for the vector of relative interest rates, we finally obtain

$$\begin{bmatrix} {}_tR_1 Z_1 \\ {}_tR_1 Z_1 \\ Z_2 \end{bmatrix} = B^{-1} \begin{bmatrix} f(\alpha) \\ g(\alpha) \end{bmatrix}$$

$$= \begin{bmatrix} \dfrac{1}{b} & \dfrac{1}{b} \\ \dfrac{-a+d}{bd} & \dfrac{b-a+d}{bd} \end{bmatrix} \begin{bmatrix} f(\alpha) \\ g(\alpha) \end{bmatrix} . \qquad (7\text{A-}21)$$

Differentiating this system with respect to α we have

$$\frac{\partial Z_1}{\partial \alpha} = \frac{1}{{}_tR_1}\begin{bmatrix} 1 & 1 \\ b & b \end{bmatrix}\begin{bmatrix} f' \\ g' \end{bmatrix} = \frac{1}{{}_tR_1}\left[-2\frac{1}{b} + 1\frac{1}{b}\right]$$

$$= -\frac{1}{{}_tR_1}\left(\frac{1}{b}\right) < 0 , \quad (7A\text{-}22)$$

and

$$\frac{\partial Z_1}{\partial \alpha}\,{}_tR_1\left(\frac{1}{Z_2}\right) - \frac{\partial Z_2}{\partial \alpha}\left(\frac{{}_tR_1 Z_1}{Z_2^2}\right)$$

$$= \left[\frac{-a+d}{bd} \quad \frac{b-a+d}{bd}\right]\begin{bmatrix} f' \\ g' \end{bmatrix} . \quad (7A\text{-}23)$$

Solving (7A-23) for the derivative of Z_2 with respect to α, we find

$$\frac{\partial Z_2}{\partial \alpha} = \frac{Z_2^2}{{}_tR_1 Z_1}\left[\frac{d-b-a}{bd} - \frac{d}{bd}\frac{1}{Z_2}\right] . \quad (7A\text{-}24)$$

It remains to be shown that the assumptions of the analysis make the sign of (7A-24) negative as well. Since we want to know the effect of an increase in the relative supply of intermediates *where, initially, the rate structure is level*, we can take ${}_tR_2/{}_tR_3 \equiv Z_2 = 1$ and, in that case, $\partial Z_2/\partial \alpha$ must be unambiguously negative. This is so because the bracketed term on the right-hand side of (7A-24) then reduces to $-(b+a)/bd$, which, since a, b, and d are all positive constants,[9] is less than zero. Since both derivatives are negative, we have demonstrated what was required in (7A-18) and (7A-19). Starting from a situation where rates on all securities are equal, an increase in the relative supply of intermediate-term issues will cause a hump in the yield curve.

7A.7 A Numerical Example

We conclude with a numerical example. We assume that, initially, money and security supplies are given by the following magnitudes: $M_T^S = 150$, $M_T^L = 150$, $S_1 = 75$, $S_2 = 150$, and $S_3 = 75$. Substituting these data and the values of the constant terms previously assumed into (7A-12), we have

$$\begin{bmatrix} \tfrac{1}{2} \\ 1 \\ \tfrac{1}{2} \end{bmatrix} = \begin{bmatrix} \tfrac{1}{2} + {}_tR_1 & -1 & 0 \\ 1 - \dfrac{{}_tR_1}{2} & 2 & -1\tfrac{1}{2} \\ \tfrac{1}{2} - \dfrac{{}_tR_1}{2} & -1 & 1\tfrac{1}{2} \end{bmatrix}\begin{bmatrix} 1 \\ {}_tR_2 \\ {}_tR_3 \end{bmatrix} .$$

[9] We also note that, given the specific parameters we have postulated in the example, which parallels the exposition of the model, $d - b - a = 0$ so $\partial Z_2/\partial \alpha < 0$, irrespective of the position from which we start the experiment.

Solving for the interest rates (which constitute the term structure), we obtain

$$_tR_1 = {_t}R_2 = {_t}R_3 = 3.50 \text{ per cent} .$$

Now let us increase the relative supply of intermediate-term issues. Let $S_1 = 50$, $S_2 = 100$, and $S_3 = 50$. The column vector of relative supplies becomes $[\frac{1}{3}, 1\frac{1}{3}, \frac{1}{3}]$ and, solving for the interest rates of the term structure, we have

$$_tR_1 = 3.50 \text{ per cent} ,$$
$$_tR_2 = 3.667 \text{ per cent} ,$$

and

$$_tR_3 = 3.50 \text{ per cent} .$$

This yield curve clearly exhibits a hump in the intermediate maturity.

CHAPTER 8

Summary and Policy Implications

DURING the 1960's, identification of the determinants of the term structure of interest rates assumed a degree of importance well beyond its significance for pure theory. As a result of the balance-of-payments difficulties of the United States and the attempts of the monetary authorities to mitigate these problems by manipulation of the rate structure, the theoretical questions discussed in this study became directly relevant to the conduct of monetary policy.

This chapter will first summarize and tie together the principal findings of this study and then examine the implications of our analysis for Treasury and Federal Reserve policy.

8.1 *A Variant of the Traditional Expectations Theory*

Our treatment began with an expectations model that differs considerably from traditional theory. Three building blocks were essential to the analysis: the mathematics of bond prices; the assumption that investors form expectations of a "normal range" of interest rates; and, finally, the introduction of expectations proper—specific anticipations about the likely course of future interest-rate movements. We examined in Chapter 3 how each of the above factors restricts the possible shape of the yield curve.

First, an examination of the mathematics of bond-price movements, by itself, helps to explain the characteristic flatness of the yield curve in the range corresponding to longer maturities. It suggests that expectations of changes in the level of interest rates will influence the yield curve mainly in the early maturities. The vulnerability of securities to capital loss and the opportunity that various issues afford for capital gains change very rapidly as maturity is extended beyond the earliest part of the maturity spectrum. Consequently, it is plausible that prices and yields of these issues are quite sensitive to changes in expectations. Conversely, the potential price fluctuations of longer-term bonds may be expected to be quite similar over a wide range of maturities. Therefore, it is not surprising that these bonds, which the mathematics show to be almost equivalent in terms of their responsiveness to changes in the level of interest rates, will sell in the market at roughly similar yields.

214

Our examination of bond-price relationships also provided reasons why the yield curve will tend to flatten even if factors other than expectations are accorded an influential role in the determination of the rate structure. For example, to whatever extent (Hicksian) liquidity premiums influence the slope of the yield curve, such premiums also have their effect mainly in the early maturities. This is so because of the sharply diminishing marginal risk to which an investor subjects himself in extending maturity further, once he gets beyond the earliest years. Finally, even if one holds that there is absolute separation of transactors in different segments of the market, as has been argued by opponents of the expectations theory, it was shown in Chapter 7 that the bond-price theorems can help to explain the limited volatility of long rates.

Next, we examined the effects that follow when the expectation of a "normal range" of interest rates is taken in conjunction with the mathematical relationships inherent in bond-price movements. We assumed that investors were uncertain about the *direction* of future rate changes, but firmly expected that whatever interest-rate variations did occur would be contained within a range experienced in the past. Treating this situation as a "game against nature" in which the investor uses a Laplace (Bayes) decision criterion, the normal-range hypothesis, together with the mathematics of bond pricing, sufficed to explain the signs of both the first and second derivative of the yield curve.

With interest rates near the upper bound of what is believed to be the normal range, investors will have more to hope than fear in terms of the possibilities for capital gains and losses. If investors seek to equalize the mathematical expectation of gain over a short horizon period, a descending yield curve will result. Alternatively, if interest rates are near the lower bound of the normal range, investors will have more to fear than hope. Possible capital gains will be small, but potential capital losses over the horizon period will loom large. In this situation, if investors seek to equalize the mathematical expectation of gain among maturities, an ascending curve will result. In either case, because equal potential changes in yields imply roughly similar changes in bond prices for most longer-term bonds, the yields of these securities will turn out to be approximately equal. Hence, whatever the slope of the yield curve in the early maturities, the curve will eventually level out.

The third factor treated was expectations proper. Expectations regarding the direction of rate changes were near-term in character and were expressed probabilistically over the whole maturity spectrum. Thus, as opposed to the traditional theory, we assumed that investors were concerned more with fluctuations of the long rate over the short run than with anticipations of the level of short rates over the long run. We argued that this view had the advantage of being in close conformity with the actual practices of bond investors. This point was later verified by interview examinations of the portfolio behavior of several institutional investors. We found that "expectations proper" may either accentuate or counteract somewhat the effects of the expectations of a normal range in determining the slope of the yield curve, but would not change the sign of the second derivative.

This model, while considerably different from the traditional formulation, is not to be interpreted as an attack on the accepted expectations theory. On the contrary, our purpose in reformulating the postulates of investor behavior was to buttress the theory, not to destroy it. The received analysis is much more than an elegant academic tour de force; it can be reformulated so that it is entirely consistent with the practices of bond traders and institutional investors. Such a reformulation is found to be both less demanding and more realistic in its assumptions, yet it is able to afford added insights into the behavior of yields of securities that differ in their term to maturity. Throughout the translation, however, the essential force of the expectations theory remained intact. We were able to show that as long as investors act to equalize the expected value of holding-period yields over one (short) horizon period, it is possible to derive the same consistent set of interest-rate relationships as were implied in the traditional analysis. Consequently, despite our amendments, the relationships of the Hicks-Lutz analysis could still serve as the foundation upon which to build amendments dealing with matters other than expectations.

In performing an empirical test of the amended expectations model, we hypothesized that investors formed expectations of a normal range of interest-rate fluctuations but were undecided on the likelihood of rates moving up or down. Investors were taken to shape their expectations of the normal range by looking both at the long-term historic range and at the average of rates over a period of more recent years. The slope of the yield curve was then postulated to be a function of the relationship between the current level of rates and the bounds of the normal range as suggested by the model. The results of tests utilizing three different sets of economic time series supported the modified expectations hypothesis. They provide independent evidence corroborating the findings of Meiselman and Kessel.

8.2 *Emendations of the Basic Model*

Despite these favorable results, it is by no means safe to conclude that expectations provide a complete explanation of the rate structure. For one thing, the pure expectations model provides no ready explanation for the fact that the portion of the yield curve relating to the shortest maturities has typically been positively sloped, even when later segments descended sharply. Moreover, humps have also been found in the intermediate maturities, a phenomenon for which the expectations theory can offer only a clumsy and implausible explanation. In addition, it remained to be shown why, at least during recent history, short rates seem "normally" to lie below long rates. Finally, on a priori grounds, we should expect of any theory that some modifications will ultimately be necessary. Consequently, it seemed appropriate to devote the remainder of the study to a series of emendations of the basic expectational analysis. These introduced transactions costs, accounted for diverse expectations, and allowed for institutional maturity preferences on both sides of the market. In building up an amended model of the determination of the rate structure, it was necessary to go into the market place to observe some characteristics of investor practices which could be integrated into the model. The analysis culminated in a synthesis of the expectations and institutional theories of the term structure.

The first modification of the pure expectations model was the introduction of transactions costs. Two types of transactions costs were introduced; new-issue costs—once-and-for-all charges incurred by the borrower at the time of the initial offering—and trading costs, incurred each time an outstanding issue is traded. The latter were assumed to be divided equally between buyers and sellers and were represented by the spread between the bid and asked prices quoted by security dealers. New-issue costs were assumed to be large relative to trading costs. We treated cases both where trading costs were equal for each maturity and where these charges increased with maturity.

The major conclusion of this portion of the analysis was that, if the term over which funds are needed by bond issuers tends to be longer than the holding periods of bond investors, the yield curve will be positively sloped (when rates are expected to remain unchanged), with the effects of transactions costs being felt mainly in the very early maturities. It was maintained that such a lack of correspondence of holding periods would be typical if most firms required relatively permanent financing. We also found that the transactions costs incurred in issuing debt securities (new-issue costs) provide a rational explanation for the maturity sectoring of bond issuers over a wide range of interest-rate differentials.

The next step was to investigate empirically the extent to which the traditional expectations hypothesis must be modified to account for institutional maturity preferences and diversity of expectations. Chapter 6 utilized aggregate data on the ownership of government securities and the results of a series of interviews and a questionnaire survey of institutional portfolio managers and bond dealers. We found that an extreme form of the institutional (or hedging-pressure) theory of the term structure was inconsistent with the portfolio practices of bond investors. However, we did find that various market partici-pants do have maturity preferences. This was stressed repeatedly dur-ing the interviews. We, therefore, reinterpreted market segmentation to mean simply that many buyers and sellers must be paid differential premiums to induce them to move from their preferred maturities. We suggested that such maturity preferences differed both among and within classes of financial institutions.

A similar investigation was performed for bond issuers. While no evidence was found that (nongovernment) bond issuers were able to alter significantly the maturity distribution of their debt in the long run, we did find significant evidence that the *timing* of long-term bond issues is strongly influenced by expectations. When long-term issues were delayed, fund requirements were met by temporarily bor-rowing at short term. Moreover, we suggested that uniformity of ex-pectations is not characteristic of a world of uncertainty and presented empirical evidence that the bond market typically involves wide di-versity of opinion. Finally, we found that institutional impediments seriously restrict the volume of speculative transactions that can be carried out by professionals. Therefore, the activities of professional speculators cannot serve as an effective substitute for absence of risk aversion and uniformity of expectations on the part of bond investors.[1]

We then constructed a partial-equilibrium model to determine the effect on the rate structure of combining maturity preferences, limited supply flexibility, and diverse expectations. The principal finding was that a non-expectations-induced change in the maturity composition of the supply of debt instruments can affect the rate structure. This is so because, as the relative supply of a particular bond maturity

---

[1] We also pointed out that professional speculators as a group are unlikely to have even nearly identical expectations. Moreover, the evidence suggests that the most knowledgeable professionals in the market, the government-bond dealers, are also (Hicksian) risk averters to some degree.

is increased, less-willing purchasers must be induced to hold the additional quantities. But it should be emphasized that a model that accounts for these influences does not vitiate the importance of expectations. On the contrary, expectations still remained the foundation of an over-all theory of the determination of the rate structure.

Finally, it should be noted that in a three-market variant of this model we were able to account easily for the humps that are occasionally observed in empirical yield curves. In a situation where the yield curve would otherwise be flat, a non-expectations-induced increase in the supply of intermediate-term issues will produce a humped curve. This construction appears to offer a reasonable explanation of the humped yield curves in the government-securities market during 1959 and 1960, which accompanied a large increase in the absolute and relative supplies of intermediates.

8.3 *"Operation Twist"*

This study then reaffirms the importance of expectations in the determination of the term structure, although our formulation of the theory differs somewhat from the traditional model. Nevertheless, we disagree with both extreme views on the matter—the one that assigns uniquely to expectations the entire role of determining the rate structure, and the other that offers them no role at all. The over-all theory presented here is essentially a syncretic one and lies closest to that suggested by Conard. The major finding of the study in terms of direct relevance for policy formulation is that exogenous changes in the relative supplies of debt instruments of different maturities will influence the interest-rate structure of different maturities. Moreover, our theoretical and empirical findings on the microeconomic level suggest that the degree of sensitivity of the rate structure to relative supplies may be greater than many economists believe.[2] Such a conclusion brings us immediately to one of the most controversial aspects of monetary policy of the 1960's—"Operation Twist."

Before we discuss the relationship between this policy and the findings of our study, it will be useful to review briefly the economic background which led to the adoption of the policy. During the late 1950's the United States emerged as a reserve-currency country suffering from both chronic unemployment and a continuing deficit in its balance of payments. This compelled a major change in the role of monetary policy. It was argued that monetary expansion, while

---

[2] As we shall indicate in Section 8.5, most other studies have suggested that relative supplies play an insignificant role in influencing the term structure.

desirable from the point of view of the domestic economy, would be particularly deleterious for the balance of payments. Through its effect in increasing national income, monetary expansion would tend to worsen the balance on current account, and, through its effect in lowering interest rates, it would tend to worsen the balance on capital account as well. On the other hand, fiscal expansion (not accompanied by an increase in the money supply), while having the same harmful effect on the current account, would tend to have a favorable impact on the capital account, since rising income would tend to raise interest rates and thereby to attract capital inflows. This argument led to a demand for a "tight money-easy fiscal policy mix."

As a corollary to this policy recommendation, it was suggested that monetary restriction should be carried out in a way least harmful to the domestic economy. This would be accomplished if the monetary authorities could successfully manipulate the rate structure so as to raise short-term rates relative to long-term rates. The higher short-term rates could be expected to inhibit short-term capital outflows (and, perhaps, attract short-term capital inflows), while the lower long-term rates would tend to encourage domestic investment and promote economic recovery. Of course, it was recognized that higher short-term rates would tend to restrain domestic activity and that lower long-term rates would encourage the outflow of capital. Nevertheless proponents of the policy alleged that the quantitative magnitude of these effects was not sufficiently large to frustrate the desired objectives. This policy has been known in the United States first as "Operation Nudge" and then (in recognition of a now obsolescent dance craze) as "Operation Twist."[3] It was begun in February 1961, when the Federal Reserve announced that it would conduct its open-market operations in both short- and long-term securities, thereby ending a decade of open-market activities confined primarily to Treasury bills.[4]

[3] This policy was recommended to President Kennedy at the beginning of his administration in reports of "task forces" headed by Paul Samuelson and Allan Sproul. See "Nudging the Capital Markets," *Monthly Letter: First National City Bank* (March 1961), pp. 28–31.

[4] The previous policy was known as the "bills only" or "bills preferably" doctrine. Arguments in favor of restricting Federal Reserve open-market operations to the bill market may be found in Winfield W. Riefler, "Open Market Operations in Long-Term Securities," *Federal Reserve Bulletin* (November 1958), pp. 1260–1274; and Ralph A. Young and Charles A. Yager, "The Economics of 'Bills Preferably,'" *Quarterly Journal of Economics* 74 (August 1960), pp. 341–373. A critique of the policy is contained in Dudley G. Luckett "Bills Only: A Critical Appraisal," *Review of Economics and Statistics* 41 (August 1960), pp. 301–306; and James Schlesinger, "Monetary Policy and its Critics,"

One's immediate attitude toward such a policy would be much influenced by the theory of the term structure to which he subscribes. A strict expectational theorist would view such an attempt to "twist" the rate structure as essentially otiose. As we have mentioned repeatedly during our expositions of the expectations theory, the relative supply of debt instruments is irrelevant for the determination of the rate structure. Institutional theorists would be far more sanguine concerning the potential effectiveness of the policy, for relative supplies play a crucial role in their theory. Because our own analysis conforms with the view that relative supplies can affect the term structure, it may be interpreted as a logical justification of Operation Twist in spite of the importance we attach to the role of expectations.

Still, our discussion leaves unsettled a central question. Is it possible to obtain a quantitative estimate of the degree of responsiveness of relative interest rates to changes in relative supplies? It is essential to determine by how much the monetary authorities must alter the maturity composition of the debt in order to change the rate structure significantly. This requires recourse to a good deal more empirical work than has been undertaken in this study. In the following sections we shall turn our attention to some attempts which have been made to bring the relevant empirical evidence to bear upon the crucial question: What is the degree of responsiveness of the rate structure to exogenous changes in the relative supply of debt instruments?

8.4 The Obstacles to Empirical Testing of the Effects of Relative Supplies

Before discussing some specific attempts[5] to isolate, empirically, the effects on the term structure of changes in the relative supplies of

---

Journal of Political Economy 68 (December 1960), pp. 601–616. The argument for "bills only" stressed that by confining its open-market operations to the Treasury-bill market (where the number of customers and volume of trading is far greater than in the long-term market), the Federal Reserve could create *a minimal disturbance in the free market and yet foster its own "independence."* The essence of the argument against "bills only" was that the policy failed to promote the objective of a "broad, deep, and resilient" market and forced the monetary authorities to give up a potentially useful instrument of control.

[5] This section relies heavily on discussions by Okun, Wood, and Meiselman of the difficulties they encountered in their own empirical studies. It should be pointed out that these authors are well aware of the enormous obstacles involved in isolating empirically the effects of changes in the relative supply of debt instruments on the term structure. See Arthur M. Okun, "Monetary Policy, Debt Management, and Interest Rates: A Quantitative Appraisal," in *Stabilization Policies,* a series of research studies prepared for the Commission

debt instruments, we wish to call attention to some general problems that beset all these studies. It is only in the light of the severity of the obstacles besetting effective empirical testing that the current unsettled status of this question can be understood.

8.4.a INADEQUACY OF THE DATA ON NONGOVERNMENT DEBT

In the first place, the available data on nongovernment debt in the United States are extremely crude. A complete maturity breakdown of the total outstanding private debt is simply not available. At best we can divide private debt into two classes: that maturing within one year and that maturing in more than one year. Because changes in the maturity composition of the debt within these categories may be expected to have important implications for the shape of the yield curve, this presents a serious deficiency.

The problem is even more critical. Data available since 1937 on the maturity of the private debt are based on original rather than current maturity. Obviously, for investors, the current maturity is the relevant one. A bond may have been issued with an original maturity of 20 years but 19 years later it is a short-term, one-year obligation and will be so regarded by the market. In addition, no maturity breakdown is available at all for many categories of private debt during certain periods. Thus, the crudeness and the incompleteness of the data on private debt constitute a serious obstacle to empirical testing of the effect of relative supplies on the term structure. Since private debt is highly substitutable for government debt in many investment portfolios, the problem cannot simply be disregarded by utilizing maturity data on government securities alone.

Finally, even if the data on private debt were consistently and accurately assembled, problems of the appropriate level of consolidation of the private sector make the data exceedingly difficult to interpret. To illustrate the difficulty, consider the following example provided by Meiselman:[6] Assume that individuals can finance instalment purchases of automobiles by borrowing either from commercial banks or from sales-finance companies, which in turn borrow the funds from commercial banks. If individuals shift their instalment loans

---

on Money and Credit (Englewood Cliffs: Prentice-Hall, 1963), pp. 331–380; John Wood, "An Econometric Model of the Term Structure of Interest Rates," a paper presented to the December 1962 meetings of the Econometric Society and revised in March 1964; and David Meiselman, *The Term Structure of Interest Rates* (Englewood Cliffs: Prentice Hall, 1962), Chapter 3.

[6] Meiselman, *op. cit.*, p. 52. See also p. 51 and pp. 65–67 for a detailed discussion of this problem.

from banks to finance companies, total measured debt will rise, yet presumably there would be no effect on market interest rates.

8.4.b PROBLEMS OF CLASSIFYING THE MATURITIES OF GOVERNMENT DEBT

Fortunately, a full maturity breakdown of the Federal debt is available. Nevertheless, a host of obstacles confronts the empirical investigator who would use these data. First, it is not clear how the maturities of different debt instruments should be categorized. Ideally, one would want as fine a maturity breakdown of the Federal debt as possible. For example, one could in principle define maturity classes by months, that is, securities maturing within 1 month, between 1 and 2 months, . . . , between 180 and 181 months, and so forth. In addition to the impracticality of such a procedure, long-run series of interest rates by such detailed maturity classifications do not exist. Thus, one must compromise and settle for a simpler classification scheme.

Assume that the investigator chooses a tripartite taxonomy, classifying the Federal debt as short-term (maturing within one year), intermediate-term (maturing in from one to five years), and long-term (maturing in over five years). Several problems arise. First, he must question whether this particular maturity classification is preferable to all alternative classifications. The question is apposite since regression results in some cases have proved sensitive to the particular scheme selected. More serious is the difficulty that any classification gives rise to abrupt and misleading changes in outstandings in the various maturity categories whenever a large issue passes from one category to another. While investors may regard securities with 5 years to maturity as essentially equivalent to those maturing in 4 years and 11 months, as the former is transformed into the latter the supply variables used in the empirical analysis will show a large decrease in long-term securities and a corresponding increase in intermediate-term issues. On the other hand, investors may not regard securities with $5\frac{1}{2}$ years to run as equivalent to 35-year bonds, yet both are treated simply as long-term debt.

One way to ease this problem is to incorporate into the analysis an average-maturity variable for the marketable debt. The continuous process of maturation would be reflected in gradual changes in the average-maturity variable. Abrupt changes in the variable could only occur when new issues were sold or when the maturity of the debt was increased via an advance-refunding operation.

The use of an average-maturity variable has been shown to have serious defects, however. To illustrate the difficulties involved, consider the following two periods during which the average maturity of the debt remained unchanged:

	Year one		Year two	
	Amount ($ billions)	Maturity (years)	Amount ($ billions)	Maturity (years)
Maturity composition of the debt	10	1	10	2
	10	9	10	8
Total debt and average maturity	20	5	20	5

At the beginning of year two, $10 billion of maturing debt is refunded into 2-year bonds. The former 9-year bonds are now one year closer to maturity. The average-maturity variable tells us there has been no change in average length of the debt. But, while we have suggested earlier that 9- and 8-year bonds may be regarded by the market as very close substitutes, such is not the case for 1- and 2-year securities. In Chapter 3 we showed that the characteristic price fluctuations for the two securities were decidedly dissimilar. Moreover, in Chapter 5 we argued that, because of transactions costs, the term structure would be very sensitive to changes in the maturity composition of the shorter maturities but insensitive to changes in the longer maturities. Thus, the average-maturity variable may conceal crucial changes in the maturity composition of the debt which are fully capable of producing substantial alterations in the term structure.[7]

8.4.c DIFFICULTIES OF DEALING WITH CALL FEATURES

The existence of optional call features presents another perplexing problem to the empirical investigator. By market convention, the first call date is considered to be the maturity date whenever a bond is selling above par, and its yield (to maturity) is calculated on that basis. The argument for such a convention is that if a bond's nominal yield (C/F) is higher than going market yields, the issuer will always take advantage of any optional call feature and redeem the issue, refunding it with a lower-coupon security. Consequently, during a period when interest rates are low, investors expect that high-coupon securities will be refunded at the earliest possible date and make their investment plans accordingly. Of course, when a bond is selling below

[7] For a good discussion of the pitfalls involved in using conventional maturity measures of the public debt, see Dudley G. Luckett, "On Maturity Measures of the Public Debt," *Quarterly Journal of Economics* 68 (February 1964), pp. 148–157.

par, the final maturity date is considered to be the relevant maturity. Since this market convention reflects the way that investors consider securities with optional call features, it has much to recommend it.

Unfortunately, there are grounds at least as strong for rejecting the convention in empirical work dealing with the term structure. The convention makes the maturity of the debt depend on security prices. Since the point of the whole exercise is to untangle the relationship between relative supplies and relative security prices, utilization of this convention would bias the results. We would, in effect, be introducing a spurious correlation between supplies of the various maturities and security prices. Consequently, neither the adoption of the market convention for defining the effective maturity date nor the choice of the final maturity date as representing the term to maturity is a wholly satisfactory alternative.

8.4.d SIMULTANEOUS-EQUATIONS PROBLEMS

A more fundamental problem is raised when one tries to recognize that changes in the relative supplies of private and government securities are endogenous, not exogenous as has typically been assumed in the models tested. As we have pointed out several times during this study, the monetary authorities and private issuers are influenced by the structure of interest rates in determining what maturity of security to issue. Since the direction of causation works both ways, it is not appropriate to posit that changes in the relative supply of debt instruments cause changes in the relationship between short- and long-term interest rates. If we take relative interest rates as the dependent variable and relative supplies as the independent variable, the basic assumption of classical least-squares regression analysis (that is, that the disturbance terms are independent of the explanatory variables) is not satisfied. Since the supplies of debt instruments depend on a fairly complicated set of relationships—such as the kinds of equipment being financed, the state of the domestic economy as seen by the monetary authorities, who happens to be the Secretary of the Treasury, and so forth—it is not surprising that the specification of an identifiable supply equation has thus far proved elusive.

8.4.e SOME ADDITIONAL COMPLICATIONS

A proper test of the implications of the institutional theory of the rate structure must also incorporate variables representing the flows of funds to the various financial institutions that are presumed habitually to place their funds in different maturity sectors. Moreover, measures of changes in the composition of liabilities within each class of investing institution must be included. Presumably, these lead to changes in the desired maturity composition of the aggregate portfolio of that institutional class, especially since changes in the relative supply of debt instruments may be related to these flows of funds. Both governmental and private issuers continually try to estimate flows of funds to various financial institutions in order to tailor their issues to appeal to those classes of institutions enjoying fund inflows. Thus far, no empirical work has accounted for these considerations.

Finally, there is a problem involved in specifying the lag structure through which changes in the relative supplies of debt instruments may be supposed to affect the term structure. Some investigators have suggested that the term structure should be influenced immediately after any change in relative supplies. Alternatively, it has been argued that changes in the spread between short- and long-term interest rates should lag behind changes in the ratio of short- to long-term debt.

I would suggest that changes in the term structure might even lead changes in the relative supply of debt instruments. Securities markets frequently discount impending future supply changes long in advance. New corporate and municipal security offerings are registered months in advance of their respective issue dates. Even (regular) refundings of the U.S. Treasury can be anticipated well in advance of the actual refunding. Consequently, the market reaction to changes in the relative supplies of different maturities may be anticipated long in advance of the actual change in supply.

In view of these difficulties, and the arbitrary decisions that they necessitate, it is not surprising that the results of empirical studies of the effect of the maturity structure of the supplies of debt instruments have been contradictory. These studies do not engender much confidence in their results, and we must conclude that the degree of sensitivity of the term structure to changes in relative supplies is still largely an unsettled question.

8.5 *Empirical Tests of the Influence of Relative Supplies*

We turn next to a review of some specific attempts to isolate the effects of changes in the relative supply of debt instruments on the term structure.

8.5.a OKUN'S STUDY

Arthur Okun's study for the Commission on Money and Credit provides a useful point of departure.[8] Okun tried to measure the

[8] Arthur Okun, *op. cit.*

alternative effects of changes in the supply of long- and short-term government securities on long- and short-government yields. Using quarterly observations for the 1946–1959 period, he estimated the parameters of the following two-equation model:

$$_tR_S = b_0 + b_1S_S + b_2S_L + B_3X ,$$ (8-1)

and

$$_tR_L = \bar{c_0} + c_1S_S + c_2S_L + c_3A_L + C_4X ,$$ (8-2)

where S_S is the supply of short-term (defined as maturing in under five years) securities, S_L is the supply of long-term (maturing in over five years) securities, A_L is the average length to maturity (in months) of all securities maturing in over five years, and X is a vector of variables including income and the potential money supply. Table 8-1 presents Okun's regression results.

TABLE 8-1
OKUN'S REGRESSION RESULTS: EQUATIONS (8-1) AND (8-2)

Dependent variable	Coefficient of S_S	Coefficient of S_L	Coefficient of A_L	R
$_tR_S$	0.058 (0.007)	0.041 (0.007)		0.948
$_tR_L$	0.022 (0.004)	0.020 (0.003)	0.005 (0.002)	0.967

We note the coefficients of the supply and average-maturity variables are positive, as would be expected. Moreover, the short rate tends to rise more when new short-term securities are issued than when new long-term issues are sold. Surprisingly, however, the coefficient of S_S in equation (8-2) is larger than the coefficient of S_L, implying that an increase in the supply of short-term debt would raise the long rate by more than would an equal increase in long-term debt. The difference between the coefficients is insignificant, however, and, since the sale of long-term bonds would tend to raise the average-maturity variable on longs (which would tend to catch some of the influence of the sale in raising long rates), this implication cannot be taken seriously. Indeed, Okun concluded that a shift in the maturity composition of the debt would have little effect on the term structure. He estimated that a simultaneous retirement of $1 billion in bills and issue of $1 billion in 20-year bonds would increase the long-short spread by only about three basis points.[9]

[9] *Ibid.*, p. 361.

8.5.b SCOTT'S ADDITION OF AN AVERAGE-MATURITY VARIABLE FOR THE TOTAL DEBT

Robert Scott criticized Okun both for combining the within-1-year and 1-to-5-year maturity categories and for neglecting to include an average-maturity variable for the short-term debt.[10] Scott proceeded to estimate the equation

$$_tR_N = d_0 + d_1(S_S + S_L) + d_2A_T + D_3X^* , \qquad (8\text{-}3)$$

where A_T is the average maturity of the total marketable debt $(S_S + S_L)$ and X^* is a somewhat different vector of macroeconomic variables. Table 8-2 presents Scott's regression results using monthly data for the 1952–1959 period.[11]

TABLE 8-2
SCOTT'S REGRESSION RESULTS: EQUATION (8-3)

Dependent variable	Coefficient of $(S_S + S_L)$	Coefficient of A_T	R
$_tR_S$	0.018 (0.013)	−0.056 (0 012)	0.831
$_tR_L$	0.004 (0.001)	−0.021 (0.006)	0.859
$_tR_L - {}_tR_S$	−0.014 (0.009)	0.035 (0.009)	0.778

Scott noted that the average-maturity variable makes a significant contribution toward explaining variation in the short rate. An increase of the average maturity of the government debt by one month is associated with a 5.6-basis-point reduction in the short rate. He concluded, then, that relative supplies do have an important influence on the rate structure. In other respects, however, the results are disturbing. In particular, a lengthening of the debt is also associated with a *decrease* in the long rate, and consequently the long-short spread is increased by less than the decrease in the short rate (see Table 8-2). Moreover, since Scott utilized a different set of data and a somewhat different set of other variables, this work does not really test which of the two models yields better predictions.

[10] Robert Haney Scott, "Liquidity and the Term Structure of Interest Rates," *Quarterly Journal of Economics* 79 (February 1965), pp. 135–145.
[11] Durbin-Watson statistics were not reported.

8.5.c WOOD'S SIMULTANEOUS-EQUATION MODEL

John Wood[12] took us a step forward in the sophistication of his tests by constructing a simultaneous-equation model aimed at isolating the effects of relative supplies on the term structure. Unfortunately, however, the quantities of government securities supplied to the public were still treated as exogenous and, therefore, independent of relative interest rates. Wood posited that the differentials between interest rates of various maturities depend upon (1) variables related to expectations of future interest-rate changes and (2) quantities of securities of the different terms to maturity.

Wood found, in a first-difference version of the model, that expectations variables do much better in explaining relative interest rates than do security supplies. Most of the coefficients of security-supply variables were not significantly different from zero, although those that were significant were generally consistent with a view that risk aversion does play a role in determining the rate structure. Of the expectations variables introduced, a weighted average of recent changes in the rate on three-month Treasury bills turned out to be the most significant. Wood concluded that "security supplies, at least of the type used in the present model, contribute very little to an explanation of ratios of interest rates on groups of securities of differing maturities when the variables are transformed in such a way as to eliminate autocorrelation in the residuals."[13]

8.5.d WALLACE'S MODEL

Perhaps the most interesting approach to testing the influence of supply variables on the rate structure has been taken by Neil Wallace.[14] Wallace broke down each long-term loan (bond) into its component short-period parts. A loan commencing now, to be repaid in one year, was taken to be a short-period bond. A 10-year bond was then considered to be made up of 10 one-year bonds: a one-year loan commencing now in period t, a one-year loan commencing next year in period $t + 1$, . . . , and a one-year loan commencing in period $t + 9$. Thus, all bonds that mature in over one year were translated into one-period loans, all bonds maturing in over two years were interpreted in part, as a supply of one-period loans during period

[12] John Wood, *op. cit.*
[13] *Ibid.*
[14] Neil Wallace, "The Term Structure of Interest Rates and the Maturity Composition of the Federal Debt," PhD dissertation, University of Chicago, 1964, Chapter 3.

$t + 1$, and so forth. Note how this breakdown copes with the passage-of-time problem.

Wallace then hypothesized that if relative supplies influence the rate structure, an exogenous increase in the quantity of one-period forward loans beginning at time $t + j$ should affect (only) the forward rate $_{t+j}r_1$. Wallace contended that this is a plausible hypothesis since "one-period forward loans to commence at one date are neither substitutes nor complements of one-period forward loans to commence at another date."[15] The quantitative effect of changes in the maturity composition of the Federal debt on the term structure of government rates is investigated by the following specific hypothesis:

$$\ln\left[\frac{1 + _{t+j}r_1}{1 + _tR_1}\right] = b_{0j} + b_{1j}\left[\frac{_tM_{j+1}}{_tM_1}\right] + b_{2j} \text{ dum }, \qquad (8\text{-}4)$$

where $_tM_{j+1}$ consists of all Treasury bonds that mature on or after time $t+j+1$, that is, that include a loan at the forward rate $_{t+j}r_1$. Quarterly observations from 1946 through 1962 were used in the regression. The dummy variable takes the value unity for observations

TABLE 8-3
WALLACE'S REGRESSION RESULTS: EQUATION (8-4)

	i	$\hat{b}_1$	R	d
Raw data	1	0.011 (0.004)	0.45	1.00
Transformed data ($\hat{\rho} = 0.50$)	1	0.010 (0.005)	0.28	1.89
Raw data	2	0.010 (0.005)	0.30	0.82
Transformed data ($\hat{\rho} = 0.59$)	2	0.008 (0.006)	0.17	1.97
Raw data	3	0.010 (0.005)	0.25	0.68
Transformed data ($\hat{\rho} = 0.66$)	3	0.010 (0.007)	0.20	2.00
Raw data	4	0.017 (0.005)	0.39	0.62
Transformed data ($\hat{\rho} = 0.69$)	4	0.023 (0.007)	0.39	1.93

[15] Ibid., pp. 29–30.

from March 1946 through March 1951, and zero for all other observations in the post-Accord period. The dependent variable is approximately equal to the difference between the forward rate $_{t+j}r_1$ and the spot rate $_tR_1$.[16] Table 8-3 presents Wallace's regression results.

Wallace found, at least for near-term forward rates, that an increase in the quantity of loans contracted at a given forward rate tends to increase that rate. This is consistent with a view that investors must be given an interest-rate inducement to lengthen the maturity of their holdings. The relationship is weak, however, particularly after a data transformation to cope with serial correlation, and the quantitative results suggest that substantial changes in the maturity structure of the debt supplied may have only very small effects on the term structure of interest rates.

8.5.e RECAPITULATION

We must conclude that the studies reviewed in the preceding sections indicate that the term structure is relatively insensitive to changes in the relative supply of debt instruments. Nevertheless, these results do not inspire much confidence. We mentioned that all empirical studies of the effects of relative supplies labor under severe obstacles. Perhaps the critical road blocks impeding further progress are the unavailability of sufficiently refined data for private debt and the difficulties of specifying an identifiable supply equation for the different maturities, particularly for the Federal government.

In connection with the latter obstacle, the following analogy attributed by Arthur Okun to Henry Wallich illustrates the complexities involved:

> The monetary authorities have consistently viewed the bond market as thin ice and they have therefore skated with great care. According to the data [Okun's], they have never fallen through the ice. Yet, it cannot be justifiably concluded that the ice is solid and the caution gratuitous.[17]

One reason for the finding that changes in the supply of debt instruments do not seem to have had large effects on the rate structure may be that there have been only very moderate changes in relative supplies. Moreover, those changes that have occurred may well have been geared to the authorities' judgment of what offerings the market would take at the time without significant changes in interest rates.

[16] For small $_{t+j}r_1$, $\ln (1 + _{t+j}r_1)$ is approximately equal to $_{t+j}r_1$.

[17] Okun, *op. cit.*, p. 350.

If it is true that one of the guiding principles of debt management in the postwar period has been not to "rock the boat," the test results reported may do nothing more than confirm that the authorities have adhered successfully to that principle. The results do not necessarily indicate that truly exogenous changes in relative supplies would have insignificant effects on relative interest rates.

During one recent period when the hands of the monetary authorities were tied because of the $4\frac{1}{4}$ per cent interest-rate ceiling, the slope of the yield curve did seem to be significantly altered by debt-management policy. During 1959 and 1960, the authorities were prevented from issuing any new long-term bonds and, therefore, had to concentrate their offerings in the 4-to-5-year maturity range to prevent a rapid and undesired shortening of the average maturity of the debt. The accompanying hump in the 4-to-5-year range of the yield curve seems to bear witness that exogenous changes in the maturity composition of the debt can have substantial effects on the rate structure.[18] Thus, in the infrequent cases where the monetary authorities were forced to "rock the boat," apparent effects on the yield curve were manifest. As we mentioned earlier, the pure expectations theory can offer only a very clumsy explanation for humps in the intermediate maturities. Of course, I am not suggesting that this one illustration be taken as proof that the importance of relative supplies has been underestimated. I would only caution against hasty conclusion from the available empirical evidence that the effects are negligible.

8.6 *The Effectiveness of Operation Twist*

The empirical work reported in the previous section would indicate that attempts by the monetary authorities significantly to twist the rate structure are likely to be frustrated. In this section we shall review the actual experience with Operation Twist and try to measure the effectiveness of the policy.

8.6.a WAS OPERATION TWIST EFFECTIVELY IMPLEMENTED?

The first difficulty to be surmounted in ascertaining whether Operation Twist was effective in altering the rate structure is that involved in measuring the extent to which the policy was actually carried out.

[18] The increase from mid-1958 to mid-1960 in the supply of bonds with maturities between three and five years (the location of the hump) was one of the most significant postwar changes in the maturity composition of the Federal debt. Incidentally, we should note that, in most of the studies reported above, the maturity categories are too crude to permit the identification of humps.

Many have questioned whether, in fact, the policy was ever given more than lip service. An examination of Table 8-4 reveals some of the reasons for this skepticism. We note that the net purchases by the Federal Reserve of securities maturing in over five years have been extremely small.[19]

The Federal Reserve has been extremely reluctant to pursue vigorously a policy designed to twist the rate structure. This reluctance can be understood only against the background of recent monetary history. It must be remembered that the "bills only" doctrine was conceived out of a complete revulsion for the postwar period of market pegging.[20] The Federal Reserve has ever since displayed a lively horror of allowing itself to be shackled again to a program of pegged security prices. Reserve officials have repeatedly stressed the necessity of creating an atmosphere where private buyers would develop an orderly market, characterized by the now-famous trinity, "breadth, depth, and resiliency." Thus, the reentry of the Federal Reserve into the long-term market was inhibited by a degree of schizophrenia. The Federal Reserve desired to reshape the yield curve, but to do so in a manner whereby it exerted no direct influence on bond prices. This conflict was resolved in favor of the very limited activity reported in Table 8-4.

While the Federal Reserve was pursuing Operation Twist with the caution of a nun undertaking the study of comparative theology, the Treasury was vigorously following a policy of advance refunding. From the beginning of 1961 to the end of 1962, the total amount

[19] It is not an easy matter to ascertain the precise magnitude of Federal Reserve purchases in the long-term maturity range of the market. This is so because the maturity summaries published on the Federal Reserve's open-market purchases do not distinguish between open-market purchases and transactions undertaken directly with the Treasury. Such direct transactions are made both for the System account and for the Trust Funds, and the published data do not break the figures down. Thus, the extent of the market activity of the Federal Reserve is even smaller than our data indicate.

A method for disentangling the System market activity can, however, be devised. Since the year-end balance sheets of the Trust Funds and the Federal Reserve give detailed breakdowns by issues held, it is possible to reconstruct the System's open-market purchases of longer-term securities. Sidney Homer has performed this calculation for the years 1961 and 1962 and finds that, for its own account, the Federal Reserve made net purchases totaling only $793 million in securities whose maturity exceeded five years. This compares with a total of $1,150 million reported by the Federal Reserve and reproduced in Table 8-4. See Sidney Homer, "Open Market Purchases of Longer Term Government Bonds by the Federal Reserve Banks and the U.S. Trust Funds," mimeographed, June 14, 1963.

[20] See Lester V. Chandler, *The Economics of Money and Banking* (New York: Harper & Brothers, 3rd. ed., 1959), pp. 438–442.

of securities outstanding in public hands whose maturity exceeded five years increased by $7,985 million (see Table 8-5). In the next two-year period an additional $4,692 million of new long-term debt was issued. Beside such a significant increase in the supply of long-term issues, the Federal Reserve's activity would appear nugatory. Such

TABLE 8-4

MATURITY DISTRIBUTION OF NET OUTRIGHT PURCHASES* FOR THE
OPEN MARKET ACCOUNT OF THE FEDERAL RESERVE SYSTEM
(Amounts in millions of dollars)

Securities maturing	1961		1962		1963		1964	
	Amt.	Per cent	Amt.	Per cent	Amt.	Per cent	Amt.	Per cent
Within 1 year	−876	−50.4	−68	−3.9	1701	54.8	1906	65.1
Within 1 to 5 years	1826	105.1	1461	83.3	794	25.6	467	16.0
After 5 years	788	45.3	362	20.6	609	19.6	553	18.9
Total net purchases	1738	100.0	1755	100.0	3104	100.0	2926	100.0

Source: *Federal Reserve Bulletins* 1962–1965.

* Net outright purchases are defined as total securities purchased in the open market less sales and redemptions.

a comparison must have been behind a statement by Harry Johnson concerning Operation Twist.

> Whatever might have been expected of this policy . . . it was not in fact pursued in any effective sense. As a result, primarily of Treasury funding operations, the maturity of the debt in public hands has in fact been lengthened appreciably, instead of shortened as the policy would require.[21]

Such a conclusion should be modified in at least one respect, however, as a closer look at Table 8-5 indicates. We note that, during the first two-year period, while the supply of long-term bonds increased, the supply of issues with a maturity under six months increased by an even greater amount, $11,599 million. Consequently, while the average maturity of the debt increased over the period, this was accompanied by a substantial increase in the total of very-short-term issues outstanding. In Chapter 5 we noted that the only

[21] Harry G. Johnson, "An Overview of Price Levels, Employment, and the U.S. Balance of Payments," *Journal of Business* 36 (July 1963), p. 286.

TABLE 8-5

MATURITY DISTRIBUTION OF OUTSTANDING GOVERNMENT DEBT AND MARKET INTEREST RATES

Maturity	December 31, 1960			December 31, 1962			December 31, 1964		
	Amount[a]	Per cent	Market interest rates[b]	Amount[a]	Per cent	Market interest rates[b]	Amount[a]	Per cent	Market interest rates[b]
Within 6 mos.	$ 41,030	26.73	2.29%	$ 52,629	32.38	2.87	$ 50,767	31.11	3.76%
6 to 12 mos.	17,580	11.45	2.71	15,324	9.43	2.96	14,565	8.92	3.91
1 to 5 year,	57,670	37.57	3.57	49,380	30.38	3.46	48,021	29.41	4.06
Over 5 years	37,235	24.26	3.90	45,220	27.82	3.87	49,912	30.57	4.13
Total	$153,514	100.00		$162,553	100.00		$163,264	100.00	

Maturity	Changes from Dec. 1960 to Dec. 1962		Changes from Dec. 1962 to Dec. 1964	
	Amount of debt	Market interest rates	Amount of debt	Market interest rates
Within 6 mos.	+$11,599	+.58%	−$1,862	+0.89%
6 to 12 mos.	− 2,256	+.25	− 759	+0.95
1 to 5 years	− 8,290	−.11	− 1,359	+0.60
Over 5 years	+ 7,985	−.03	+ 4,692	+0.26
Total	+$ 9,039		+$ 712	

Source: *Treasury and Federal Reserve Bulletins*, 1961–1965.

[a] Amounts are in millions of dollars and exclude those bonds held in government accounts or by the Federal Reserve Banks. Figures may not add because of rounding.

[b] Averages of 3 months centered on Dec. The within-6-months rate is taken to be the 3-months bill rate (market yield). The 6- to 12-months rate is taken to be the yield on 9- to 12-month issues. The 1- to 5-year rate is the rate on 3- to 5-year issues. The over 5-year rate is the average rate on bonds maturing in over 10 years.

large equilibrium rate differentials ascribable to transactions costs are those necessary to induce investors with very short holding periods to buy longer issues. That is to say, if investors with a 5-year holding period have to be induced to buy 40-year issues (by virtue of a Treasury debt-management operation which replaces 5-year with 40-year bonds), the yield differential which must be offered them is insignificant (see Column 6, Table 5-3). If, however, some 30-day investors have to be induced to hold a 1-year bond, the yield differential which must be offered is considerable (see Column 1, Table 5-3).

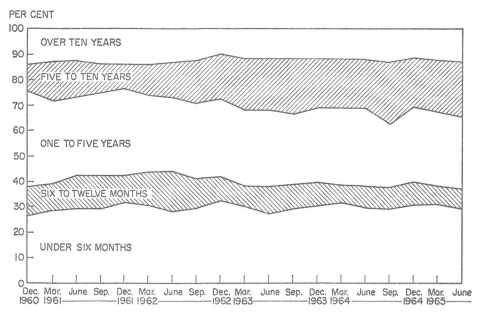

FIG. 8-1. Maturity distribution of outstanding government bonds. (Excluding securities held in government accounts or by the Federal Reserve Banks.)

Hence, it follows (from the effect of transactions costs alone) that the increase in the supply of short issues might be expected to have a far greater effect on the term structure than the increase in long maturities outstanding.

Thus, at least during the first two-year period, the over-all pattern of Treasury financing operations was not at cross purposes with Operation Twist. On the contrary, the Treasury successfully managed to lengthen the average maturity of the debt while still increasing the relative supply of very-short-term securities. During the second two-year period, however, the pattern of changes in the relative supplies of bonds was clearly perverse (Table 8-5). Perhaps a clearer picture of the over-all change in the maturity distribution of outstanding government bonds may be obtained from Figure 8-1, which depicts the maturity composition of the debt from December 1960 to June 1965. It is clear that the only persistent and significant change over the period was the increase in the relative supply of bonds maturing in over five years. We must conclude that, despite some increase in the relative supply of very-short-term issues, for the period as a whole the combined effect of Treasury and Federal Reserve policy on the maturity composition of the debt was not consistent with the objectives of Operation Twist.

8.6.b THE BEHAVIOR OF THE RATE STRUCTURE, 1961–1964

We turn now to an examination of the behavior of the rate structure in the four years since the abandonment of "bills only." The starting point for such an examination has typically been a direct look at the changes in long and short yields over the period. We note in Table 8-5 that from December 31, 1960, to December 31, 1964, bill yields rose 147 basis points while bond yields rose only 23 basis points. It would appear, therefore, that the monetary authorities were successful in engineering a substantial increase in short rates while restraining the rise in long rates. Perhaps a more striking comparison can be made for the first two-year period, to December 31, 1962. We find that there was a considerable alteration in the term structure of interest rates. Short rates rose at the same time that intermediate rates fell, while long rates remained at approximately the same level. Moreover, these yield changes appear to be broadly consistent with the changes that occurred in the maturity composition of the outstanding debt. We have noted that, during the first two-year period, the combined effects of Federal Reserve and Treasury policy should have put short rates under relatively greater upward pressure, particularly as compared with intermediate rates.

Unfortunately, such naïve comparisons between yield curves at two widely separated points in time can be quite misleading. To illustrate this point we might note that during October 1959 the market yield on three-month bills was 4.05 per cent while the yield on long-term bonds was 4.11 per cent. If we now compare these data with the yields for December 1964, we might be tempted to conclude that the policy was a total failure. From October 1960 to December 1964, short yields fell 29 basis points while long-term yields fell only 2 basis points. The point is that short-term yields always rise more than long-term rates when yields are rising and fall more when rates are falling. The crucially important question is how the rates on bonds of different maturities would have behaved in the absence of Operation Twist. We cannot hope to answer this question without an understanding, supported by empirical evidence, of the determinants shaping the yield curve.[22]

8.6.c THE MODIGLIANI AND SUTCH TEST OF THE EFFECTIVENESS OF TWIST

We have seen that naïve comparisons of the interest-rate structure at two different time periods are inadmissible. The *cetera* are simply not *paria* and no heroic assumption can make them so. The task of assessing the success of Operation Twist is much more difficult, requiring the use of a theoretically grounded and empirically tested model. An attempt to provide such a test has been undertaken by Franco Modigliani and Richard Sutch.[23]

The theoretical underpinnings of the work of Modigliani and Sutch (hereafter M & S) consist of an eclectic theory of the term structure containing many of the elements included in the preceding chapter. The empirical form of the test utilizes an estimating equation similar to (4-8), with the addition of variables measuring the relative supply of debt instruments in different maturity categories. Regarding the expectational elements in the specification employed by M & S, two changes distinguish their approach from the one we used in Chapter 4. First, M & S used a much shorter period of market history and a different weighting procedure to form the average of past rates. Secondly, they employed current and past values of the short rather than the long rate on the right-hand side of the estimating equation.

It will be helpful first to present briefly the M & S method of estimating the lag structure of past rates, since it rests, in part, on theoretical and statistical considerations we have not discussed previously. The imaginative work of Frank de Leeuw provided the motivation for the basic approach employed.[24] In specifying an expectations

---

[22] This point has also been stressed by Modigliani and Sutch, whose work is discussed in the next section. See Franco Modigliani and Richard Sutch, "Innovations in Interest Rate Policy," a paper presented at the 78th annual Meeting of the American Economic Association, December 30, 1965.

[23] Modigliani and Sutch, *op. cit.*

[24] Frank de Leeuw, "A Model of Financial Behavior," Chapter 13 in J. Duesenberry, G. Fromm, L. Klein, E. Kuh, eds. *Brookings Quarterly Econometric Model of the United States Economy* (Chicago: Rand McNally; Amsterdam: North Holland Publishing, 1965), pp. 465–530.

mechanism, de Leeuw considered two hypotheses: The first is what we have called the "normal-range" hypothesis. It asserts that the market expects future interest rates to tend toward a "normal level" of rates that can be estimated on the basis of past experience. The second, offered by James Duesenberry, suggests instead that an increase in rates may lead the market to expect a further rise.[25] The first hypothesis implies that the spread between long and short rates $(L - S)$ should be negatively related to the difference between the long rate and the average of past long rates $(L - L_A)$. It also suggests that the values of λ (the weighting factor in forming the average of past rates) ought to be close to unity, since rates in the more distant past should have substantial weight in determining the normal level. We found support in Chapter 4 for both of these implications. On the other hand, the Duesenberry hypothesis suggests, first, that λ should be small (since nearby rates should be weighted most heavily and distant rates should not significantly influence the average) and, secondly, that the coefficient of the difference between the current and past average of long rates thus formed should be positive (since rates would be expected to continue moving in the same direction).

De Leeuw commingled the two hypotheses. Both the normal-level variable $(L - L_A$, high $\lambda)$ and the Duesenberry expectations variable $(L - L_A$, low $\lambda)$ were used as explanatory variables of the long-short spread. Employing a systematic searching to select the most satisfactory values of both λ's, he found that the coefficients of the two expectational variables had the proper sign and were statistically significant.

M & S accepted de Leeuw's basic formulation of the problem, but they combined both expectational elements into a single lag structure. Since de Leeuw's formulation suggested that the lag distribution should rise to a single peak and then fall, they concluded that a fourth-degree polynomial could satisfactorily reproduce the true structure. The method employed to estimate the lag structure was one developed by Shirley Almon.[26] Lags of three to six years were tested, and the best results were obtained for a lag of around four years.

M & S's empirical work differs from that reported in Chapter 4 in yet another respect. A weighted sum of short rates was used on the right-hand side of the estimating equation. Thus, investors are hypothesized to form their expectations of future interest rates

[25] James Duesenberry, *Business Cycles and Economic Growth* (New York: McGraw-Hill, 1958), p. 318.
[26] Shirley Almon, "The Distributed Lag between Capital Appropriations and Expenditures," *Econometrica* 33 (January 1965), pp. 78–96.

on the basis of past values of the short rather than long rates. The equation finally estimated by M & S, omitting the relative supply variables, is shown below.[17]

$$L-S = a_1 + a_2 S + a_3 S_A \qquad (8\text{-}5)$$
$$= 1.239 - 0.684S + 0.679S_A \qquad R = 0.987$$
$$(0.028) \quad (0.030) \quad (0.039)$$

The results obtained by M & S have important implications for our study of the term structure, in general, and for a proper appraisal of the success of Operation Twist, in particular. In the first place, we see that the authors have been extremely successful in explaining interest-rate differentials in the government-securities market over two decades. Their work substantially extends de Leeuw's original results and confirms that, while important, the normal-range hypothesis is not the only factor explaining the generation of expectations. Secondly, the authors found that the addition to equation (8-5) of variables measuring the change in the relative supply of short- and intermediate-term debt did not improve the results. M & S concluded that " . . . *the change in short or the intermediate debt appears to have no significant detectable influence on the spread*" [italics theirs].[28] This result confirms those summarized earlier in the Chapter. In view of the enormous difficulties in isolating the effects of supply changes, discussed in Section 8.4, such a finding is not surprising.

Perhaps the most important implication of the work of M & S lies in the use of their empirical estimates to judge the effectiveness of Operation Twist. The authors used the parameter estimates of equation (8-5) to extrapolate predictions for the long-short spread from 1962 through the third quarter of 1965. Comparing the actual spread with the value obtained by extrapolation, they found little evidence that Twist had a significant effect on the rate structure, at least until mid-1964. "With but a couple of exceptions, the error is within ten [basis] points or less than the standard error; beginning with the second quarter of 1962, however, the spread is consistently smaller than the computed value and, beginning with 1964-IV, the difference becomes impressive, four to six times the standard error. Thus, the best that could be said on the basis of . . . [8-5] is that the twist policy was slightly to moderately successful."[29]

---

[27] Data from the first quarter of 1942 to the fourth quarter of 1961 were used.
[28] Modigliani and Sutch, *op. cit.,* p. 41.
[29] *Ibid.*

8.6.d THE RESULTS OF SOME ALTERNATIVE SPECIFICATIONS
OF THE EXPECTATIONS-FORMING MECHANISM

While the empirical work of M & S makes a convincing case that
Operation Twist had only a very limited effect, we should be careful
not to conclude that any attempts deliberately to alter the term structure must necessarily fail. In the first place, as we remarked above,
the policy was not vigorously pursued—indeed, it was hardly carried
out at all. Secondly, there exist alternative empirical tests that suggest
that the commitment of the monetary authorities to Twist may have
had somewhat more influence on the expectations-forming mechanism
than M & S found. Several alternative and equally legitimate specifications of the expectations hypothesis can be found which fit the
data reasonably well during the pre-Twist period. With their specification, M & S can also explain the post-Twist observations and thus
they conclude that the effect of Twist was insignificant. With other
specifications, however, it can be shown that the underlying structure
generating the observations has changed in the post-Twist period and
that relative interest rates have been altered significantly. Since both
types of specifications can explain the pre-Twist data, and since there
seem to be no compelling reasons to choose among the models on
a priori grounds, it is difficult to feel comfortable that we have obtained a decisive answer to the policy question at hand.

We shall illustrate this point with two examples: One is taken
from the work of Neil Wallace[30] and the other utilizes the empirical
tests developed in Chapter 4. Using quarterly postwar data on government yields from 1946 through 1962, Wallace first developed parameter estimates for Meiselman's error-learning equation (2-14a) and
for (2-14a) supplemented by an additional term measuring the effect
of changes in the maturity composition of the Federal debt. He then
used these parameter estimates (together with 1963 data on one-year
spot rates and on the maturity composition of the debt) to predict the
rates on four-year government bonds during 1963. The predictions
reveal that the monetary authorities have been far more successful
in twisting the rate structure than would have been predicted by
the regression results. When the rising short-term rates of 1963 were
used to generate predictions of the four-year rate, Wallace found that
the four-year rate was consistently overestimated.[31] For example, the

---

[30] Neil Wallace, *op. cit.*, pp. 45–47.
[31] When Wallace estimated the four-year rate with the parameter estimates
of the equation combining the Meiselman error-term and an additional term

difference between the four-year and one-year rate in September 1963 was 27 basis points. The regression results predict a difference of about 59 basis points. Wallace's results suggest that the monetary authorities have been more successful in twisting the rate structure than is indicated by the M & S tests.

An extension of the empirical work reported in Chapter 4 also supports the possibility of deliberate alteration of the rate structure. There we tested our own variant of the expectations theory by assuming that the slope of the yield curve would be determined by the relationship between the current level of (long) rates and bounds of the normal range (as determined by the past history of interest-rate fluctuations). Table 4-3 reported the results of these tests using data from the government-securities market in the post-Accord period. We pointed out that one factor which militated against the usefulness of our work was that the change in monetary policy from "bills only" to Operation Twist may have altered the expectations-forming mechanism. Such a change could have interfered with our attempt to isolate a stable relationship through time. The question whether, in fact, this was the case can be easily formulated as a testable hypothesis.

There exists a standard test, developed by G. C. Chow, to determine whether a relationship remains stable during two consecutive time periods.[32] The hypothesis that the same model generated the observations in both time periods may be tested by calculating the F-ratio,

$$F = \frac{Q_3/k}{Q_2(m+n-2k)} \, , \qquad (8\text{-}6)$$

with $(k, m+n-2k)$ degrees of freedom. In (8-6) k is the number of coefficients to be estimated, Q_2 is the sum of the squared residuals from the least-squares estimate of the coefficients based on the first n observations plus the sum of the squared residuals from the least-squares estimate of the coefficients from the second m observations, and $Q_3 = Q_1 - Q_2$, were Q_1 is the sum of the squared residuals from the fitted function to all $n+m$ observations. Applying the test

---

measuring changes in the maturity composition of the government debt, the predictions overestimated the four-year rate by slightly more than those obtained from the simple Meiselman error-learning equation. This is not surprising since there was a relative increase in the supply of intermediate- and long-term issues during this period; that is, the supply changes were perverse.

[32] See Gregory C. Chow, "Tests of Equality between Sets of Coefficients in Two Linear Regressions," *Econometrica* 28 (July 1960), pp. 591–605. An excellent description of the test procedure may be found in J. Johnston, *Econometric Methods* (New York: McGraw-Hill, 1963), pp. 137–138.

to the sub-periods, January 1957–January 1961 (pre-Twist), and April 1961 to April 1965 (post-Twist),[33] we find in Table 8-6 that we should reject the hypothesis that the post-Twist observations were generated by the same structure as the first set.[34]

TABLE 8-6

CHOW TEST TO DETERMINE WHETHER INTEREST-RATE RELATIONSHIPS IN THE
GOVERNMENT-SECURITIES MARKET REMAINED STABLE AFTER
THE INTRODUCTION OF OPERATION TWIST

| Sub-periods | Weights for in calcu- lating mov- ing avg. (λ) | Computed F | Critical F Significance level (per cent) | |
			1	5
I/1957–I/1961	1	11.41	4.54	2.93
II/1961–II/1965	0.95	7.90		

We see that the particular specification of the expectations hypothesis chosen has an important bearing on our estimates of the extent to which the interest-rate structure has been altered. But, while there is disagreement on the extent of the quantitative effect of the Twist, the qualitative results of the three tests reported are the same. They all indicate that short rates have risen relative to long rates. This in itself requires some explanation. Since we have seen that the actual changes in the relative supply of bonds of different maturities were not consistently in the direction called for by the policy, one wonders why the rate structure should have been affected at all. In the final section we shall address ourselves to this question.

8.7 Factors Responsible for Altering the Term Structure

In this section we advance the hypothesis that whatever alteration in the interest-rate structure occurred after the introduction of Opera-

---

[33] Our test may be criticized on the grounds that only four years of observations are included in estimating the pre-Twist relationship. As was emphasized in Chapter 4, we did not want to include interest-rate observations during the period before the Treasury-Federal Reserve Accord in forming the average of past rates. We felt it was not reasonable to assume that investors formed their ideas of a normal level of rates from observations taken from the pegging period.

[34] We must warn the reader that, while these results are highly suggestive, we cannot really make any probabilistic statement about the hypothesized structural change. This is so because, as we indicated in Chapter 4, Durbin-Watson statistics show that the residuals from the least-squares regressions are highly autocorrelated.

tion Twist can be explained largely by two factors unrelated to the actual changes in the relative supply of the different maturities of Federal debt outstanding. The first factor is the concomitant development of the negotiable certificate of deposit and the manipulation of the ceiling interest rates imposed under Regulation Q. The second is the influence of the announced policy objectives of the monetary authorities on the formation of expectations.

8.7.a NEGOTIABLE CERTIFICATES OF DEPOSIT AND
BANK-PORTFOLIO MANAGEMENT

As we mentioned earlier, an important objective of the monetary authorities during the 1960's was the retention of foreign funds in the United States in order to mitigate the hemorrhage of U.S. gold reserves. In support of this objective, Regulation Q ceiling rates on time deposits were raised several times, beginning in January 1962. These successive increases in permissible rates of interest stimulated a spectacular growth in one particular form of deposit, the negotiable certificate of deposit (hereafter referred to as the CD). Introduced in 1961, $16 billion of CD's were outstanding by the end of 1965. This important financial innovation and the removal of restrictive ceiling rates on time deposits had a significant influence on bank-portfolio management and, therefore, on the interest-rate structure.

Easing of restrictions on the rate commercial banks could pay to attract time deposits made the banking system better able to fulfil its intermediary function of arbitraging the usual spread between short-term interest rates and expected holding-period returns from long-term securities. Banks were able to attract large quantities of corporate funds that otherwise might have been invested in Treasury bills. The banks in turn invested such funds in longer-term issues and thus contributed to closing the long-short spread. The availability of a new instrument that could be used to attract short-term funds also had an important effect in altering the accustomed "liquidity ratios" that had been considered a sign of prudent bank-portfolio management.

Before the development of the CD, banks relied on a secondary reserve of short-term liquid assets (typically Treasury bills) to meet any sudden increase in loan demand or any large deposit withdrawal. After commercial banks began issuing CD's, however, they felt that there was less need for a secondary (or so-called liquidity) reserve of short-term liquid assets. Instead, these bankers relied more heavily on the creation of new liabilities than on the sale of short-term government bonds as a source of funds. Thus, the development of the CD has supported a lengthening of the maturity of bank assets. Especially noteworthy has been the increase in the granting of term loans and the substantial increase in the holdings of intermediate-term tax-exempt securities. Thus, perhaps the most noticeable effect of the CD and increases in Regulation Q ceilings has been the reduction in the spread between the yields of Federal government and tax-exempt bonds that occurred during the 1962–1965 period.

8.7.b OPERATION TWIST AND THE FORMATION OF EXPECTATIONS

Thus far, we have neglected an additional and very important route by which actions of the monetary authorities may alter the term structure. It may well be that the Federal Reserve's very commitment to the idea of Twist may itself influence the formation of expectations.[35] The actual presence in the market of a buyer with essentially unlimited resources, and an announced willingness to employ them in pursuit of a specific objective, is likely to exert a psychological impact which can be far more important than the actual number of dollars committed. In this section, we shall present some additional evidence which suggests that, in fact, the activities of the Federal Reserve have had considerable effect on the formation of expectations.

One direct method of investigating whether the monetary authorities have influenced the views of market participants is to ask them. During the course of the interviews described in Chapter 6, I asked each portfolio manager the extent to which his interest-rate expectations had been altered by Operation Twist. Of 48 individuals contacted, 40 reported that the abandonment of "bills only" made an important difference in their views concerning the likely future course of events in the government-securities market; 4 reported that the change in policy had no effect on their expectations; and the remaining 4 could not give an unambiguous answer to the question.

The 40 portfolio managers whose expectations were altered were then asked specifically how the policy change related to Operation Twist. The answers indicated to me that the influence of the monetary authorities on expectations is most clearly perceived in terms of their effect in shaping investors' views of our construct of the "normal

---

[35] Several writers have suggested that the monetary authorities may exert considerable influence on the formation of expectations. See, for example, Edward J. Kane and Dudley G. Luckett, "The Use of Monetary Policy: Comment," *Southern Economic Journal* 29 (April 1963), pp. 326–330; and Harry G. Johnson, "Issues in Monetary and Fiscal Policies," *Federal Reserve Bulletin* 50 (November 1964), pp. 1400–1413, especially p. 1410.

range of interest rates." The typical response to my question viewed the Federal Reserve's activities as imposing a floor on the "normal range" for short rates and a ceiling on the "normal range" for long rates. For example, one portfolio manager answered, "Given the current international situation you can be sure that the Federal Reserve wouldn't dare let short rates fall below 3.50 per cent." Another responded, "This is a rigged market. Long rates will not be allowed to rise much above current levels." As was indicated in Chapter 3, such changes in expectations could be expected to alter the term structure in the desired manner.[36]

In sum, both the direct evidence and the indirect tests reported in Section 8.6.d suggest that the formation of interest-rate expectations in the bond market may be extremely sensitive to the "open mouth" policy of the monetary authorities. Perhaps, in this last argument, we may be accused of coming perilously close to proposing a bootstrap theory of price determination.[37] Such an objection can be answered, however. The ability of the monetary authorities to influence the term structure through their effect in altering expectations must ultimately rest on the market's belief that the Federal Reserve can (and will, if necessary) manipulate the rate structure in accordance with their objectives by directly changing the relative supplies of debt instruments. Consequently, the Federal Reserve could peg the rate structure for periods during the 1940's without engaging in any open-market transactions at all. As long as the market was convinced that the monetary authorities would use their unlimited resources to whatever extent was necessary to back up their desires for a particular rate structure, then rational investors would formulate

[36] An even better method of measuring the effectiveness of the monetary authorities in altering expectations would have been to conduct questionnaire surveys of interest-rate expectations both before and after the inception of "Operation Twist." The single survey, conducted during April 1965, and described in Chapter 6, cannot be used to determine the influence of the monetary authorities on expectations. Nevertheless, some gratuitous comments, made in letters accompanying the return of the completed questionnaires, suggest that the commitment of the monetary authorities to the goals of Operation Twist may itself have had a considerable effect on the expectations held by many market participants. Consider, for example, the following comments: "The government-bond market has degenerated to a reflection of government convictions." "As I am sure you well know, the structure of interest rates will be governed by what the Federal Government wants it to be." Such comments imply that the policy objectives of the monetary authorities play an important role in the formation of expectations.

[37] John R. Hicks has complained that some formulations of expectational theories leave the rate of interest uncomfortably hanging by its own bootstraps. See his *Value and Capital* (New York: Oxford University Press, 2nd ed., 1946), p. 164.

expectations accordingly. But note again that even the Federal Reserve's ability to change expectations rests on the proposition that relative supplies can influence the rate structure. Thus, some type of eclectic theory such as we have presented in this book must be considered the only rational explanation of the apparent success of the monetary authorities in reshaping the yield curve. As Mrs. Robinson has argued, today's price of any long-lived object with negligible carrying costs must be strongly influenced by expectations about what its price will be in the future as determined by anticipated supply and demand conditions.[38] If bond yields hang by their bootstraps, then so does the price of a painting by Miró.

[38] Joan Robinson, "The Rate of Interest," *Econometrica* 19 (April 1951), p. 103.

Advance Refunding: A technique, used primarily for marketing Treasury bonds, whereby holders of short- and intermediate-term securities are given the option of exchanging their bonds for longer-term issues.

Arbitrage: The simultaneous purchase and sale of equivalent securities in the same or different markets. Arbitrage differs from speculation in that the arbitrage transaction yields an assured profit.

Asked Price (Yield): The price (yield), net of transactions charges, at which a dealer will sell a security to the buyer.

Baa Rating: See bond ratings.

Backwardation: The condition in the spot and forward markets where spot prices exceed forward prices. In reference to interest *rates* (rather than *prices*), forward rates would exceed spot rates; hence, the yield curve would be positively sloped.

Basic Yield: The yield, as of a given date, of the highest-grade bonds outstanding with a given term to maturity.

Basis Book: A book of bond values giving the appropriate bond price for different combinations of coupons (C), yield to maturity (i), and term to maturity (N).

Basis Point: A hundredth of one per cent (0.01 per cent).

Bid Price (Yield): The price (yield), net of transactions charges, at which a dealer will purchase a security from the seller.

Bond Ratings: Quality ratings of bonds assigned by investment-advisory agencies. In the rating scheme used by Moody's Inc., Aaa bonds are judged to have the highest quality, i.e., they have the least credit risk. Baa bonds are considered to be of medium quality.

Broker: An agent who executes orders to buy and sell securities. For this service he receives a commission.

Call Date: The earliest date prior to maturity when a callable bond may be redeemed by the issuer.

Call Feature: See Callable bond.

Call-money Rate (Call-loan Rate): The rate of interest on loans made on a day-to-day basis and payable on demand one day following the time contracted.

Call Price(s): The price (or schedule of prices) at which a callable bond may be redeemed prior to maturity.

Call Provisions: The terms upon which a bond may be redeemed prior to maturity.

Callable Bond: A bond that may be redeemed at the option of the issuer at a date prior to the final maturity date.

CD: See Negotiable Certificate of Deposit.

Commercial Paper: Short-term unsecured notes issued by industrial corporations and finance companies.

Compensating Balance: A deposit balance required to be held at a commercial bank to compensate the banker for services rendered.

Consol: A bond paying a fixed-interest coupon in perpetuity. The term was originally applied to consolidated loans of the British government.

Contango: The condition in the spot and forward markets where forward prices exceed spot prices. In reference to interest *rates* (rather than *prices*), spot rates would exceed forward rates; hence, the yield curve would be negatively sloped.

Conversion Feature: See convertible bond.

Convertible Bond: A bond that may be converted into a specified number of common shares at the option of the holder.

Coupon (C): The evidence of the bondholder's right to semiannual (or annual) interest payments. The coupons for (bearer) bonds are detachable from the bond itself and become payable when due.

Coupon Rate: The ratio of the annual coupon (C) to the face value of the bond (F).

Credit Risk: The risk that there may be a default in interest or principal payments.

Current Yield: The annual coupon (C) expressed as a percentage of the market price (P).

Dealer: An individual or firm in the securities business who acts as a principal rather than as an agent (broker). The dealer may execute orders for customers, but he buys securities for his own account and sells from his own inventory. The dealer's profit (or loss) is the difference between the price he pays and the price he receives for the same security.

Dealer Spread: The difference between the bid and asked prices quoted by the dealer.

Default: The failure to pay interest or principal in the full contractual amount when due.

Discount: A bond is said to sell at a discount if its market price is below par. The size of the discount is measured by the difference between the market price and par value.

Dollar Averaging (Dollar-cost Averaging): The portfolio practice of investing a fixed dollar amount at regular intervals. When bond prices are low, the investor buys more bonds than at high prices, thus assuring himself of a lower average cost per bond than the simple average of bond prices.

Face Value (F): The principal amount of the bond which becomes due and payable upon maturity.

Governments (Treasury Securities): Interest-bearing debt obligations of the United States Treasury.

Holding-period Return (Yield): The yield realized by an investor over the time period during which he has funds to invest.

"Inside-market Spreads": The bid-and-asked spread at which the dealers trade among themselves or with their largest and best customers.

Intermediates (Intermediate-term Securities): A rather elastic term often referring to securities maturing in from 3 to 5 years, or thereabouts.

Line of Credit: A statement by a bank that it is prepared to lend up to a stated maximum amount to a prospective borrower.

Long Position: A trading position in which the trader owns more securities than he has contracted to deliver. By extension, it refers to any person owning an inventory of securities.

Longs (Long-term Securities): By convention, securities maturing in 10 years or more. Long (long-term) interest rates (yields) refer to the yields on such securities.

"Magic Fives": The nickname of the Treasury securities that were issued on November 15, 1959 with a 5 per cent coupon rate, which was considered unusually high at the time. This issue matured on August 15, 1964.

Margin: A purchase of securities is said to be "on margin" when the buyer puts up only a portion of the purchase price (the margin) and borrows the remainder, using the security as collateral.

Market Risk: The risk of capital loss that may be suffered if there is a change in the level of market interest rates.

Mid-point Yield: The yield corresponding to a bond price midway between the bid and asked price.

Negotiable Certificate of Deposit (CD): A negotiable time deposit at a commercial bank with a specific maturity date and rate of interest. The deposit is evidenced by a contract (certificate) that may be resold in the secondary market.

New-Issue Cost: The once-and-for-all charges incurred by the borrower at the time of the initial offering of (debt) securities.

Optional Maturity: See callable bond.

Par Value: The face amount of a bond (typically $1,000). A bond selling at par sells at 100 per cent of its face value.

Pegging: Holding prices or quotations at a fixed level.

Portfolio: The inventory of securities held by an individual or institution.

Premium: A bond is said to sell at a premium if its market price is above par. The size of the premium is measured by the difference between the market price and par value.

Regulation Q: The Federal regulation prescribing maximum interest rates that can be paid on time deposits including CD's.

Repurchase Agreements (RP's): Short-term arrangements between government-bond dealers and (usually) corporations for the financing of the dealers' inventory. They are often executed by making a specific sale contract covering a part of the dealer's inventory, together with an agreement to "buy back" the securities at a specific price at a future date. RP's are also effected with the Federal Reserve Bank (at the initiative of the Reserve Authorities).

Secondary Market: The trading market for securities once they have been issued.

Short Position: A trading position in which the trader has sold securities that he does not own in the hope of being able to buy them later at a lower price.

Short Sale: The sale of securities that the seller does not possess.

Shorts (Short-term Securities): By convention, securities maturing within one year. Short (short-term) interest rates (yields) refer to the yields on such securities.

Sinking Fund: A fund of cash (held by a trustee) that has been accumulated by periodic payments for the purpose of purchasing or otherwise redeeming bonds before or at maturity.

Speculation: The maintenance of a long, short, or hedged (long and short) position in the anticipation of future profit. Speculation by means of a hedged position in different securities differs from arbitrage in that the anticipated profit is not assured.

Term to Maturity (N): The date when the face value of the bond becomes due and payable.

"Thin" Market: A market in which there are comparatively few bids to buy, or offers to sell, or both. Consequently, a market where the sale of a block of securities of given size will result in a relatively large change in price.

Trading Costs: The sum of all charges incurred by the purchaser or seller of securities in the secondary market.

Treasury Bills: Short-term debt securities issued by the United States Treasury on a continuing basis. Treasury bills do not carry coupons, as do regular Treasury bonds. Bills are sold at a discount from their stated (face) value and mature at par.

Yield Curve: A graphic device for examining the relationship between the yield and term to maturity of comparable debt securities.

Yield to Maturity (i): The (annual) interest rate that makes the present value of the stream of future coupon payments and of the face value repayable at maturity equal to the purchase price.

BIBLIOGRAPHY

Alchian, Armen A., "The Rate of Interest, Fisher's Rate of Return over Cost and Keynes' Internal Rate of Return," *American Economic Review* 45 (December 1955), pp. 938–943 (reprinted in *The Management of Corporate Capital*, Ezra Solomon, ed.).

Almon, Shirley, "The Distributed Lag Between Capital Appropriations and Expenditures," *Econometrica* 33 (January 1965), pp. 178–196.

American Bankers Association, *The Commercial Banking Industry*, a monograph prepared by the Commission on Money and Credit (Englewood Cliffs: Prentice-Hall, 1962).

Bailey, Martin J., "Discussion," *American Economic Review, Papers and Proceedings* 54 (May 1964), p. 554. (Discussion of B. G. Malkiel, "The Term Structure of Interest Rates," *American Economic Review* 54, May 1964, pp. 532–543.)

Baumol, William J., "The Transactions Demand for Cash: An Inventory Theoretic Approach," *Quarterly Journal of Economics* 66 (November 1952), pp. 545–556.

Baumol, William J., Malkiel, Burton G., and Quandt, Richard E., "The Valuation of Convertible Securities," *Quarterly Journal of Economics* 80 (February 1966), pp. 48–59.

Baxter, Nevins D., *The Commercial Paper Market*, Econometric Research Program Research Memorandum No. 69 (Princeton: October 1964), mimeographed.

Baxter, Nevins D., and Shapiro, Harold T., "Compensating-Balance Requirements: The Results of a Survey," *Journal of Finance* 19 (September 1964), pp. 483–496.

"The Behavior of Consumer Credit," *Monthly Review*, Federal Reserve Bank of New York, 42 (March 1960), pp. 50–54.

Chandler, Lester V., *The Economics of Money and Banking* (New York: Harper & Brothers, 3rd ed., 1959).

────── *Inflation in the United States, 1940–1948* (New York: Harper & Brothers, 1951).

Chow, Gregory C., "Tests of Equality between Sets of Coefficients in Two Linear Regressions," *Econometrica* 28, (July 1960), pp. 591–605.

Cochran, John A., "Postponement of Corporate and Municipal Bond Issues, 1955–1957" (August 1957), unpublished.

Commission on Money and Credit, *Impacts of Monetary Policy* (Englewood Cliffs: Prentice-Hall, 1963).

────── *Money and Credit* (Englewood Cliffs: Prentice-Hall, 1962).

Conard, Joseph W., *Introduction to the Theory of Interest* (Berkeley: University of California Press, 1959).

Culbertson, John M., "Discussion: Econometric Studies in Money Markets II," a paper presented to the Econometric Society, Pittsburgh, December 1962.

———— "The Term Structure of Interest Rates," *Quarterly Journal of Economics* 71 (November 1957), pp. 485–517.

———— "The Use of Monetary Policy," *Southern Economic Journal* 27 (October 1961), pp. 130–137.

de Leeuw, Frank, "A Model of Financial Behavior," Chapter 13 in J. Duesenberry, G. Fromm, L. Klein, E. Kuh, eds. *Brookings Quarterly Econometric Model of the United States Economy* (Chicago: Rand McNally; Amsterdam: North Holland Publishing, 1965), pp. 465–530.

Duesenberry, James, *Business Cycles and Economic Growth* (New York: McGraw-Hill, 1958).

Durand, David, *Basic Yields of Corporate Bonds, 1900–1942,* Technical Paper 3 (New York: National Bureau of Economic Research, 1942).

———— "A Quarterly Series of Corporate Basic Yields, 1952–1957, and Some Attendant Reservations," *Journal of Finance* 13 (September 1958), pp. 348–356.

Durand, David, and Winn, Willis J., *Basic Yields of Bonds, 1926–1947; Their Measurement and Pattern,* Technical Paper 6 (New York: National Bureau of Economic Research, 1947).

The Economic Almanac, 1953–1954 (New York: Thomas Y. Crowell Company, 1953).

Federal Reserve Charts on Bank Credit, Money Rates and Business, Board of Governors of the Federal Reserve System (October 1963).

Fisher, Douglas, "The Structure of Interest Rates: A Comment," *Economica* 31 (November 1964), pp. 412–419.

Fisher, Irving, "Appreciation and Interest," *Publications of the American Economic Association* 2 (August 1896), pp. 23–29; 88–92.

———— *The Nature of Capital and Income* (New York: The Macmillan Co., 1906).

———— *The Theory of Interest* (New York: The Macmillan Co., 1930).

Fisher, Lawrence, "Determinants of Risk Premiums on Corporate Bonds," *Journal of Political Economy* 67 (June 1959), pp. 217–237.

Freeman, Harold, *Introduction to Statistical Inference* (Reading: Addison-Wesley, 1963).

Friedman, Milton, *A Theory of the Consumption Function* (Princeton: Princeton University Press, 1957).

Goldsmith, T., *Goldsmith's Washington Service* (1958–1965).

Gottlieb, Manuel, "Cyclical Timing of Municipal Bond Issues," *Quarterly Review of Economics and Business* 1 (May 1961), pp. 67–75.

Grant, J. A. G., "Meiselman on the Structure of Interest Rates: A British Test," *Economica* 31 (February 1964), pp. 51–71.

Gurley, John G., and Shaw, Edward S., *Money in a Theory of Finance* (Washington: The Brookings Institution, 1960).

Hawtrey, Ralph G., *A Century of Bank Rates* (London: Longmans, Green and Co., 1938).

Hickman, William B., *The Term Structure of Interest Rates: An Exploratory Analysis* (New York: National Bureau of Economic Research, 1943).

Hicks, John R., "Mr. Hawtrey on Bank Rates and the Long Term Rate of Interest," *Manchester School of Economics and Social Studies* 10, No. 1 (1939), pp. 21–37.

———— "A Suggestion for Simplifying the Theory of Money," *Economica* 2 (1935), pp. 1–19, reprinted in American Economic Association, *Readings in Economic Theory* (Homewood: Irwin, 1951), pp. 13–22.

———— *Value and Capital* (London: Oxford, Clarendon Press, 1939, 2nd ed., 1946).

Hirshleifer, Jack, "On the Theory of the Optimal Investment Decision," *Journal of Political Economy* 66 (August 1958), pp. 329–352. (Reprinted in *The Management of Corporate Capital*, Ezra Solomon, ed.)

Homer, Sidney, *A History of Interest Rates* (New Brunswick: Rutgers University Press, 1963).

———— *An Analytic Record of Yields and Yield Spreads* (New York: Salomon Brothers and Hutzler, 1963), supplements.

———— "Comparative Price Opportunity and Price Risks from Various Issues of Long-Term United States Government Bonds," Memorandum to Portfolio Managers from Salomon Brothers and Hutzler, June 2, 1965.

———— "Open Market Purchases of Longer Term Government Bonds by the Federal Reserve Banks and by the U.S. Trust Funds," mimeographed (June 14, 1963).

Hunt, P., Williams, C. M., and Donaldson, G., *Basic Business Finance* (Homewood: R. D. Irwin, 1961).

Johnson, Harry G., "An Overview of Price Levels, Employment, and the U.S. Balance of Payments," *Journal of Business* 36 (July 1963), pp. 279–289.

———— "Issues in Monetary and Fiscal Policies," *Federal Reserve Bulletin* 50 (November 1964), pp. 1400–1413.

Johnston, J., *Econometric Methods* (New York: McGraw-Hill, 1963).

Kaldor, Nicholas, "Speculation and Economic Stability," *The Review of Economic Studies* 7 (October 1939), pp. 13–16.

Kalecki, Michael, *Essays in the Theory of Economic Fluctuations* (London: G. Allen & Unwin, Ltd., 1939).

Kane, Edward J., and Luckett, Dudley G., "The Use of Monetary Policy: Comment," *Southern Economic Journal* 29 (April 1963), pp. 326–330.

Kane, Edward J., and Malkiel, Burton G., "The Term Structure of

Interest Rates: An Analysis of a Survey of Interest-Rate Expectations" (Princeton: February 1966), mimeographed.

Kessel, Reuben, *The Cyclical Behavior of the Term Structure of Interest Rates,* Occasional Paper 91 (New York: National Bureau of Economic Research, December 1965).

Keynes, John Maynard, *The General Theory of Employment, Interest and Money* (New York: Harcourt, Brace, 1935).

———— *A Treatise on Money* (London: Macmillan, 1930, and New York: Harcourt, Brace, 1930).

Lerner, Abba P., *The Economics of Control* (New York: Macmillan & Co., 1944).

Liviatan, Nissan, "Consistent Estimation of Distributed Lags," *International Economic Review* 4 (January 1963), pp. 44–52.

Lorie, James H., and Savage, Leonard J., "Three Problems in Rationing Capital," *Journal of Business* 28 (October 1955), pp. 229–239. (Reprinted in *The Management of Corporate Capital,* Ezra Solomon, ed.).

Luce, R. Duncan, and Raiffa, Howard, *Games and Decisions* (New York: John Wiley, 1957).

Luckett, Dudley G., "Bills Only: A Critical Appraisal," *Review of Economics and Statistics* 41 (August 1960), pp. 301–306.

———— "Maturity Measures of the Public Debt," *Quarterly Journal of Economics* 78 (February 1964), pp. 148–157.

———— "Professor Lutz and the Structure of Interest Rates," *Quarterly Journal of Economics* 73 (February 1959), pp. 131–144.

Lusher, David W., "The Structure of Interest Rates and the Keynesian Theory of Interest," *Journal of Political Economy* 50 (April 1942), pp. 272–279.

Lutz, Friedrich A., "The Structure of Interest Rates," *Quarterly Journal of Economics* 55 (November 1940), pp. 36–63; reprinted in American Economic Association, *Readings in the Theory of Income Distribution* (Homewood: R. D. Irwin, 1946), pp. 499–529.

Macaulay, Frederick R., *The Movements of Interest Rates, Bond Yields, and Stock Prices in the United States since 1856* (New York: National Bureau of Economic Research, 1938).

Machlup, Fritz, "Marginal Analysis and Empirical Research," *American Economic Review* 36 (September 1946), reprinted in Richard Clemence, ed., *Readings in Economic Analysis,* II (Cambridge: Addison-Wesley, 1950); and Fritz Machlup, *Essays in Economic Semantics* (Englewood Cliffs: Prentice-Hall, 1963), pp. 519–554.

Malkiel, Burton G., "Expectations, Bond Prices and the Term Structure of Interest Rates," *Quarterly Journal of Economics,* 76 (May 1962), pp. 197–218.

————, "The Term Structure of Interest Rates," *American Economic*

Review: Papers and Proceedings, 54 (May 1964), pp. 532–543.

Malkiel, Burton G., and Kane, Edward J., "U.S. Tax Law and the Locked-In Effect," *National Tax Journal,* 16 (December 1963), pp. 389–396.

"Market Interest Rates and Maturity of Issues," *Monthly Review,* Federal Reserve Bank of Kansas City (August 1954), pp. 3–8.

Markowitz, Harry, *Portfolio Selection: Efficient Diversification of Investments* (New York: Wiley, 1959).

Marx, Daniel, Jr., "The Structure of Interest Rates: Comment," *Quarterly Journal of Economics* 56 (November 1941), pp. 152–156.

Mead, E. S., and Grodinsky, J., *The Ebb and Flow of Investment Values* (New York: D. Appleton-Century, 1939).

Meiselman, David, "Discussion: Econometric Studies in Money Markets II," a paper presented to the Econometric Society, Pittsburgh, December 1962.

——— *The Term Structure of Interest Rates* (Englewood Cliffs: Prentice-Hall, 1962).

Meltzer, Allan H., and von der Linde, Gert, *A Study of the Dealer Market for Federal Government Securities* (Washington: Government Printing Office, 1960).

Michaelson, Jacob B., "Holding Period Yields on U.S. Government Securities and the Term Structure of Interest Rates," *The Journal of Finance* 20 (September 1965).

——— "The Term Structure of Interest Rates: Comment," *Quarterly Journal of Economics* 77 (February 1963), pp. 166–174.

Milnor, John W., "Games Against Nature," in Thrall, Coombs, and Davis, eds., *Decision Processes* (New York: John Wiley, 1957).

Modigliani, Franco and Sutch, Richard, "Innovations in Interest Rate Policy," a paper presented at the 78th Annual Meeting of the American Economic Association, December 30, 1965.

Moody's Bond Survey (1958–1965).

Morris, Frank E., "A Study of Municipal Bond Sales Postponed During the Past Nine Months," *IBA Statistical Bulletin,* No. 3 (April 1957).

——— "The Impact of Monetary Policy on State and Local Government: An Empirical Study," *Journal of Finance* 15 (May 1960), pp. 232–249.

Musgrave, Richard A., *The Theory of Public Finance* (New York: McGraw-Hill, 1959).

"Nudging the Capital Markets," *Monthly Letter: First National City Bank* (New York, March 1961), pp. 28–31.

Okun, Arthur M., "Monetary Policy, Debt Management, and Interest Rates: A Quantitative Appraisal," in *Stabilization Policies,* a series of research studies prepared for the Commission on Money and Credit (Englewood Cliffs: Prentice-Hall, 1963), pp. 331–380.

Olyphant, Murray, "Government Bonds," *Banking, Journal of the American Bankers Association* 50–58 (1958–1965).

Orcutt, G. H., and James, S. F., "Testing the Significance of Correlation between Time Series," *Biometrika* 35 (1948), pp. 397–413.

Parks, Robert H., "Income and Tax Aspects of Commercial Bank Portfolio Operations in Treasury Securities," *National Tax Journal* 11 (March 1958), pp. 21–34.

Patinkin, Don, *Money, Interest and Prices* (Evanston: Row Peterson, 1956).

Porter, Sylvia, *Reporting on Governments* (1958–1965).

Phelps, Charlotte Demonte, "The Impact of Monetary Policy on State and Local Government Expenditures in the United States," in *Impacts of Monetary Policy*, a series of research studies prepared for the Commission on Money and Credit (Englewood Cliffs: Prentice-Hall, 1963), pp. 621–647.

Pickering, Richard C., "Effects of Credit and Monetary Policy Since Mid-1952 on State and Local Government Financing and Construction Activity" (April 1955), unpublished.

—— "State and Local Government Bond Financing During the First Half of 1958" (May 1959), unpublished.

Renshaw, Ed, "A Note on the Arithmetic of Capital-Budgeting Decisions," *Journal of Business* 30 (July 1957), pp. 193–201. (Reprinted in *The Management of Corporate Capital*, Ezra Solomon, ed.).

Riefler, Winfield, "Open Market Operations in Long-Term Securities," *Federal Reserve Bulletin* 44 (November 1958), pp. 1260–1274.

Robertson, D. H., "Mr. Keynes and the Rate of Interest," *Essays in Monetary Theory* (London: P. S. King and Son, 1940), pp. 1–38; reprinted in American Economic Association, *Readings in the Theory of Income Distribution* (Philadelphia: The Blakiston Co., 1951), pp. 425–460.

Robinson, Joan, "The Rate of Interest," *Econometrica* 19 (April 1951), pp. 92–111; reprinted in Joan Robinson, *The Rate of Interest and Other Essays* (London: Macmillan, 1952), pp. 3–30.

Robinson, Roland I., *The Management of Bank Funds* (New York: McGraw-Hill, 1951).

—— *Postwar Market of State and Local Government Securities* (Princeton: National Bureau of Economic Research, Princeton University Press, 1960).

Robinson, Romney, "The Rate of Interest, Fisher's Rate of Return over Cost, and Keynes' Internal Lack of Return: Comment," *American Economic Review* 46 (December 1956), pp. 972–973.

Rolph, Earl R., "Principles of Debt Management," *American Economic Review* 47 (June 1957), pp. 302–320.

Say, J. B., *A Treatise on Political Economy* (Philadelphia: Lippincott, Grambo & Co., 1853).

Schlesinger, James, "Monetary Policy and its Critics," *Journal of Political Economy* 68 (December 1960), pp. 601–616.

Scott, Ira O., Jr., *Government Securities Market* (New York: McGraw-Hill, 1965).

———— "The Availability Doctrine: Theoretical Underpinnings," *Review of Economic Studies* 25 (October 1957), pp. 41–48.

Scott, Robert Haney, "Liquidity and the Term Structure of Interest Rates," *Quarterly Journal of Economics* 79 (February 1965), pp. 135–145.

Securities and Exchange Commission, *Costs of Flotation of Corporate Securities, 1951–1955* (Washington: Government Printing Office, June 1957).

Shackle, G. L. S., *Decision, Order and Time in Human Affairs* (Cambridge: Cambridge University Press, 1961).

———— *Uncertainty in Economics* (Cambridge: Cambridge University Press, 1955).

Sidgwick, Henry, *The Principles of Political Economy* (London: Macmillan, 1887).

Sloane, Peter E., "Determinants of Bond Yield Differentials," *Yale Economic Essays* (Vol. 3, No. 1, Spring 1963), pp. 3–55.

Solomon, Ezra, ed., *The Management of Corporate Capital* (Illinois: Free Press of Glencoe, 1959).

———— "The Arithmetic of Capital-Budgeting Decisions," *Journal of Business* 29 (April 1956), pp. 124–129. (Reprinted in *The Management of Corporate Capital* Ezra Solomon, ed.).

Stone, Robert W., "Federal Reserve Open Market Operations in 1962," *Federal Reserve Bulletin* 49 (April 1963), pp. 429–457.

Tintner, Gerhard, *Econometrics* (New York: John Wiley & Sons, 1952).

Tobin, James, "The Interest Elasticity of Transactions Demand for Cash," *Review of Economics and Statistics* 38 (August 1956), pp. 241–247.

———— "Liquidity Preference as Behavior Toward Risk," *Review of Economic Studies* 25 (February 1958), pp. 65–86.

Treasury-Federal Reserve Study of the Government Securities Market (Washington: Government Printing Office, 1959), Part I.

United States Treasury Department, *Treasury Bulletins,* 1952–1965.

Van Horne, James, "Interest-Rate Risk and the Term Structure of Interest Rates," *Journal of Political Economy* 73 (August 1965), pp. 344–351.

von Neumann, John, and Morgenstern, Oskar, *Theory of Games and Economic Behavior,* 3rd ed. (Princeton: Princeton University Press, 1953).

Walker, Charls E., "Federal Reserve Policy and the Structure of Interest Rates on Government Securities," *Quarterly Journal of Economics* 68 (February 1954), pp. 19–42.

Wallace, Neil, *The Term Structure of Interest Rates and the Maturity Composition of the Federal Debt* (Ph.D. dissertation submitted to the University of Chicago, December 1964), unpublished.

Wilks, S. S., *Mathematical Statistics* (Princeton: Princeton University Press, 1945).

Williams, John Burr, *The Theory of Investment Value* (Amsterdam: North-Holland Publishing Co., 1956; 1st printing 1938).

Wood, John H., "An Econometric Model of the Term Structure of Interest Rates," a paper presented to the Econometric Society, Pittsburgh, December 1962; revised March 1964, unpublished.

——— "The Expectations Hypothesis, the Yield Curve, and Monetary Policy," *Quarterly Journal of Economics* 78 (August 1964), pp. 457–470.

——— "Expectations, Errors, and the Term Structure of Interest Rates," *The Journal of Political Economy* 71 (April 1963), pp. 160–171.

Young, Ralph A., and Yager, Charles A., "The Economics of 'Bills Preferably,'" *Quarterly Journal of Economics* 74 (August 1960), pp. 341–373.

INDEX

casualty insurance companies, *see* fire and casualty insurance companies

certainty, *see* income certainty; principal certainty

certificate of deposit, *see* negotiable certificate of deposit

Chandler, Lester V., 85n, 233n

Chow, Gregory C., 242

Cochran, John A., 156n

commercial banks, maturity preferences of, 10, 145, 147–153, 158–164, 183–185; ownership of Public Housing Authority securities, 139–140; ownership of U.S. Treasury securities, 147–153; maturity data on portfolios of, 148–149; portfolio-management policies of, 158–164; survey on expectations of, 172n; influence of tax law on behavior of, 177–179; and negotiable certificates of deposit, 244–245

commercial-loan theory, 132n

commercial paper, costs of issuing, 130–131, 133–134

commercial-paper rate, understates borrowing costs, 130–131

Commission on Money and Credit, and risk aversion of dealers in government securities, 116

comparative-statics analysis, used in synthesis of term-structure theories, 181

compensating-balance requirements, and new-issue costs, 130–131; on bank loans, 131–132

Conard, Joseph W., expectations theory of the term structure, 18, 30, 39–40, 181n–182n, 219

consols; price changes of, 51, 53, 56–57; yields of, relative to long-term issues, 66–67

consumer credit, 132n

convertibility features, affecting bond-yield differentials, 1n

corporate bonds, yield curves for, 4–11; default risk on, 12, 137; transactions costs on, 105, 112–113, 137; survey of issuers' behavior, 166–168; lack of data on maturity composition of, 222; anticipation of market reaction to new issues, 226

corporate issue period, 132

corporations, *see* nonfinancial corporations

coupon rate, effect on bond-yield differentials, 1, 34n; effect on relationships among yield to maturity, holding-period yield, and forward rates, 44–49; effect on bond-price changes, 56–57. *See also* yield; rate

credit risk, *see* default risk

Culbertson, John M., 35, 73, 183n; criticism of expectations theory, 24, 39; hedging-pressure hypothesis of the term structure, 27–28, 39, 145; empirical test of the expectations theory, 29

debt management, *see* debt-management policies under U.S. Treasury

decision-making under risk, 65–67

deep-discount bond, *see* discount bond

default risk, effect on bond-yield differentials, 1; effect on Durand yield curves, 12, 137n; on corporate bonds, 137; on PHA obligations, 137; on U.S. Treasury securities, 137

de Leeuw, Frank, 238–240

discount bonds, 53–55, 58n, 79–81; call protection feature of, 67n, 72; tax advantages of, 72

dollar-averaging, by institutional investors, 165

Duesenberry, James, 238–239

Durand, David, bond prices in theory of the term structure, 51n. *See also* Durand basic yields

Durand basic yields, 4–15, 34, 37, 52n, 77, 82, 102; construction of yield curves, 5, 10–13, 34; presence of credit risk in, 12, 137n; calculation of forward rates from, 48–49; use of, in testing reformulated expectations hypothesis, 83–94, 96, 98–100

duration, defined by Macaulay, 57n

Durbin, G., 88, 91, 92, 98, 228, 243

error-learning model, use of, in testing expectations theory, 30–38; applied to Durand data, 30–33; applied to U.K. Treasury securities, 34; applied to U.S. Treasury securities, 35

expectations, in traditional theory of the term structure, 18; and imperfect

ory, 103–104, 106, 108; and maturity of issue, 104, 106–112, 118–123, 135–142, 143; and transactions costs, 104, 106–112, 118–123, 135–142, 143; equation for, with transactions costs, 107–108; used in constructing indifference yield curve, 109–112

internal yield (internal rate of return): used in computing holding-period yields, 19; relation of, to yield to maturity, 41–42. *See also* yield to maturity

nominal yield: defined, 53; relation of, to bond price, 53–59, 79–81; relation of, to years to maturity, 53–59, 79–81; relation of, to yield to maturity, 53–59, 79–81

yield to maturity: defined, 2n, 53; of U.S. Treasury securities, 12–14; of commercial paper of General Motors Acceptance Corporation, 13, 14; relation of, to long and forward short rates, 40–49; mathematical expression for, 41; ambiguities in concept of, 41–42; relation to (Hicksian) average long rate, 42–43, 44; relation of, to holding-period yield, 44–48, 120; relation of, to coupon size, 44–48; relation of, to bond price, 53–59, 79–81; relation of, to years to maturity, 53–59, 79–81; with transactions costs, 120; affected by compounding practice, 123n; calculation of, in presence of call provisions, 224–225

yield curve, defined, 2; construction of, 2–3; types of, 3, 4; for corporate bonds, 4–11; for U.S. Treasury securities, 12–14, 35, 139, 142; "normal" positive slope in twentieth century, 12, 14–16, 102, 136; cyclical behavior of, 12–16, 145; for securities of General Motors Acceptance Corporation, 13–14; for U.K. Treasury securities, 14–15; in nineteenth century, 15n; in medieval and Renaissance times, 15–16; "shoulder" of, 16, 59n, 65; game-theoretic explanation of typical shapes, 63–65; shape influenced by risk-aversion, 69–71, 136; influenced by special call features, 72; influenced by special tax features, 72; kinks in empirical curves, 72; conditions for zero slope, 103, 187; positive bias caused by transactions costs, 104, 112, 127–129, 133, 136–143, 217–218; relation to indifference yield curve, 109–112 118–129; as an equilibrium solution, 120n, 123–129; "riding the yield curve," 121n; typical shapes, given non-zero transactions costs, 124–129; affected asymmetrically by trading costs, 128–129; sensitivity to changes in relative supplies, 128–129, 191–192, 199, 201, 221–232, 238–244; positive bias possible from issuers' preferences, 133–136; empirical tests of influence of transactions costs, 136–140; for Public Housing Authority securities, 139, 140n; explained by hedging-pressure hypothesis, 145; effect of degree of uniformity of expectations, 191–192, 199, 201; relation to holding curve, 199–200; changes in, may precede changes in relative supplies, 226; behavior of, during "bills only" era, 233, 242; behavior of, during 1961–1964 period, 237–238; influenced by development of negotiable certificates of deposit, 244–245; influenced by monetary authorities' impact on expectations, 245–247. *See also* indifference yield curve; Durand basic yields; securities *under* U.S. Treasury

"humped" yield curves: defined, 3–4; of U.S. treasury securities, 13; of General Motors Acceptance Corporation, 13–14; hump in intermediate maturities, 102; explanation of, by pure expectations theory, 102, 201–202, 217; explanation of, by transactions costs, 140–142; business-cycle explanation of, 201–202; explanation of, in three-market model of term structure, 201–204, 210–213; and hedging-pressure hypothesis, 201–204, 210–213; influence of relative bond supplies, 201–204, 210–213, 232; empirical curves of 1959 and 1960, 204

Young, Ralph A., 220n

Ingram Content Group UK Ltd.
Milton Keynes UK
UKHW022312230623
423960UK00008B/321